For

DAWNY

&

in memory of

STEVEN MICHAEL ZIMRING,

free spirited, pure hearted, hilarious

and inspiringly kind

Praise for Towpath

Towpath is one of the reasons I live in London. It's a jewel-like, dream of a place. Somewhere to sit and watch the world go by. A treat for each one of the senses. This book is an invite into their magical world.
KEIRA KNIGHTLEY

Lori & Laura are a magical team with the ability and flair to know what is right, beautiful and tasty. Laura cooks an incredible, culinary juggling act – as she battles with crazy cyclists, the weather and a canal. This book is packed full of food you want to know and cook. I suggest you dive in and cook up a Towpath feast for your friends and family.
FERGUS & MARGOT HENDERSON

I want to go full-on 'Julie and Julia' on it and cook a dish every day until I have cooked every single one. This is a cookbook that absolutely everyone should possess. It's a life-changing kind of thing that you'd want to pass on to your children. The only tricky thing about this book is that I will cook so much from it, I will probably have to get one each year as it will be cooked from to death.
OLIA HERCULES

When people ask about my favorite restaurants, I instantly think of Towpath. Warm, quirky, intimate, it's a restaurant you never want to leave. This cookbook is the same: personal, inviting and filled with fantastically appealing food.
RUTH REICHL

I find myself transported. Your voices, my dears, are as clear as bells, the words float off the pages like the coots of the canal. The sense of place and time, wonder and friendship, the sheer joy of generosity and giving and pleasing are all beautifully woven together. The love and respect you have for each other shines through on every page as you recall adventures and dishes and people and instances galore. This book, inspiring as it is useful, is a masterclass in the good things in life.
JEREMY LEE

A book of stories and recipes for honest, unfussy food that sings of its season, and of the intelligence, love and companionship that is at the heart of Laura and Lori's Towpath.
RACHEL RODDY

Family, community, friendships, sensational food in an unlikely spot. Lori and Laura create canal-side magic. It's my family's happy place. This book is beautiful. The recipes are not daunting to copy which is wonderful for someone like me. I love all the stories of how hard it was to start something like this. It's funny and human and you get the sense of what hard work it is too. It's great that people all over the world will get to have a little slice of the magic.
TRACEY ULLMAN

Towpath is my absolute favourite place in London to eat out and pass time. This book is the perfect reflection of it and will sit close to my stove forever, becoming more stained, splattered and thumb-worn as each season passes. It's an incredible gift to us that we can now cook Laura's food at home too.
ED SMITH

Towpath is the definition of community and has become our veritable home away from home. This book conjures memorable days and nights spent canal-side at the thoughtful oasis they have generously conceived.
PETER DOIG

Towpath

RECIPES & STORIES

LORI DE MORI & LAURA JACKSON

FOREWORD BY JOJO TULLOH

CHELSEA GREEN PUBLISHING
WHITE RIVER JUNCTION, VERMONT
LONDON, UK

Project Editor: Muna Reyal
Designer: Will Webb
Photographers: Scott MacSween and Joe Woodhouse
Proofreader: Anne Sheasby
Indexer: Hilary Bird

Printed in the United States of America.
First printing September 2020.
10 9 8 7 6 5 4 3 2 1   20 21 22 23 24

Library of Congress Cataloging-in-Publication Data
Names: De Mori, Lori, author. | Jackson, Laura, 1981- author.
Title: Towpath : recipes and stories / Lori De Mori & Laura Jackson ;
foreword by Jojo Tulloh.
Description: White River Junction, Vermont : Chelsea Green Publishing,
2020. | Includes index.
Identifiers: LCCN 2020029370 (print) | LCCN 2020029371 (ebook) | ISBN
9781645020127 (hardcover) | ISBN 9781645020134 (ebook)
Subjects: LCSH: Cooking, Italian. | LCGFT: Cookbooks.
Classification: LCC TX723 .D336 2020 (print) | LCC TX723 (ebook) | DDC
641.5945—dc23
LC record available at https://lccn.loc.gov/2020029370
LC ebook record available at https://lccn.loc.gov/2020029371

Chelsea Green Publishing
85 North Main Street, Suite 120
White River Junction, Vermont, USA

Somerset House
London, UK

www.chelseagreen.com

Contents

Foreword

It's hard to imagine a life without Towpath, yet there was a time when this stretch of canal offered only a blank wall. Now on sunny days the lunchtime scene is a piece of street theatre, the narrow space thronged with people, a line snaking back from the counter, waiting staff calling out names and bearing plates to the tables, old friends meeting, dogs and toddlers getting under foot, runners trying to bash their way through the throng and amidst all this hospitable melee, Lori at the wooden counter greeting both new and familiar faces with equal warmth, pouring wine and making coffee while simultaneously describing what you might like to eat or drink with her own special grace. In the next alcove along Laura is in the kitchen, head down, pinny on, toiling with such fierce concentration, putting all her considerable skill and intellect to use for our benefit.

It seems so right and inevitable that it should be here and yet the beginning was a leap of faith. How can you have a restaurant without a front door, without walls or windows to keep out the weather (or to hold back the hordes on busy sunny days)? It might seem a bit mad to look at a bleak stretch of post-industrial canal and project a vision of an unassuming yet highly ambitious eatery. It is a happiness in life that wonderful things sometimes occur spontaneously and so it was with Towpath. It came about almost by accident when three newly converted units at the base of a warehouse came up for sale soon after Lori left Italy to begin her new life as a Londoner. Towpath's starting point, like all unrepeatable successes, was deceptively straightforward. A 'small is beautiful' approach inspired by the winning simplicity of a hole in the wall bar in Florence and Lori's realisation that people want less, done better.

When Lori met Towpath's cook and co-proprietor, the modest yet enormously talented Laura Jackson, the alchemy of a truly great partnership was forged. A mutually strong work ethic, an approach to food that is serious but worn lightly, a commitment to sourcing ingredients that are grown or made with care (both for the quality of the product and the environment) and personalities that are contrasting yet complementary mean that together they make one extraordinary whole.

Any words will fail when placed against a plate of Laura's food, which somehow manages to be simultaneously exciting and comforting. Laura has a great talent for putting a few simple ingredients together so that they sing. I know of no other chef who has her way with vegetables (my favourite, a plate of asparagus and ajo blanco). But there is so much else, her homemade soft scoop ice creams, the cordials, the impeccable crumbly pastry of her tarts, the carefully planned menus for long evening meals where delight follows on delight till you rise from the table late at night, replete and a little bit tipsy.

Towpath is special in so many ways, but one element makes it unique, its position, tucked away from traffic by the water gives it a secret, off radar appeal. On still days, the canal is a deep green vault of mirrored clouds; cormorants pierce the surface with serpentine grace while plucky coots defend their patch. In May,

creamy elderflowers froth against the warm old brick of the bridges; beneath the arches glitter with refracting light while above roses climb the wall. At night the water, dark and silent, provides a shimmering backdrop for those candlelit suppers. Eating so well yet being outside makes a kind of magic. I have a particular fondness for grey, drizzly days when Towpath shines its welcome from afar, a beacon of warmth where good food and hospitality await.

The recipes in the book you are holding have developed over ten years and like all slowly maturing things they are rich and deep in flavour. For those who love Towpath (and I am certainly one) this book will provide solace in the cold and lonely months from November to March when this restaurant, so open to the elements, is closed. For anyone who cannot visit physically, it is a chance to experience at one remove what makes this a place to cherish.

JOJO TULLOH

nota bene
Like all things Towpath, this book is a wholly collaborative effort.
The 'I' of the recipes is Laura.
The 'I' of the stories is Lori.

Hello

A lot has changed since Towpath first rolled up its shutters more than ten years ago on the Regent's Canal in Hackney and everything but the toasted cheese sandwich was cooked from home across the bridge. And a lot hasn't. It is still as much a social experiment as an admittedly unusual set-up from which to try our very best to satisfy your hunger. A place where seasonality means we close every year in November because England's cold, dark winters are incompatible with hospitality from our little perch beside a shallow, man-made waterway that snakes through East London. Where we don't offer takeaway coffees, in the hope that people will decide to stay awhile and watch the coots skittering across the water. And where we are still without a phone or a website, because we'd rather you all just show up like hungry kids at a playground.

We've learned a lot in our time at Towpath about what makes people happy. It's the simple things really. We thrive on connection. On honest, unfussy food that sings of its season. Our eyes brighten near water, wildlife and sky. I am writing this from home on the kind of crisp spring morning our customers would call, 'a perfect Towpath day'. Except that it is March 2020 and we are closed, like so many others during this surreal time, sheltering at home. Laura is at her house writing recipes for some of our purveyors, which they will pass on to their customers with fresh ideas for what to cook from their home kitchens. The days are bewildering in their uncertainty. And sometimes spacious too. We've never had so much time to think about what matters. There is solace in the smallest pleasures. Our dreams of being back out in the world have a childlike simplicity. We long to see our friends and our families. To sit together at the table and share a meal.

This book will be born into not quite the world it was imagined for. We've asked ourselves if it could still be relevant — not as a nostalgic relic from more carefree times, but in whatever future we'll be awkwardly feeling our way into. Yes, we say, humbly! Towpath has always been not only our most heartfelt offering of joy and deliciousness, but also a kind of social and gastronomic response to the malaise running alongside all our first world striving. And what we've cared about all along — connection, community, simplicity — feels more important than ever. This book is filled with tales of our adventures and misadventures. We hope they will inspire you to approach your own work, your neighbourhood and your community with whatever your version of that spirit may look like.

You can use this book to learn to cook beloved Towpath recipes. But it is our real wish that you take a page from Laura's honest, unfussy and comforting approach to the table: one that celebrates the flavours of every season, wastes nothing, delights in cooking with whatever is at hand, and finds inspiration everywhere — so long as it's about making the ingredients shine.

Here's to when we meet again. Or meet for the first time. Or perhaps never meet at all, but raise our glasses to each other all the same.

LORI & LAURA

March

The Towpath Year

The Towpath year begins the first Tuesday in March and ends (with fireworks, music and much carousing) in the wee hours of the Monday nearest to Guy Fawkes night in November. Or at least it's meant to.

I am writing from home on the Sunday morning of what was meant to be the last day of our first week back from Towpath's 2018 winter hibernation. Laura, Towpath's other half, and the tireless creative force behind the deliciousness that comes from its kitchen, is spending an unexpected day at home with her husband Alex – probably the last he'll see of her on a Sunday until winter returns. The temperature reads -1°C. There are dusty patches of snow on the ground and the sky is a dull, steely grey. Cakes have been made. Yoghurt and Seville marmalade too. Not to mention slow simmering stews and all manner of hearty fare to welcome in another Towpath year. Nonetheless, after much discussion, the metal shutters on the four little kiosks we call home remain firmly shut. We'd already delayed opening by a week this year in the hopes of escaping the 'Beast from the East', a polar vortex which spiralled in from the Arctic to trumpeting headlines. Who knew it would be so swiftly followed by this mini-Beast?

We have learned a thing or two over the years, one of which is that we will always lose an arm wrestle with winter. On days like today our little patch of the Regent's Canal in East London is no place to be. Coots and ducks still skitter across the water and the occasional intrepid jogger lopes past. But anyone with half a bit of sense is not at an outdoor café on the canal, however warm the welcome and delicious the food. We'd made a valiant effort yesterday – four of us dressed for a polar expedition, setting up tables and flowers, chalking up the menu, stomping our feet behind the counter while snow flurries blew across the water. In truth, we did have a few customers – almost all of them Towpath friends, bless them, coming out to keep us company and offering to sign a permission note, if we needed one, to close up shop and go home.

Strange end to a week that began with so much delight, under warm(ish) sunny skies and the near constant refrain that, 'If Towpath is open it must mean winter is OVER!' It is a lovely thing to be compared to swallows. Or daffodils. To be seen as a sign of something as joyful as spring. This dire weather is not meant to last. We will roll up the shutters and begin again on Tuesday.

MARCH

PORRIDGE, WALNUTS, BROWN SUGAR AND BUTTER

It's the start of the Towpath year. As we prepare to open, people cycle, walk and run by shouting in excitement, 'Towpath is opening, so Spring must be here'. It's time to dust off the cobwebs, open the shutters and gently wake up Towpath. There is something lovely about putting Towpath to sleep for a few months and then re-opening invigorated and enthusiastic. Hopefully the customers feel the same. Every year I have the same conversation with Lori just before opening. Will we still have any customers? Surely, they will have found somewhere better to go? Do I remember how to cook? Will people still want to eat my food? It is a constant worry, but I'm always surprised when people turn up on the first day, so excited about our return.

Porridge is a breakfast staple. It's been on the menu since day one. It's perfect for an early March day when it's most likely to still be very cold. Nothing warms you up more than porridge.

The great thing about porridge is the limitless toppings and how wonderfully they can follow the seasons. Seasonal fruits either fresh, poached or stewed. Rhubarb, quince, blackberry and cherry. An overripe plum or some squishy strawberries that would be too sad to eat uncooked make for a delicious compote to add to your porridge. Our most popular porridge is with toasted walnuts, brown sugar and salted butter. I use pinhead oats, which have a much more toothy texture than rolled oats and a nutty flavour.

Serves 4

180g/6¼oz pinhead oats
pinch of salt
750ml/1⅓ pints full-fat milk
60g/2¼oz salted butter
100g/3½oz walnut halves, toasted
30g/1¼oz muscovado or
    rapadura brown sugar

Put the oats in a saucepan with 1 litre/1¾ pints water and the salt.

Bring to the boil and cook until almost all the water has evaporated and the mixture has a cement-like consistency, stirring from time to time. This normally takes around 20–25 minutes. Unlike milk, the water will not catch or burn. Add the milk, bring to the boil and turn down very low, stirring regularly until the oats are cooked but not mushy – about another 20 minutes.

To serve, divide between four bowls. Dot blobs of butter over the top, scatter over the walnuts and sprinkle over the brown sugar. Pour a bit of hot milk on top, if desired. Serve immediately.

The Fruits of Winter

There's a little game that Laura and I play right before we open where she has me try to guess what will be on the menu for those very first days.

Here's what I know. Among other things, there will be Scottish pinhead oats for breakfast. This has, in fact, been a staple on our breakfast menu since Towpath's first kitchen-less days, when we cooked from home across the canal (more on this later). Laura would always choose a fried egg over porridge to start her day, but she understands that this is the ultimate comfort breakfast for a frigid morning on the cusp of spring. The seasonality part of this equation has to do with what she'll put on it. Apple compote? Poached rhubarb? Blood orange and muscovado sugar?

Apples (and potatoes, for that matter) are to the English garden what tomatoes are to the Italian. So many varieties! Such nuanced understanding about their qualities, flavours and behaviours! Certainly not, as I used to think, nature's dowdiest fruit. We get our apples from Chegworth Valley, some for cooking with cinnamon and butter, others to slice, crisp and raw, over granola and yoghurt.

Rhubarb, despite its bright pink stalks and tart sweetness, is actually a vegetable pretending to be a fruit. I've only recently made friends with it. Until moving to London I had a vague notion that it was poisonous (actually only the leaves are) and no recollection of ever having seen it in any market in California or Italy where I'd lived. Laura poaches it in apple juice with bay leaves, aniseed, peppercorns, orange peel and rosemary. We use the poaching liquor to make a cordial, which we serve at the bar with sparkling water and ice.

Oranges in winter, especially when you live in a damp, cold, sun-deprived part of the northern hemisphere, are a revelation. The closest thing there is to edible sunshine. Blood oranges are the best version of an already extraordinary thing. We juice them at the bar and sometimes scatter slices of them over our porridge.

Bitter Seville oranges we love for the particularly British reason that they are the best of all oranges from which to make marmalade. They have only the briefest season – around 6 weeks in January and February when they are picked in Andalusia and shipped to the UK. Their arrival in London precipitates a marmalade-making frenzy in those predisposed to such winter diversions. My friend Hilary and I made 25 litres of it at her house this February. Two days of juicing, chopping and packing pith and seeds into little pectin-rich muslin balls, each step dutifully followed according to recipe, except for foolishly boiling the whole lot in one giant, never-to-fully-set but nonetheless delicious batch. 'Surely it's almost there?' we kept repeating to each other as it bubbled endlessly on the stove and then failed, again and again, the famous 'saucer test'. Finally, I sent Laura a little video of our efforts. She was 10,000 miles away in Sydney visiting her parents. She pinged back a wide-eyed emoji… then patiently rebottled our marmalade in small batches in the Towpath kitchen on her return. Moral of the story is don't bottle more than six litres in one batch or it will never set. And be thankful if you have a Laura in your life to correct your mistakes.

THE MAKING OF MARMALADES, JAMS AND JELLIES

I love the idea of being able to preserve something that's only in season for a short time and then appreciating it in a different form at another time of year. The joy of eating a mouthful of raspberry jam in the thick of winter is such a blessing. A little reminder of the long, balmy, sunny days where we top our granola with fresh raspberries, make a raspberry cordial for a thirst-quenching drink or bake a simple raspberry frangipane tart.

Another reason that I love making preserves is that it allows me to use up the week's excess fruits. A purist would probably be upset with this as they would only use the freshest ripest fruits, but for example, I might get in 10kg (22lb) of strawberries for the week and then on Friday realise that it's going to rain solidly all weekend and I won't use them all up.

Making marmalades, jams or jellies in large quantities is a labour of love. Every batch comes out differently. I use a thermometer as a guide. Once the jam reaches a temperature of 104.3°C/220°F, it should set. However, this is not always the case, so I rely on the saucer test. Put a plate in the fridge before you start. When you think the jam is at setting point, use the thermometer as a guide, then put a teaspoon on the cold plate. Leave in the fridge for 5 minutes and then run a finger through to see if the jam has set – if it has the jam will wrinkle rather than run.

Making marmalade in large quantities is problematic as Lori discovered. It will never set, it will reduce and turn very dark in colour. It must be done in smaller batches. One must be so patient.

SEVILLE ORANGE OR BLOOD ORANGE MARMALADE

Makes 1 litre/1¾ pints marmalade

1kg/2¼lb Seville or blood oranges
100ml/3½fl oz lemon juice
800g/1¾lb caster sugar

Notes

Some general rules when making marmalades, jams and jellies:

Always add lemon juice because it contains pectin which helps set the fruit. As you heat the fruit, the proteins change and form scum. Sometimes it is impossible to get rid of all the scum just by skimming it. If you add small blobs of butter on the scum and whisk it in, the butter reacts with these proteins and gets rid of the scum.

When sterilising for personal use, soak the kilner jars in hot, soapy water, then rinse with hot water and place the jars upside down in a low oven (around 100°C/212°F) to air dry. Put the marmalade, jam or ketchup into the warm, dry jars and seal immediately.

Wash the oranges, remove the buttons at the top, cut in half and juice.

Keep the juice in one container and any pulp that came out with the juice in another container. Spoon the remaining pith out of the juiced oranges (Seville oranges are much pithier than blood oranges) and add to the pulp container.

Lay a muslin cloth in a bowl and tip the pith/pulp mixture into it. Tie the cloth up tightly.

Using a sharp knife, thinly slice the orange peel halves into thin pieces. Place in a bowl and cover with the orange juice and 2.5 litres/4½ pints water. Add the pith and pulp tied up in their cloth and leave overnight or for up to 24 hours in the fridge or cool place.

The next day, place in a preserving pan along with the muslin bag, bring to the boil and then simmer until the peel is soft, mixing from time to time. This will take 1½–2 hours. Continue simmering until the contents of the pan are reduced by about one third. Remove the muslin bag and place in a bowl. When it is cool enough to handle, squeeze as much liquid from the bag into the preserving pan as possible, scraping the sides with a spatula. The pectin released will help the marmalade set.

Add the lemon juice and sugar. If I am using blood oranges, I add less sugar – about 600g/1lb 5oz – because they are sweeter than Seville. Stir and bring to the boil, making sure all the sugar dissolves. Skim off any scum that forms on the top. This will appear white and frothy on the surface of the marmalade.

Cook rapidly until setting point is reached – around 30–40 minutes. Use the saucer test (see page 19) to see whether the marmalade is set. If not, keep boiling, but remember to stir frequently so it doesn't catch. Once the setting point is reached, skim off any remaining scum and pour immediately into hot, sterilised jars.

RHUBARB JAM

This recipe can be used with forced rhubarb or field rhubarb. Field rhubarb is just as delicious and far more economical, but I love using forced rhubarb as it produces such a vibrantly coloured jam. Forced rhubarb literally means rhubarb that has been forced to grow. Initially the plants are grown normally outdoors for at least 2 years. They are then forced to grow indoors in dark sheds, excluding light to speed up growth and encourage thinner, longer and less woody stalks. It is brighter in colour, sweeter and more delicate than field rhubarb. By forcing it to grow, it is ready to eat about 6–8 weeks before the natural season. This normally lasts from January to the beginning of March. In the UK, most forced rhubarb is grown in the 'Yorkshire triangle', an area between Wakefield, Morley and Rothwell.

Makes 1 litre/1¾ pints

1kg/2¼lb forced rhubarb
600g/1lb 5oz jam sugar
100ml/3½fl oz lemon juice
large piece of ginger, peeled and
    sliced thinly (optional)

Wash and trim the rhubarb and cut into 3cm/1¼in pieces. As rhubarb varies in size, make sure to cut the rhubarb so it is all of similar size for even cooking. Put into a preserving pan or other non-reactive pan.

Add the sugar, lemon juice and ginger, if using. Mix well and leave overnight or for up to 48 hours.

Bring the mixture to the boil. Boil rapidly for about 12 minutes, removing any scum, then test for the setting point using the saucer test (see page 19).

Depending on how close you are to the setting point, cook for another 15 minutes and check again.

Once set, remove from the heat and immediately pour into hot, sterilised jars.

WILD GARLIC REVUELTOS

For me, wild garlic signifies the start of spring. The punchiness and brightness of wild garlic tells us that the days are getting longer. In season, wild garlic is so abundant that you see it everywhere. I'll go out foraging for it and many customers bring in bagfuls for me, so it appears on our menu all the time. I love serving this dish for breakfast or lunch. Revueltos is Spanish and is a cross between an omelette and a scrambled egg. It's a quick and delicious dish to make – the combination of the wild garlic, smoked paprika and lemon go so well together.

Serves 1

1 tablespoon olive oil, plus extra
    for frying revueltos
generous handful of wild garlic,
    washed and dried
2 eggs, plus 1 yolk
dash of double cream
salt and pepper
sweet smoked paprika, to sprinkle
wedge of lemon, to serve

Heat a small frying pan with the olive oil over a high heat. Quickly sauté the wild garlic in the pan and remove once it has wilted. Place to one side.

Mix the eggs, egg yolk and cream in a bowl, season with salt and pepper and beat well. Be cautious with the amount of salt you use.

Using the same frying pan, add enough olive oil so it generously coats the pan. Heat over a high heat and when the pan starts smoking, pour the egg mix into the pan. Let the egg mix sizzle and quickly move it around using a spatula so it looks like a cross between an omelette and scrambled eggs. When the eggs are still a bit wet on top, turn the pan off as the residual heat will continue to cook it.

Scatter the wild garlic over the top, then sprinkle with smoked paprika. Season. Turn out onto a plate so the wild garlic is on top. Place a wedge of lemon on the side.

Serve with hot toast and butter.

Notes
Wild garlic is great as a sauce, drizzled over beetroot and braised lentils. Blanch the garlic (or use raw) and blitz with lemon juice, olive oil and salt and pepper.

You can also make a delicious wild garlic pesto to toss through pasta or serve on the side with meat or fish.

Make a wild garlic aioli or add it raw to steamed clams and chorizo.

It's delicious chopped through a savoury tart or frittata.

MARCH

POACHED RHUBARB WITH BLOOD ORANGE

The combination of rhubarb with blood orange is a seasonal delight. At this time of year, often after a long and miserable winter, a little pick-me-up is a good thing. The vibrancy of rhubarb with the punchiness of blood orange makes everything feel better. This is perfect served on granola or porridge, and I also love it just with yoghurt and some seeds scattered over.

750g/1lb 10oz rhubarb, leaves
    trimmed away
6 bay leaves
handful of black peppercorns
1 cinnamon stick
4 whole allspice berries
4 star anise
½ vanilla pod, seeds scraped or
    1 teaspoon vanilla extract
2 sprigs rosemary
juice of 4 blood oranges, peel of 2
juice and peel of 1 lemon
250g/9oz sugar

Preheat the oven to 140°C fan/325°F/gas mark 3.

Rinse the rhubarb and cut into 5cm/2in pieces. Since rhubarb comes in different thicknesses, make sure the pieces are cut into similar sizes to make for even cooking.

Add the bay leaves, black peppercorns, cinnamon stick, allspice berries, star anise, vanilla pod and seeds or extract, rosemary, orange juice and peel, and lemon juice and peel. Dredge the fruit in the sugar.

Cover with foil and bake until the rhubarb is soft but not falling apart. This could take anywhere between 30–60 minutes, depending on the type of rhubarb, so check after 20 minutes.

Notes
This is a perfect example of making a cordial by poaching the fruit. If you want to make a rhubarb cordial, just add more liquid before poaching – I add in 500ml/18fl oz. You could either squeeze more blood oranges, add water or apple juice or a combination of all three. Since rhubarb acts like a sponge, a lot of liquid will come out of the fruit. Once cooked, strain the liquid – though keep some for the poached rhubarb. This is something I do whenever I'm poaching fruit. It's a no-brainer – two recipes in one!

FENNEL, CITRUS, RADICCHIO AND CAPER SALAD

This is another of our odes to winter citrus. I love the freshness of citrus in winter. It's like an instant zing, a wake-me-up for those dreary, dull days. This salad has become something of a tradition for our opening week each year – when I look back at all my menus over the last 10 years, this salad always appears. It's fresh, light, nourishing and easy to make.

Serves 4

1 head fennel, outer leaves
    removed
½ medium head radicchio,
1 grapefruit
3 blood oranges
3 clementines if in season
75ml/3fl oz best olive oil
1 lemon, juiced
1 tropea onion or 2 spring onions,
    thinly sliced on an angle
1 heaped tablespoon capers,
    drained
generous handful of flat-leaf
    parsley, roughly chopped
salt and pepper

Cut the fennel in half and thinly slice by hand or with a mandoline. If preparing in advance, coat the fennel lightly in some lemon juice to prevent the fennel from going brown and losing its lovely bright colour.

Cut off the end of the radicchio, remove the core and break into pieces.

Cut away the peel and pith from the grapefruit, oranges and clementines. Do this over a container as some of the juices will leak. Squeeze the peel into this container – you will be surprised by how much juice comes out of the discarded peel.

Thinly slice the fruit on the cross section. It becomes harder to slice as you get towards the end of the fruit. Separate the perfect-looking slices from the less-perfect slices.

Whisk together the olive oil, lemon juice and any juice from the container.

In a bowl, toss together the fennel, radicchio, tropea onion or spring onions, capers, parsley and the less-perfect citrus with the dressing and season.

Scatter the perfect slices of citrus on top and serve.

Notes
You could also scatter toasted hazelnuts over the top.

Roast the fennel first if it is very cold and grim out.

Substitute thinly sliced kohlrabi and radishes for the fennel or use all three.

A Bit of History

The Regent's Canal in East London, where Towpath makes its home, is a very different place to what it was in the nineteenth century when horses walked the narrow path along the water pulling everything from coal to fruit and even ice from Norway. In those days, the buildings along the canal were mostly red-brick warehouses, factories and wharves. The canal itself was strictly for business, a no man's land snaking through the city below street level.

During the infamous 'Big Freeze' in the winter of 1962-3, the canal froze so solidly that barges were trapped in a layer of ice for weeks. By the time it thawed, freight was being moved over land and the heyday of commercial canal navigation was effectively over. What ensued in East London was the slow dereliction of the canal and of many of the buildings running alongside it. Fast forward roughly 40 years. . .

The photographic studio/flat where I came to live with my then-husband Jason Lowe was a stone's throw from the Regent's Canal, although I didn't realise it in the winter of 2000 when I first came to visit him from Italy where I was living when we met. Jason liked to call our part of town 'the ass-end of London'. Even better were the words, 'East Fucking London', graffitied in bold on the wall outside the flat. My kids found this hilarious.

In so far as our little neighbourhood was concerned, Jason was visionary, and bold in a Fitzcarraldo kind of way. He foresaw its transformation and wanted to be a part of it. In the summer of 2009, he noticed something interesting happening directly across the canal from us. While most of the old warehouse buildings and factories nearby were being replaced by shiny modern new builds, the 1930s art-deco Bankstock building was being not so much restored as reimagined. The former factory had been stripped down to its original concrete-and-brick bones and its old accretions removed and replaced by a two-storey zinc, glass and wood rooftop addition. At the building's canalside feet, four metal roller-shutters and a 'For Sale' sign had appeared. Jason asked me to find out what was behind them.

The funny thing about physical spaces is that they almost always look smaller as bare empty shells than when they're crammed full of things. This was certainly the case regarding 'Kiosks 1, 2 and 3' as Beverly, the estate agent, referred to them. (The fourth kiosk, which to make matters more confusing was really the first kiosk counting left to right, was not at this point for sale, though it would eventually become our kitchen.) Kiosks 1 and 2 were roughly five metres wide and two metres deep

with grey breezeblock walls and rough concrete floors. Kiosk 3 was four metres wide, as shallow as its siblings and likewise a breezeblock and concrete rectangle, smaller than your average bus shelter and just as exposed to the elements. The ground outside the shutters was unpaved, scrabbly earth. The kiosks were separated from each other by thick concrete columns, not of the attractive design feature variety, but of the holding-up-the-building kind. There was no way of opening the whole thing up, no

hope of knocking down walls to make the three little spaces into a single smallish one. It was not exactly inspiring, but somehow full of possibility.

In the beginning, Jason was going to buy them with Flo Bayley, an incredibly talented designer and an even better friend. There was talk about opening a shop selling random things that Flo (an artful magpie) had collected and that Jason had picked up on his wanderings as a food photographer, but as ideas do, this one morphed into something else, in a sequence of events that went vaguely like this: Beverly the estate agent told us we'd lost our bid for the kiosks to someone who'd made a higher offer; Flo said something like, 'That's fine actually, I really liked it all better as a dream than a reality'; Jason asked Beverly to relay to the buyers that he'd be happy with only one of the kiosks if they didn't want them all. Time passed…

I was driving our little white Fiat 500 from London to Tuscany when, somewhere in Switzerland, my mobile rang and it was Beverly, saying that the buyers had backed out and we could have all three kiosks if we still wanted them. I rang Jason and he renewed the offer. It was accepted.

I don't remember the moment the shop idea gave way to the café or when exactly I started thinking to myself, 'I'll do this', but sometime over the next few weeks I did. There was only one problem. Well, two really, the first being that the spaces were way too small to house anything resembling a kitchen. This we resolved by deciding that any cooking that needed to be done would happen in the flat. The remaining dilemma was that now the kiosks had been purchased, there was not enough money to transform them into anything remotely inviting. Actually, there was no more money at all.

And so I asked my parents for a loan. We emailed them photographs. Subjected them to endless fantastications. Asked them to imagine what we were envisioning while staring at a picture of three tiny concrete boxes on a dusty patch of a disused canal. It was only years later (and yes, I've repaid them) on a visit to London, that my father took me aside and said he had to tell me something. 'Sweetie, hats off to you. I want you to know, way back in the beginning, when you told us what you wanted to do, I didn't see it. I just couldn't see it happening.' And so bless them doubly, my parents, whom I love infinitely for a thousand other reasons. That they put their money on a vision they couldn't fathom – because anything I wanted so much, they wanted for me.

FENNEL AND BERKSWELL GRATIN

You will see throughout the book that I love to use things up and not waste anything. This is the perfect dish for doing so. Berkswell is a raw sheep's milk cheese that is not dissimilar in taste to Parmesan and in texture to manchego. I often have Berkswell on the menu and so I end up with lots of bits and pieces. Melting them in a gratin is the perfect solution.

You can prepare this in advance and leave in the fridge until you are ready to cook. It is quite robust and can easily be reheated – it is lovely served the next day and will also last 2–3 days.

Serves 6–8

200g/7oz unsalted butter
2 tablespoons olive oil
4 onions, sliced
8 heads fennel, thinly sliced or
    shaved on a mandoline
4 cloves garlic, minced
4 bay leaves
2 sprigs thyme
75ml/3fl oz white wine
75ml/3fl oz full-fat milk
75ml/3fl oz double cream
250g/9oz Berkswell cheese,
    grated
½ lemon, juiced
salt and pepper

Notes
If you have a mixture of different cheese ends to use up, feel free to substitute for the Berkswell. I often use Parmesan, Lancashire, Cheddar, Ticklemore, blue cheese or a mix of these.

Preheat the oven to 210°C fan/450°F/gas mark 8.

Melt the butter and olive oil in a large saucepan over a medium heat.

Add the onions and sweat down until softened but not coloured – about 10 minutes.

Add the fennel, garlic, bay leaves and thyme. Cook for 5–10 minutes on a low heat to start softening the fennel, but don't soften too much as the gratin will be cooked again in the oven. It's just a lovely way to start the cooking process and get all the different flavours to know one another.

Now add the white wine and bring to the boil. Cook for a few minutes.

Add the milk and cream and bring to the boil so the milk and cream start to reduce and thicken. You want the liquid to be quite thick.

Once the liquid has reduced, season with salt and pepper, take off the heat and add a couple of handfuls of the grated Berkswell. Stir in the lemon juice. Check the seasoning again.

Take a 30 x 20 x 6cm/12 x 8 x 2½in rectangular roasting tray and put in a layer of the fennel mix. Season and sprinkle over a layer of Berkswell.

Keep on layering until the tray is full and all the mix is used up. Finish with Berkswell so it will go brown and crispy on top.

Bake for around 40 minutes, until the fennel is completely cooked. If it looks like it is getting too brown, turn down the heat.

Serve with a crisp, fresh lemony salad.

ROAST CROWN PRINCE SQUASH, RAINBOW CHARD, CHICKPEA AND SAFFRON STEW

This stew is a regular on the menu at the beginning and end of our season. It feels hearty and warming yet at the same time an injection of health. Substitute any other greens, squash and pulses for the rainbow chard, squash and chickpeas. This dish is vegan, but if you are not vegan, I recommend grating some Parmesan over the top before serving.

Serves 6–8

For the chickpeas
250g/9oz dried chickpeas, covered and soaked overnight in water or 550g/1¼lb cooked
1 head garlic, cut in half horizontally
2 red chillies, whole
nice glug of olive oil
handful of peppercorns
3 bay leaves
2 sprigs rosemary
2 sprigs thyme
salt and pepper

For the roast squash
650g/1lb 7oz crown prince squash, peeled, seeds removed and cut into 3cm/1¼in pieces
4 tablespoons olive oil

Preheat the oven to 210°C fan/450°F/gas mark 8.

Start by draining the chickpeas (which you've soaked overnight). Place in a saucepan – the chickpeas will expand quite substantially during cooking so make sure you use a large-enough saucepan. They will also cook more evenly if not overcrowded. Cover with 1.5 litres/2¾ pints water.

Bring to the boil and remove all scum. Add in all the other ingredients for the chickpeas (don't hesitate to use any other leftover bits in the fridge that would be good for the stock). Turn down to a simmer and cook until the chickpeas are tender but not mushy, around 1–1½ hours. At this point, season with salt and pepper.

While the chickpeas are cooking, prepare the squash. I like to cut my squash at different angles for aesthetic reasons, but just make sure they are all a similar size so that they cook evenly. Coat the squash with olive oil, and season. Roast the squash on a high heat to get a lovely caramelisation and colour. Make sure you don't overcrowd the roasting tray as the squash will end up steaming rather than browning. The squash should cook within 25–35 minutes – you want the squash to be cooked through but still holding its shape, otherwise it will go mushy once in the broth.

In another large saucepan, sweat down the onions and garlic in the olive oil over a low heat until soft and sweet – about 10 minutes. Add the red chillies.

Add the rainbow chard stalks and continue to cook on a gentle heat for around 5 minutes until they too soften. Season.

Add the saffron and its liquid. If you have excess saffron strands left in your container, swirl around with a little water and pour in – don't waste any of that delicious flavour.

For the broth

4 red onions, sliced

4 cloves garlic, minced

4 tablespoons olive oil

2 red chillies, whole

7 stalks of rainbow chard, stalk
and leaf separated and stalks
cut into 1.5cm/¾in slices.

20 saffron strands, soaked in
100ml/3½fl oz boiling water
for at least 10 minutes

300g/10½oz tinned whole plum
tomatoes, blitzed or mashed

1 lemon, juiced

salt and pepper

Add the tinned tomatoes and cook for another
10 minutes until it is slightly reduced.

Now add the cooked chickpeas and their liquid,
but remove any stocky bits that were thrown into the
chickpea cooking liquid. Bring to a boil and simmer
for around 25 minutes.

At this point, add the roasted squash and cook for
another 25 minutes, so all the ingredients get to know
one another. Season as you go, and at the end, check
the seasoning and add enough lemon juice to cut
through the richness.

When ready to serve, add the chopped rainbow
chard leaves. They will only take a few minutes to cook
in the hot broth.

Serve with a drizzle of olive oil.

Notes
If you use a lot of Parmesan, always keep the rinds.
They are perfect for a recipe like this, where you
can include the rinds with the onions and garlic when
preparing the broth to add a delicious, nutty, creamy flavour.

CHICKEN DUMPLING BROTH

I have vivid memories of my mum serving me chicken broth and dumplings as a kid whenever I was coming down with something. It really is so nurturing and soothing, and warms your whole body up, making you feel better instantly. The origins of this dish come from when the Jews had to flee Egypt from persecution and they literally had to run with their unleavened bread – matzo – and so the matzo ball evolved. A way of using the unleavened bread by blitzing it to form fine breadcrumbs.

For me, dumplings epitomise comfort. Put any type of dumpling in front of me and you will hear shrieks of pure joy. Wonton, pierogi, ravioli, manti, gyoza, khinkali, any type of dim sum… I could eat them all day. Plus, I love a sauce and so the fact that most dumplings come with a sauce on the side makes it even more exciting, especially when in combination with broth (arguably the ultimate sauce) – it doesn't get much better!

Serves 4, makes 16–20 dumplings

For the dumplings

4 eggs, beaten
4 tablespoons cold fizzy water
2 tablespoons beef, chicken
  or duck fat, melted (or veg oil)
2 tablespoons vegetable oil
140g/5oz matzo meal
¼ teaspoon baking powder
2 teaspoons salt
pepper

3 litres/5¼ pints chicken stock
  (see below)

Combine the eggs, fizzy water, fat and vegetable oil.

In a separate bowl, mix the matzo meal, baking powder, salt and some pepper.

Pour in the egg mixture and mix gently until combined, being careful not to overmix.

Leave, uncovered, in the fridge for at least 1 hour.

When ready to cook, bring the stock to the boil. While the stock is warming, roll the dumpling mix into 3cm/1¼in- sized balls.

Place the balls into the stock, bring to the boil and then simmer, covered, for 40–60 minutes until cooked through (cut one in half to check). Check the seasoning of the broth.

When ready, ladle the broth into bowls, add three dumplings to each and a generous grind of pepper. I always start with three but the matzo mix will make extra and you'll definitely want to go back for more!

Notes

At Towpath, chicken is often on the menu, so I always have a large container of chicken stock in the fridge, made using the carcasses from the roast chickens and the leftover veg and herbs.

Place chicken bones and/or carcasses in a pan with any type of veg scraps you have on hand. We have a container that sits in the fridge at Towpath and is constantly topped up with veg scraps we don't use during the day. Cover the pan with water and bring to the boil. Skim off any scum, turn the heat down to a really low simmer and very gently cook for at least 4 hours. Strain, cool and use.

You may even get enough chicken fat from the top of the stock to use when making your dumplings and thus not be wasting anything at all!

If you want to make stock but do not have any leftover bones, you can always pick up chicken bones for nothing, roast them in the oven beforehand and you are ready to go.

OLIVE OIL CAKE

This is the perfect accompaniment to a coffee. Light, fluffy and moist, this cake is delicious served morning, day and night. We have it on the counter every day and the recipe is based on one from Lori's book *Beaneaters & Bread Soup*. The recipe comes from Lisa Contini Bonacossi, the late matriarch of the wonderful Capezzana winery which sits on ancient farmland that has been producing wine and olive oil as far back as the time of Charlemagne. When we are lucky enough, we use their olive oil at Towpath. And there is nothing better for this cake.

Serves 12

butter, for greasing
3 eggs
300g/10½oz caster sugar
175ml/6fl oz best quality olive oil
180ml/6¼fl oz full-fat milk
1 orange, zested and juiced
325g/11½oz self-raising flour,
    plus extra for dusting

Preheat the oven to 160°C fan/350°F/gas mark 4.

Line, butter and flour a 24cm/9½in cake tin.

In a large mixing bowl or mixer, beat together the eggs and sugar until pale yellow. This should take about 5 minutes.

Slowly, in a continuous stream and on a high speed, pour in the olive oil, milk, orange zest and juice. You may need to lower the speed towards the end to prevent the mix from splattering everywhere.

Gently fold in the flour, until fully incorporated.

Pour the batter into the prepared tin. Bake for about 45 minutes, until golden brown and a toothpick or skewer inserted into the centre comes out clean. Leave to cool in the tin.

April

A Realm of One's Own

We've come to think of Towpath as our own tiny realm. A dustmote in the Big Smoke. But nonetheless not without its own vision, values and what's evolved into a rather long list of what we do – and what we don't. Even though we opened with no clear business plan beyond, 'let's see what we can do with this funny little space', from the very beginning we were all on the same page about the big things. Which is good, because after all, this was where we would be spending our days and, as Annie Dillard writes, 'how we spend our days is, of course, how we spend our lives.' No small matter.

We wanted to create a place with a small-town sense of friendliness and belonging, but also a vibrancy – a bit like a schoolyard at lunchtime, where you could just turn up and know that, at least until the bell rang, there would be an escape from the tedium of being pinned to a desk with a pencil in your hand trying to learn long division. We dreamed of a place where every table would not be occupied by someone staring into a device, lost to the world around them. So, we asked ourselves, what kind of invitation could we offer, above and beyond what we put on people's plates and in their glasses, that would entice them to put it all down and rest a bit? Like on a porch in Alabama.

First of all, it meant taking a decidedly low-tech approach ourselves. This proved easy enough since we had zero enthusiasm for spending our energies creating a website, blogging, instagramming, tweeting or doing whatever else one does to establish an 'on-line presence'. We wanted to be in the world doing physical things. More like on a farm than in an office. Laura wanted to be cooking and I (less usefully but with equal enthusiasm) wanted to create homely little still lifes from the daily objects that surrounded us, arrange flowers in old metal jugs and have interesting conversations with whoever ambled up to our counter.

In practical terms this meant that there would be no website, no phone number, and no wifi. More controversially, though not intentionally so, there

would be no takeaway cups with their attendant paraphernalia, which we had visions of being crammed into the already overflowing (and woefully insufficient) bins along the towpath or sunken like shipwreck on the murky bottom of the canal. And anyway, we wanted people to stay – even if that just meant standing at the bar for a few minutes with a cappuccino, Italian style.

As for the coffee itself, from the very beginning we decided to keep it simple. Beans from our friend Alessandro Staderini of Piansa. *Dieci Magnifici Più Uno* he calls the blend – 10 arabica beans sourced from all over the world for their aroma, flavour and balance, plus one robusta for that little kick and beautiful crema, roasted in small batches at Piansa's *torrefazione* just outside of Florence. To the dismay of some, there would be no decaf (as we only had room for one grinder). And no filter coffee or cold brew. Just the best possible Italian-style coffees we could make with the wonderful Marzocco machine Alessandro gave us when we told him we wanted to bring our favourite coffee to London. To the utter horror of others, we decided to use only one type of milk – rich, sweet, full fat and delicious, which we get from Northiam Dairy in Sussex. No semi-skimmed. No soy, oat, almond, rice or other 'non-milk milk'. More on this in a moment.

Simplicity suited us both practically and temperamentally. The former, because after all, at least at the very beginning, we were cooking from home and operating out of a space that was roughly the size of a market stall – a set-up that was proving complicated enough as it was. The latter, because we were of the opinion that there might already be a tad *too* much choice out in the world. We didn't want to be the place that offered everything, any way you wanted it.

I don't think we're the only ones who find supermarkets exhausting. All that wandering around fluorescent-lit aisles only to find yourself glassy-eyed in front of the yoghurt section and its orderly arrangement of varieties with their various flavours, fat contents, milk bases, container sizes and expiration dates, searching for the one little pot to take home. We took our cue from friends like Leila McAlister whose café and grocery is a prayer answered for anyone prone to being overwhelmed by choice. Here is a person deeply passionate about all things gastronomic (not to mention social, artistic and political), who has winnowed through all manner of edibles to offer up a very personal, and in our opinion, wondrous collection of delights. Florets of rosy pink radicchio, sticky sweet prunes from France, strings of Polish sausages, big yellow tins of strong, loose tea. Ahhh, we say. Thank you.

This approach is not for everyone. Perhaps that's exactly the point. Nothing is. Surely there are more than enough places in this big city to satisfy every proclivity. The way we see it, trying to please everyone ends up turning your rich broth into something that, as they'd say in Italy, *non sa di nulla.* Tastes of nothing. Hence our funny little queendom that reflects the things that make our hearts sing. Which in turn gives us the energy to get out of bed on a rainy morning and do what we do as if we really cared. Because we do.

We have occasionally changed our minds about some things. Debit cards, for example. For years we didn't take them because somehow the notion of card machines got tangled up with our general aversion to the virtual, rather than the physical world. But after the umpteenth time we found ourselves pointing someone in the direction of the nearest cash point, in an increasingly cashless world, we asked ourselves, why? What did we have against cards? Nothing, it turned out.

This year we had a serious look at what we call, 'the milk question'. What about alternative milks? Semi-skimmed cow's milk? We have nothing but admiration for vegans – ok, except maybe the ones who are either smugly or militantly so. Our hearts go out to everyone living with food allergies. And despite tempting them mercilessly, we wholly commiserate with the weight conscious. But when we sat around, talked about it and played out the logistics, we began to imagine the customer who would only drink almond milk or perhaps oat milk or only Oatly oat milk, and the special jugs we would have to have to make sure they were not contaminated with cow's milk, and on and on until we were cross-eyed at the Sisyphusness of it all. We also couldn't get our heads around the fact that oat milk – made from oats (one of the least expensive ingredients in a kitchen), water and rapeseed oil – costs exactly twice as much as milk from our dairy's lovely single-herd cows grazing in open fields, living in barns and being milked twice a day.

I don't think we're being intentionally negative. On a fundamental level, we're responding to something we'd collectively learned in all the years standing out on the towpath trying to make people happy – whatever we do, whatever we offer, there will *always* be someone who wants it slightly otherwise. And so, with that thought in mind, though not engraved in stone and with no malice intended, we've stuck with our one beautiful full-fat milk. But, who knows, we might try our hand at making our own oat milk one day. *

If only the laptop dilemma could be so easily resolved. Perhaps with a big sign, as many have suggested, next to the chalked-up lunch menu and the flowers my friend Hilary brought from her garden: 'PLEASE, NO LAPTOPS DURING BUSY MEALTIMES'. This sign could go next to the other signs people have asked us to post about our lack of decaf, our no takeaway drinks (*unless* you bring your own cup) and our no hot drinks after 5pm. This is a country that loves to be told the rules. Go to any park and it's the first thing you see when you walk past the gate. A great big list of everything you can and can't do. We wish it could simply be a matter of common sense.

All this is not to minimise the fact that, to grossly generalise, most of us, most of the time, seem to feel overwhelmed with all that is on our metaphorical plates – so much so that when we stop to sit down in front of an actual meal, we instinctively feel like it's also the perfect time to carry on with our work, catch up on emails, 'like' someone's post or Google that forgotten name. Tick a few things off the infinite list. In a perfect world, we wish we could all allow ourselves to take a minute to just look out on the water and see what the coots are up to, gaze up at the sky, actually taste our food or, at the very least, consider the notion that the stranger sitting across from us might not want to spend their lunch staring at the back of our laptop.

More than one customer has accused us of being up ourselves – to our faces or occasionally, as my son Julien once delighted in showing me, in a righteously indignant online rant. We've been asked more than once to justify the fine print of our unwritten rules: 'Why is it ok to write in a notebook but not on a laptop? Read an old-fashioned book? Draw on paper?' For no reason that can easily be stated in words. Because we're luddites? Control freaks? Because it just feels different? To us, it somehow does.

There's an upside to our not having all those signs with rules on them – it encourages us to talk to each other, however awkwardly, about how we want to live in this modern world. We don't pretend to know. But we're interested in the question. And it makes us happy to be a place that invites the conversation.

* Since writing this, the kitchen's been experimenting with making our own oat milk. It's a lovely, pale biscuity colour and tastes, well, oaty. It can only be served cold because there's nothing added to it to keep it from separating when steamed. Not everyone is happy.

GRANOLA

This is one of Towpath's breakfast staples. As the seasons change so will the fruit served with granola. At the beginning of the Towpath season I like to serve it with rhubarb, blood oranges, apples or pears, either fresh, poached or as a compote. As we move into spring-summer, I use all types of berries as well as cherries and other stone fruits. In autumn, it's quinces, apples and pears again. You can also choose any other nuts or seeds or in different combinations. Perfect for using up any that are floating around and need using up.

This recipe makes quite a large quantity and it lasts for weeks in an airtight container. Judging from our regular customers who come daily or at least several times a week for breakfast, the ones who order granola ALWAYS order granola. If you are a lover of granola, you are going to want to eat a lot of it, so be sensible and make a large batch! If you want to make your own yoghurt to eat with the granola, see overleaf.

Makes about 2kg/4½lb

175ml/6fl oz sunflower, vegetable
   or a neutral oil
600g/1lb 5oz honey
100g/3½oz brown sugar
few drops of vanilla extract
2 pinches of cinnamon
1 teaspoon salt
800g/1¾lb jumbo oats
250g/9oz whole almonds,
   in their skins
250g/9oz pumpkin seeds
250g/9oz sunflower seeds
2 handfuls of raisins

Preheat the oven to 145°C fan/325°F/gas mark 3.

In a medium-sized saucepan, put in the oil, honey, brown sugar, vanilla extract, cinnamon and salt. Slowly bring to the boil – if you do this over a high heat, the mixture will overflow unless you watch it at all times.

Gently stir as it comes to the boil. Check that the sugar has completely dissolved and you have a smooth liquid.

Place the oats, almonds, pumpkin seeds and sunflower seeds in a big heatproof bowl or tray.

Pour the liquid mixture carefully over the oats, nuts and seeds. Give it a good stir, making sure the oats, nuts and seeds are evenly mixed and coated.

Spread thinly on greaseproof-lined flat baking trays. I normally use two large trays for this quantity. The thinner the layer the more evenly it will cook and the quicker it colours, which will make your life much easier as you won't have to constantly take the granola out of the oven and turn it.

Bake for around 25–40 minutes until the granola is golden and caramelised. You may need to turn it over if one side is browning more than the other.

Remove from the oven and leave to cool slightly for around 5–10 minutes. Break up the granola using your hands – the warmer the granola is the easier it is to break up. Add the raisins and mix thoroughly.

Serve with yoghurt and seasonal or poached fruit or compote on top.

YOGHURT

Before opening Towpath, Lori and I had endless conversations about what we should and shouldn't offer. One thing we felt strongly about was trying to make everything ourselves (excluding the bread. Best leave that to the professionals!). Up until a few years ago we were only serving our own yoghurt. I had discovered that making yoghurt was so easy and so satisfying – it became my pride and joy. Every few days I would swaddle up the jars of yoghurt in a cosy green blanket, place them somewhere warm and say 'night night'. This would always bring a smile to my face.

The recipe we use is from a Harold McGee piece in the *New York Times* exclaiming the wonder and delight of making one's own yoghurt. We buy our milk from Northiam Dairy and as we've become much busier, their yoghurt too. It is so delicious, rich and creamy, but when I can, I will still make our own.

Makes 1 litre/1¾ pints

1 litre/1¾ pints full-fat milk
3 heaped tablespoons yoghurt
(from an earlier batch or
shop-bought if you are
starting fresh)

Thermometer

Heat the milk in a saucepan to between 82–88°C/180–190°F, just before it comes to a boil. It will form a thin skin on the top. Leave the milk to cool until it reaches between 46–49°C/115–120°F.

Once the milk has cooled, in a separate bowl, mix together the yoghurt with a small cup of the warm milk using a wooden spoon. Mix well. Add this to the saucepan of warm milk. From this point onwards you need to be very gentle! Carefully stir the mixture and pour into a clean glass jar with a lid. We use 1-litre/1¾-pint kilner jars.

Wrap the jar in a couple of tea towels or a small blanket and set it to rest in a warm place (taking care not to jiggle the jar) for 6 hours. You'll notice in winter when the outdoor temperature is cooler that the yoghurt will take longer to set. Sometimes I even leave it overnight. In summer, if you leave it out too long it will become very tart.

Store in the fridge and eat within a week, taking care to hold back 3 tablespoons for your next batch!

Don't despair if the yoghurt comes out quite differently from batch to batch. I can sometimes make yoghurt for weeks and it sets beautifully, then the next time it's all gloopy and claggy. If this happens, I start again with a fresh starter.

PEAS AND BROAD BEANS IN THEIR PODS WITH TICKLEMORE

A regular at Towpath will know that my style of cooking is very simple. I don't like to mess with the ingredients. If you have something beautiful and seasonal, why on earth would you want to do too much to it? What you want to do is showcase this single ingredient and let it shine. The perfect example of this is my homage to the very first of the season's peas and broad beans. Giacinta and Alberto, our Italian suppliers who turn up with a van of produce every Tuesday from Italy, always deliver the first broad beans and peas. The peas and broad beans are so sweet, fresh and crunchy at the beginning of the season that they have to be served as is. As the season continues they change, toughening so they need to be cooked – they become a completely different vegetable.

The sweetness of the peas and broad beans with the saltiness of Ticklemore is one of utter deliciousness. Ticklemore is a pasteurised goat's cheese, young and fresh, with a chalky texture and a slight lemony flavour. I used to always serve the peas and broad beans with ricotta until one day Neal's Yard Dairy ran out. I asked them what would be a good replacement and they recommended Ticklemore. It was a next-level suggestion. Thank you, Neal's Yard, for putting an English twist on this dish!

Serves 2

250g/9oz peas and/or
   broad beans in their pods
   (must be the first of the season)
75g/3oz Ticklemore (or ricotta)

Very simply, place everything on a plate and serve with fresh bread and butter.

CONFIT GARLIC AND GOAT'S CURD

This is a beautiful use of early spring wet garlic, which is the first of the season garlic that hasn't been hung to dry and so is much sweeter and milder than normal garlic. Save the remaining confit oil for cooking or to confit more garlic. The oil can be reused up to three times for confiting the garlic.

Serves 4

8 heads wet garlic
around 750ml/1⅓ pints olive oil
4 sprigs thyme
4 sprigs rosemary
4 bay leaves
handful of peppercorns
4 slices sourdough bread
400g/14oz goat's curd
    (or other goat's cheese) at
    room temperature
salt and pepper

Preheat the oven to 130°C fan/300°F/gas mark 2.

Cut the top two-thirds of the stalks off the garlic heads and discard. Wash the heads if necessary (sometimes they can be a bit gritty). Place them snugly in a heavy-bottomed casserole dish, bottoms down. Pour in enough olive oil to cover the garlic heads entirely. Add the herbs, peppercorns and a pinch of salt. Over a low flame, bring the oil to a gentle boil.

Remove the casserole from the heat. Cover with a cartouche (a piece of greaseproof paper cut to the size of the casserole) and then a tight-fitting lid. Bake until the garlic is soft – about 45 minutes–1½ hours. To test whether the garlic is cooked, remove one head from the casserole using a pair of tongs. If all the cloves are soft, it is cooked. Remove from the oven and leave to cool until warm.

Right before serving, toast the bread, cut the slices in half, then cover generously with goat's curd. Sprinkle with salt and pepper. Place the toast on a platter or individual plates. Place one garlic head on top of each half piece of toast. Drizzle over some of the confit oil and serve with a finger bowl. You can also scatter the bay leaves and herbs over the top.

The best way to eat this is to squeeze the head of garlic until the cloves fall out and then spread the soft cloves over the cheese.

APRIL

KOHLRABI, BROWN SHRIMP, CAPERS, MINT AND ROCKET

Kohlrabi is also known as a German turnip and is part of the cabbage family. It is an extremely versatile vegetable and is all about crispness and texture. This recipe is inspired from the salad we used to make at Rochelle Canteen, which in turn came from Fergus Henderson of St. John. I love how fresh this salad is, but it's also robust, so people still love to order it even on a cooler day.

Serves 4

3 kohlrabi, peeled, halved and
    thinly sliced (use a mandoline
    if you have one)
2 spring onions, sliced thinly
    on an angle
2 tablespoons capers, drained
2 handfuls of mint, picked and
    chopped
150g/5½oz brown shrimp
4 handfuls of rocket
1 lemon, juiced
3 tablespoons best olive oil
salt and pepper

Put the kohlrabi, spring onions, capers, mint, brown shrimp and rocket into a bowl. Dress lightly with lemon juice and olive oil. I always dress my salads lightly so I don't use all of the dressing to begin with. Give the salad a good toss and season with salt and pepper. Taste and add more dressing accordingly. You want it to taste punchy.

Gently pile up on individual plates, making sure all of the components are visible.

Notes
Since kohlrabi is more about texture than full of flavour, it can be paired with many things. Serve it with radishes, spring onions, goat's curd or feta. Add to fennel. Flake through smoked mackerel instead of brown shrimp. Add in some pickled cucumber. Make a coleslaw with it and dress with mayonnaise.

MONK'S BEARD, MARINDA TOMATO TONNATO

A few years ago monk's beard was almost unknown in English kitchens. In Tuscany it's referred to as agretti (literally 'little sour' things). It is reminiscent of samphire, similar in its crunch and texture, but definitely not in taste – not salty at all and tastes more like spinach.

Tonnato sauce is traditionally seen in vitello tonnato, a sublime summery dish of cold, thinly sliced roast veal that is smothered in the sauce. The sauce can also be served with thinly sliced pork or used to dress the monk's beard and served with a soft-boiled egg. I love to dip crudités into the tonnato sauce or simply spread it on fresh bread.

Serves 4, makes 475g/1lb 1oz

For the tonnato sauce

1 egg
1 tablespoon Dijon mustard
200g/7oz tinned tuna in brine
3 anchovy fillets
½ tablespoon red wine vinegar
½ tablespoon lemon juice
225ml/8fl oz sunflower, vegetable, or a neutral oil
salt and pepper

To serve

6 marinda tomatoes, eyes removed, thinly sliced on the cross section
400g/14oz tonnato sauce (see above)
handful of capers, drained
300g/10½oz bunch monk's beard, pink woody tips removed, washed thoroughly
½ lemon, juiced
2 tablespoons best olive oil

To make the tonnato sauce, place the egg, mustard, 150g/5½oz of the tinned tuna, the anchovy fillets, vinegar and lemon juice with 1 tablespoon of water in a Magimix or large bowl. Blend or whisk together well.

Slowly pour in the oil till you have a thick, rich sauce. You may need to add more lemon or water if the emulsification is getting too thick. Season with salt and pepper and blitz in the last 50g/2oz of tinned tuna.

Place the tomatoes on a platter, slightly overlapping each piece. Thickly smother the tonnato sauce over the tomatoes. Sprinkle over the capers. Season with pepper (not salt!).

Blanch the monk's beard in boiling water for 3 minutes. Drain well and season with salt and pepper and dress with lemon juice and olive oil before adding on top of the salad.

Home Cooking

However challenging our set-up might seem today, it's positively luxurious compared to the one we first opened with one frigid grey February morning in 2010. That first year our three little kiosks were configured thus: bar, seating, micro bike shop (from which my daughter's then boyfriend James built terrifying and beautiful fixies for the brave to cycle around London in). Noticeably absent from this equation was a kitchen, which in truth was not so much lacking as hidden just over the bridge on the other side of the canal in Jason's and my flat. Which already doubled as his photographic studio. An awkward arrangement. But it made a family of us and taught us a kind of flexibility and resourcefulness that would have been hard to learn any other way.

Mornings were like musical chairs. Laura would show up at the flat just as I was setting off to roll up the shutters on the canal. Two second-hand Lucozade fridges hummed in the sitting room next to wooden crates of oranges and 25-kilo sacks of flour and sugar. Jars of homemade pickles and marmalade lined shelves where once there were books. Sometimes the kitchen was already occupied by another cook, someone like Mark Hix, whose food Jason photographed for a weekly column in the late, lamented *Independent* newspaper. Usually Laura had help – Jason's assistant Joe perhaps or my daughter Micky – but insofar as the Towpath kitchen was concerned, she ruled the roost. No small feat in a household with no shortage of strong opinions, gastronomic or otherwise. In short order, Laura had our respect and our attention for both her insane work ethic – the girl was a Trojan – and because she responded to the constraints of her kitchen like a bull to a matador's red cape. What could we do but step aside?

On a practical level, this meant that she satisfied her need to make people feel properly, lovingly fed, even from a distance, by having us make everything we could ourselves. Marmalade, compotes, jellies and jams. Granola with oats and toasted nuts inspired by her time at Melrose and Morgan. Yoghurt from Harold McGee's *On Food and Cooking,* a lesson in thermometers and patience, resulting in big glass jars of the stuff that she swaddled in a soft green blanket until it set just so. In lieu of fried eggs, she made tortillas with potatoes and onions, and savoury tarts with the most buttery of crusts. And that was just breakfast. She brewed ginger beer from a recipe Harry Lester gave her when they cooked together at his auberge in the Auvergne. When it was ready, she decanted it into flip-top bottles to keep at the bar. It was so lively we handled it like an explosive.

While Laura was cooking at the flat, we at the bar were delegated a few culinary tasks of our own. These we carried out with some trepidation (we never knew when Laura would pop over to see how we were doing) and the help of one portable electric burner (which sat on a shin-high metal shelf behind the counter), a large pot-bellied urn, a Dualit toaster and a reconditioned panini press we'd found off Brick Lane.

We used our little burner in the mornings to make porridge (pinhead oats, which when properly creamy and nutty were transferred to the urn) and at lunch to warm some sort of topping for a crostino (braised cavolo nero for instance). At approximately 12.30 a soup or stew took porridge's place in the urn. The toaster was used for the obvious. There was always some kind of salad at lunch, the assembly of which inevitably required frequent sprints to the house for handfuls of chervil or some other ingredient we'd run short of. The panini machine was busy all day long toasting cheese sandwiches – the bane of Laura's existence.

Towpath's grilled cheese sandwich deserves a paragraph all its own. Maybe even a whole page.

We spent ages before we opened doing two things: deciding what we would call ourselves (which was no easier than naming a child) and dreaming up what we would serve to our imaginary customers. Back when I was still based in Tuscany, Jason would sometimes surprise us with a giant wedge of Montgomery's Cheddar from Neal's Yard Dairy. We thought it was sublime – England's answer to Italy's *parmigiano*. The appearance of this cheese in our lives coincided with my obsession with bread making and Jason's decision to make jelly from the quinces in our garden. I'd always loved the trees with their pale pink blossoms and strange, fuzzy, pear-shaped fruits that looked like something out of a renaissance still life and smelled like some heavenly mixture of apples and roses, guava and musk, but I hadn't the faintest idea what to do with them, beyond putting them in a bowl to be admired.

The making of quince jelly requires a patient cook. First there is the chopping and boiling of the rock-hard fruits. Then the molasses-slow straining of pulp through muslin. Drip… drip… drip. And finally the painstaking boiling of the resulting juice with sugar until the exact moment it reaches its fabled (though hardly obvious) setting point. The reward is a deep garnet-hued jelly, tasting of honeyed apple, pear and rose.

Since grilled cheese sandwiches are a staple comfort food of many American childhoods, mine included, and we were all fans of Bill Oglethorpe's Borough Market stall, which had taken the toasted cheese sandwich to new heights, it was only a matter of time before we came up with a version of our own. Which happened one cold autumn day in Tuscany when we heated up a big cast-iron skillet, buttered slices of homemade sourdough, filled them with grated Montgomery's Cheddar and spring onion and fried them on both sides until they were crisp and golden and oozing cheese. Lastly, we cut our sandwiches in half, put them on plates and, in a play on the Spanish manchego and membrillo theme, heaped great spoonfuls of quince jelly on the side. Swoonworthy. And *exactly* the thing we could imagine people eating out on the canal on a cold, damp London day.

Everything about these sandwiches miraculously evoked that lovely woozy childhood feeling of full-bellied contentment. Like Pooh and his honey pot. Yet it was grown up too. Elevated, possibly, by the delightful surprise of the sweet, tangy jelly. And by the fact that (unlike the grilled cheese sandwiches of my youth) each ingredient was exceptional in its own right. Not to mention the happy discovery that our cheese sandwich begged to be quaffed down with a tannic red

wine. We hoped that people would like it as much as we did. But then as they say – be careful what you ask for.

It took a minute, but we at the bar eventually realised that making each sandwich to order (from slicing the bread to grating the cheese) was neither charming nor efficient. And so we handed the prepping of the sandwiches back to the kitchen, which was when Laura realised that the shape of our lovely round loaves of sourdough made it impossible for the sandwiches to be a standard size; that cutting the bread in neat uniform slices was as hard as drawing a perfect circle for anyone but her; that it took eons to grate the amount of cheese we were going through and that we would need industrial quantities of quince jelly to make it through the year.

Eventually these issues were resolved – or at least resolutely faced. The lovely Ben MacKinnon of e5 Bakehouse asked Laura for a paper cutout of her ideal loaf and he made us just that. We've invested in a series of commercial graters. (They never live long in our kitchen.) The very good news is that said kitchen is now just where it should be – right out on the towpath with the rest of us. Which means that there are now fried eggs *too*. And lamb chops, roast chicken, fish pies and a thousand other delights that Laura's dreamed up. So, in actual fact, we don't really need to make cheese sandwiches any more. Except that somehow we all feel that we do. Even Laura. It's part of our origin story. Which is why every year after Towpath has been tucked up and put to bed for winter, she finds herself all alone in the kitchen making a 100 litres of quince jelly. A year's supply of honeyed sweetness.

ARTICHOKES, COCO BEANS, CIME DI RAPA AND AIOLI

Spring is the season for the morellini artichoke, which is not a baby artichoke but a particular variety that has an incredibly sweet aftertaste and works wonderfully with the bitterness of the cime di rapa. It feels like spring in a mouthful. If you can't find smooth-skinned morellini artichokes, use any small artichoke you can get your hands on.

This recipe has many variations. Since the beans and artichoke base are cooked separately, you can replace the beans with farro, chickpeas or lentils. You can also swap the cime di rapa with cicoria, puntarella leaves, rocket leaves or spinach.

Serves 8

For the artichokes
8 tablespoons olive oil
1 teaspoon coriander seeds
1 teaspoon fennel seeds
2 onions, thinly sliced
½ leek, sliced on a slight angle, soaked in cold water to remove any grit
2 celery sticks, sliced on a slight angle
1 medium carrot, sliced on a slight angle
½ head fennel, outer hard pieces removed, sliced on a slight angle
4 cloves garlic, minced
4 bay leaves
½ teaspoon chilli flakes
10–15 morellini artichokes
2 tablespoons white wine vinegar
200ml/7fl oz white wine
3 tablespoons lemon juice, plus ½ lemon, sliced, for the artichoke water
salt and pepper

Warm 4 tablespoons of the olive oil for the artichokes in a large saucepan over a medium heat. When warm, add the coriander and fennel seeds, onions and leeks and cook over a gentle heat until softened but not coloured – about 10 minutes. Season.

Now add the rest of the olive oil with the celery, carrot, fennel, garlic, bay leaves and chilli flakes. Continue to cook over a gentle heat for 15 minutes until the rest of the vegetables start softening. Season.

While the veg is cooking, prep the artichokes. Fill a bowl with water and the sliced lemon. This is for the prepped artichokes so they don't turn brown. Cut the top third of the artichoke leaves off. Remove the outer hard leaves until you reach the light green softer leaves. Cut off the bottom two-thirds of the stem and, with a peeler, remove the woody tough green skin from the base of the artichoke and the stem – I find using a peeler for the stem is best and a small paring knife to smooth down and remove the tough bits at the base. Cut into quarters lengthways so you still see the lovely shape of the artichoke. As you are using baby artichokes, you won't need to remove the chokes because the hairs are immature and soft.

Add the artichokes to the saucepan and mix well. Cook for a few minutes.

Add the white wine vinegar, white wine, lemon juice and enough water to just cover the veg. Season with salt and pepper and bring to the boil.

Cover with a cartouche (a piece of greaseproof paper cut to the size of the pan), turn the heat down very low and cook until the artichokes are tender but just cooked. This should take about 35 minutes.

For the stew

200g/7oz cooked arrocina or
    other small white beans and
    their liquid (see Courgette,
    Saffron and White Bean Stew,
    page 158)
100g/3½oz cime di rapa, washed
    and sliced into strips
1 tablespoon aioli per person
    (see recipe below)
100g/3½oz croutons
50g/2oz parsley, roughly chopped
best olive oil, to finish

Check the seasoning and acidity. Add the cooked white beans and their broth into the artichokes and cook all together for 20 minutes (without the cartouche). Check the seasoning again.

When ready to eat, add the cime di rapa and cook for another 5 minutes until wilted.

Serve with a blob of aioli, a scattering of croutons and the parsley. Finish with a generous glug of olive oil.

AIOLI

I love a sauce on the side and I love how aioli can brighten up a dish. I remember making aioli at Rochelle Canteen and Margot Henderson would always say 'Add more garlic. You literally want your mouth to be on fire'. She would make us use 15–20 cloves in a single batch, if not more. It was pretty punchy to say the least but if you were feeling a bit run down, you'd have a big spoonful of aioli. An instant cure. My recipe below has less garlic. I still love the taste of the garlic but more as an afterthought to the accompanying dish.

Makes 500ml/18fl oz
(lasts up to a week in fridge)

1 egg, plus 1 yolk
4 cloves garlic, minced
1 tablespoon Dijon mustard
1 lemon, juiced (you might not
    need it all)
100ml/3½fl oz water (you might
    not need it all)
550ml/19fl oz sunflower,
    vegetable or a neutral oil
salt and pepper

Place the egg, egg yolk, garlic, mustard, 1 tablespoon lemon juice and 1 tablespoon water in a Magimix or bowl. Blend or whisk until it is well amalgamated. Add the oil in a slow steady stream, mixing constantly.

When it starts to emulsify or thicken, taste and either add more water or lemon juice (or both) to loosen the mixture. Continue to pour in the rest of the oil until fully incorporated. The thickness of the consistency should resemble Greek yoghurt. Season.

Notes
I love the versatility of aioli. It can be used to dress a salad or as a dip for crunchy vegetables. It's great on the side of a roast chicken, fish or rare piece of beef, or on broths, stews or deep-fried battered artichokes. Often if I want a quick snack in the kitchen, I'll simply eat it with fresh bread. It is an all-round excellent sauce and one you will often see on the Towpath menu. I love it!

FRENCH ONION SOUP

Every year when I go to Australia I always visit my dear friends, Marta and Felix, who moved from London to the Adelaide Hills a few years ago to be close to Felix's family.

While visiting, I have got to know their community well. They are a tight-knit group of people, making natural wine and living sustainably. When they heard that Lori and I were working on a book they insisted on testing recipes. We set up a test kitchen in Felix's aunt, Mary Broderick's house. I gave each person a recipe to try out, constructively criticise or add any general comments. This soup was the first one made and tasted. I want to thank Marta, Felix, Mary, Judy and Jackie for testing. I also want to include a great tip that Mary told me. She asked me if I knew how to get rid of the smell of garlic and onions on your hands? To which I responded 'no'. With a cheeky smile, she said, 'Wipe them on stainless steel and the smell will disappear'. It really does work and I promised I would write about it in the book. Thanks Mary!

Serves 4

200g/7oz unsalted butter
8 brown or red onions, thinly
    sliced
4 cloves garlic, minced, plus
    1 clove for serving
6 sprigs thyme
3 bay leaves
1.25 litres/2 pints 2fl oz chicken
    stock
2 slices sourdough bread
350g/12oz Montgomery Cheddar,
    grated
salt and pepper

Notes

If you are vegetarian, this soup can be made with vegetable stock or water instead of chicken stock. If you are dairy free, substitute the butter for olive oil and just place a garlic toast in the soup instead of a cheesy one. Although the butter and chicken stock add intensity, it is the caramelisation of the onions that brings the most flavour to the soup.

Melt the butter in a large saucepan over a medium heat. Once melted, add the onions, garlic, thyme and bay leaves. Lightly season and cook for 1 hour, stirring regularly to prevent the onions from catching. You want the onions to caramelise. This will add a sweetness to the soup and is the most important stage. If the onions start to catch, pour in a splash of water, stir and then scrape the bottom of the pan. The liquid will remove all that goodness stuck to the bottom and add more flavour to the soup.

At around 40 minutes the onions will start to caramelise faster, so stir more regularly and turn the heat down for the remaining 20 minutes if necessary.

Pour in the stock. Bring to the boil, then lower to a simmer and cook until the liquid is thick and caramelised. This should take another hour. Season. Depending on how rich you like the soup you may want to skim some of the butter off the top once it settles.

When you're ready to serve, preheat the grill. Toast the bread, cut in half then rub each slice with the garlic clove. Generously cover the toast with the grated cheese and grill until the cheese has melted.

Place each toast in the bottom of each soup bowl. Ladle the onion soup over the top and sprinkle generously with black pepper.

ROAST CHICKEN

My favourite thing in the world to cook. I love a good roast chicken so much I could eat it every day and the juices from the roasting tin to me is the best gravy you can have. About three years after opening Towpath I had to give up dairy for a while for health reasons. Up until this point I would smother my chicken in butter and roast, but then I stopped using butter. What I found was that I actually preferred roasting a chicken without butter. The skin crisps up better as you can have the oven piping hot and not worry about the butter burning. The key to a perfect roast chicken is to get the skin super crispy on a high heat and then finish off the cooking on a very low heat. Always serve your chicken with something that soaks up the gravy. I love to serve it with a farro salad.

Serves 6

1 x 2.5kg/5½lb organic or free-
  range chicken, get the best
  quality available
1 head garlic, cut in half
  horizontally, skin on
3 bay leaves
6 sprigs tarragon
1 lemon, halved
100ml/3½fl oz olive oil
coarse sea salt and pepper

Notes
The great thing about roasting a chicken is that you get several other meals out of it.

When I roast and carve a chicken, I am always amazed how much meat there is left on the carcass and I always pick the meat off the carcass to use for a salad or in a broth. Then I make a stock from the bones and use it for any kind of broth, stew or soup (see Notes on page 34).

Preheat the oven to 210°C fan/450°F/gas mark 8.

Remove any giblets or offal from the inside of the chicken. Save the offal for making a pâté and the giblets for a stock. Remove any excess fat from inside the chicken.

Place the chicken in a suitable roasting tin – you want something with a lip to collect all the juices.

Stuff the chicken cavity with the head of garlic, bay leaves and tarragon. Squeeze the lemon juice over the top of the chicken. Don't worry too much about the pips. Stuff one half of the lemon into the cavity too.

Pour the olive oil over the top and season generously with salt and pepper and then, using your hands, rub the chicken all over with the oil and the lemon juice and seasoning that has collected in the tin.

Roast for 25 minutes until the skin has browned and gone crispy. If it needs a bit longer to crisp up, leave for another 10 minutes, but make sure you deduct that time from the overall cooking time.

Reduce the heat to 130°C fan/300°F/gas mark 2 and roast for another 35 minutes. The chicken is cooked when the juices from a skewer inserted between the leg and thigh run clear.

Rest for at least 15 minutes before carving.

Serve the chicken on top of a farro, broad bean and pea salad (see page 64). Make sure you pour the juices all over the top so the farro soaks up all the delicious juices. Serve some aioli (see page 60) on the side.

FARRO, BROAD BEANS, PEAS AND TROPEA ONIONS

Farro is not something I had ever cooked with until meeting Lori. I love the nuttiness of the grain and its versatility. In the UK, the closest grain to it would be barley, although to me farro is far superior. It is such a great grain for making fresh salads and I always feel like it is doing something good for my body when I eat it!

Serves 8

200g/7oz farro
100g/3½oz podded broad beans
100g/3½oz podded peas
½ bunch of parsley, picked and
   coarsely chopped
½ bunch of mint, picked and
   coarsely chopped
2 tropea onions or 4 spring
   onions, thinly sliced on a
   slight angle
75ml/3fl oz best olive oil
1 lemon, juiced
salt and pepper

To prepare the farro, place it in a medium saucepan and rinse several times to get rid of the starch. Farro is incredibly starchy so this could take up to 8–10 rinses of really swirling it around with your hand each time. Drain, return to the saucepan and cover with water.

Bring to the boil, remove the scum and drain. Rinse thoroughly with cold water to remove any starch. Now cover again with cold water and bring to the boil. Remove any scum. Turn down to a simmer and cook for about 20 minutes until it has a little bite but is cooked.

Drain and again rinse with cold water to remove any more starch. You will be amazed how much starch there is left. Leave in a colander to get rid of any excess water.

While the farro is cooking, prepare the broad beans and peas. Broad beans and peas at the beginning of the season are super tender, fresh and sweet and definitely do not need cooking, but the best way to test this is to try them. If they taste delicious, do nothing. If they taste a bit older, cook them.

To cook, blanch in water separately for a couple of minutes, drain and place in a bowl of iced water. This will keep the bright green colour, but don't leave in the water for too long as this will remove the flavour. If the broad bean skins are tough, you might want to peel the skin after they have been blanched.

Now mix the farro, broad beans, peas, herbs, onions, olive oil, lemon juice and season. You want the salad to be punchy, so add more of whatever it needs depending on taste.

Either eat as is or with a blob of aioli (see page 60).

ONGLET, WATERCRESS, PICKLED WALNUTS AND BEETROOT

A pickled walnut is simply delicious and Opies to me is the Rolls Royce of pickled walnuts. In fact, it is the only pickled walnut to eat. There are certain things which shouldn't be replicated. For example, the only tomato ketchup to eat is Heinz. No other brand competes. I feel the same about Philadelphia cream cheese, HP brown sauce and Lea & Perrins Worcestershire sauce.

I have tried to pickle walnuts on a couple of occasions. It was something I got super excited about. On the first occasion, I picked them too late – they still had a green shell, but at that time I didn't know how to test to see if a shell had formed. As a result, I had to discard them. A few years later I tried again, making sure I picked them when the shell hadn't yet formed. You can check this by sticking a pin in the end where the flower was. If the shell has started forming you will feel resistance from the pin. I then brined them for several weeks, dried them out for a week and then pickled them. It worked but it just didn't taste as good as an Opie. I am definitely not a believer of cutting corners, but sometimes you have to accept your loss and leave some things to someone else who does it better.

Serves 4

For the salad
4 medium beetroot, cooked
  (see Beetroot Borani, page 80)
6 pickled walnuts and their brine
  – definitely Opies!
2 banana shallots, sliced thinly on
  a slight angle
handful of capers, drained
handful of parsley, roughly
  chopped
1 clove garlic, minced
1 tablespoon merlot red wine
  vinegar (or a red wine vinegar
  with a pinch of sugar added)
2 tablespoons best olive oil
200g/7oz watercress
salt and pepper

oil, for frying
4 x 250g/9oz onglet pieces,
  trimmed
120g/4¼ oz horseradish cream,
  to serve

An hour or so before you want to eat, marinate the beetroot. (If you do not have time, it will still taste delicious.)

Cut the beetroot into odd-shaped wedges, about 2cm/¾in in size. Halve two pickled walnuts and thinly slice. Add to a bowl with the beetroot wedges, shallots, capers and parsley. Add the garlic, vinegar, olive oil and 1 tablespoon of the pickled walnut brine.

Give the salad a big mix and season. Set aside until ready to assemble.

Fill a pan with a generous amount of oil so it's almost 0.5cm/¼in deep. Place over a high heat until it's smoking hot. Carefully put in the pieces of onglet. It should sizzle as the meat goes in. Season. Leave for about 3 minutes, until crispy and brown. Turn over and repeat. Season again. Turn off the heat and leave in the pan for 2 minutes to continue cooking. Place on a plate and leave to rest for 5 minutes.

While the meat is resting, get the salad ready. Mix the watercress gently through the marinating beetroot. Taste and check for seasoning, balance of acidity and oil.

Place in a bowl to serve or on individual plates. Put a whole pickled walnut on each plate along with a blob of horseradish cream. Slice the onglet against the grain on a slight angle. Plate and pour the juices over.

MEXICAN WEDDING CAKES
(RUSSIAN TEA CAKES)

These cookies have been on the counter at Towpath since day one. I remember that before we opened, Micky (Lori's daughter) and I messed around with lots of different cookie recipes. We made these and instantly loved them. They were particularly nostalgic for Micky as she associated them with her childhood as a special treat. They are small and crumbly – a little morsel that doesn't feel too indulgent. The difference between a Mexican wedding cake and a Russian tea cake is in the nut. The Mexican wedding cake specifically uses pecans whereas a Russian tea cake can contain any type of nut, although never mixed nuts. We always use pecans in ours.

Makes 18 cookies

125g/4½oz unsalted butter, softened
25g/1oz caster sugar
¼ teaspoon vanilla extract
⅛ teaspoon fine salt
140g/5oz plain flour
60g/2¼oz pecans, coarsely chopped
icing sugar, sifted, for dusting

Preheat the oven to 160°C fan/350°F/gas mark 4.

Cream the butter, caster sugar, vanilla extract and salt together until soft and fluffy. Gently fold in the flour and pecans. Do not overmix.

Roll the dough into tablespoon-sized balls or weigh out 18g/generous ½oz per piece. Keep the cookies rounded rather than flattened, like a ping-pong ball. If the mixture is too warm to shape, place in the fridge for 30 minutes to firm up. (The mix will keep well in the fridge for up to a week, and you could also roll into balls and freeze.)

Place onto a baking sheet lined with greaseproof paper. Bake for 15–20 minutes until they are firm enough to move around on the tray.

Leave the balls to cool, then generously dust with icing sugar before serving.

May

Taking Orders

Moving our kitchen from across the canal to right next door to the bar felt like the answer to all our prayers. The sardine days, shoulder to shoulder behind the bar, making coffees, taking orders, grilling sandwiches, stirring porridge, washing dishes and running food, while Laura and her team were someplace else entirely, were over. Looking back, I don't know how we ever did it. Our new configuration felt luxurious. Streamlined. Surely we were on our way to becoming an impeccably well-organised version of our formerly chaotic selves. It was all very exciting.

We rolled up our sleeves to help get the kitchen ready. With great enthusiasm and minimal expertise, we tiled walls and painted the concrete floor. Paintbrushes and trowels in hand, we dreamed up systems for our new, improved set-up. This exercise was strangely less straightforward than we'd imagined.

Some of the seemingly simplest questions were full of hidden implications. Like, how were we going to get orders from the bar to the kitchen, separated as they are by an impenetrable concrete wall? Should we have one of those systems where an order placed at the bar magically appears on a ticket printed out in the kitchen? Or possibly better yet, it appears on a screen in the kitchen, doing away with paper altogether? Interesting. Of course, our till, which was little more than a glorified calculator with a cash drawer, was not equipped to do either of these things. These were the days before we even took debit cards. We were about as untechnologically organised as a business could be.

Here's the solution we came up with: customers would deliver their own ticket (which would have both their order and their name on it) to the kitchen, and then sit down and wait for their food to be brought to them. We smiled at the thought that this little minuet could also become a means of introducing everyone to each other, and of keeping the kitchen from becoming an isolated hive of activity that never crossed paths with the beneficiaries of their labours.

It wasn't until we put our system into play that the gremlins emerged. Let's say you, the reader, are the customer. We've learned that just because we look you in the eye and ask you to do something (for instance, take your ticket to the kitchen) and you nod your head in assent, that doesn't mean you're actually going to do it. You might just pop the ticket into your wallet, sit down and potentially wait for an eternity. We've gotten very good at spotting the sort of vacant nod which means, 'I may look like I'm listening, but I'm not.'

Then there is the minor awkwardness of you having to deliver a ticket to a very busy kitchen that doesn't have a designated ticket receiver. This you do by standing at the entrance to said kitchen and trying to catch someone's eye – usually the person washing dishes and/or running food. First-time customers can be a bit bemused by this arrangement, but not you. Your ticket, once handed over, is put at the end of a row of existing orders, on the back wall if it's breakfast, or the front if it's lunch or dinner.

When your food is ready, it is brought out of the kitchen by a runner who calls your name. Granted, it would be easier if they already had some way of

knowing where you were sitting, but you probably didn't know that either at the time you placed your order. It is definitely easier if the runner is not so shy as to be unable to raise their voice above the sound of a butterfly's wings flapping.

But even if your name rings out loud and clear, potential pitfalls lurk. There are days when all of our customers seem to go by one of four names. You'd be surprised by how many people will take a bowl of granola when they've ordered fried eggs so long as they hear their name called. They will especially take a cheese sandwich if someone who shares their name has ordered one. Equally puzzling are the people who will answer to any name so long as the person calling it is carrying the thing they've ordered. That's what hunger can do to you.

Every so often we think about modernising this aspect of our operation. Especially on days when the ticket minuet has gone awry. We talk among ourselves and ask our regulars what they think we should do. 'Nothing!' they all say. 'We like it this way.' They still want to peek into the kitchen and give Lindy their ticket. The kitchen still wants to say hello. It seems we'd all rather be a name than a number.

MARINDA TOMATOES AND MOJO VERDE

This is one of our Towpath breakfast staples. Although marinda tomatoes now seem to be available all year round, they are traditionally a winter tomato, green, tart and firm. They are a great vessel for a variety of sauces because of their robust nature and immense flavour; delicious served with smoked paprika and garlic, all kinds of pesto or with caramelised chilli sage butter. Even just sliced on buttered toast, drizzled with olive oil, salt and pepper, they are a joyful thing.

My favourite combination though is with mojo verde. This sauce goes delightfully with fried eggs as well. I became obsessed with this sauce when I first ate it at Morito with fried potatoes. I asked them what was in it and they gave me a list of ingredients. This is my interpretation.

Serves 2

For the mojo verde
1 green pepper, deseeded and
    roughly chopped
2 bunches of coriander, with
    stalks, roughly chopped
2 cloves garlic, minced
2 jalapeños, roughly chopped
6 pinches of ground cumin, seeds
    toasted whole, then finely
    ground
2½ tablespoons sherry vinegar
250ml/9fl oz olive oil
salt and pepper

4 slices of sourdough bread
butter, for spreading
4 marinda tomatoes, thinly sliced
    on the cross section (you could
    also use up any tomatoes you
    have at home)
best olive oil, to finish

Place the green pepper, coriander, garlic, jalapeños and ground cumin with some salt and pepper to season into a blender. I use a Magimix for this, but any food processor or blender will work. Or you could dice everything into a chunky salsa or make in a pestle and mortar.

Blitz till you have a paste, scraping down the sides from time to time. Add the sherry vinegar and then, while you have the motor running, slowly pour in the olive oil so that it amalgamates. Check the seasoning and acidity. Jalapeños can be quite mild so add more if there is no kick – you want a punchy, spicy fresh salsa.

To serve, toast the bread and then butter. Spread or smother the mojo verde over the top and lay the sliced tomatoes over, slightly overlapping them. Season with salt and pepper and drizzle over olive oil.

Notes
The amount of mojo verde you make will be far more than is needed for the tomatoes. Store in the fridge for up to a week, making sure it's at room temperature before serving.

It's delicious with fried eggs, scrambled eggs and omelettes, or you could also serve with crispy potatoes, roast cauliflower or friggitelli peppers as well as on top of curries or roast meat, chicken or fish.

TARAMASALATA

Taramasalata is one of my favourite things and when cod's roe is in season I have it on the menu constantly. I often have it on toast for breakfast and I always have a small container in my fridge at home for a little snack. It's so addictive and I know other people feel the same – the thought of not being able to eat it for one day is slightly distressing. Our dear friend Davo, who cooked with us for two years, taught me this recipe. Every time I make it, I think of him and what he is getting up to in Queensland.

Serves 4, makes 500g/1lb 2oz

150g/5½oz smoked cod's roe,
    peeled and veins removed
1 clove garlic, minced
½ lemon, juiced
40g/1½oz pitta bread or white
    bread soaked in water, then
    squeezed out
275ml/9½fl oz sunflower oil,
    in a jug
salt and pepper

Put the cod's roe, garlic, 2 tablespoons lemon juice, pitta bread and 2 tablespoons water in a food processor (a hand blender or liquidiser will work as well). Blitz together until well combined.

When the mixture is very smooth, slowly drip in the oil, with the motor running, to emulsify the mixture. Do not add all the oil at once or it will split. The mixture will thicken as you go and will appear not to want any more oil. Add another tablespoon or two of water and/or lemon juice to loosen and continue to add the oil slowly. Season to taste, but it rarely needs salt as the cod's roe is naturally salty.

Serve with pitta bread or toast and a handful of crunchy radishes.

Notes
The easiest way to peel the cod's roe is to soak it in cold water for at least 30 minutes, which will soften the skin, but even then the skin can be a complete nightmare to peel – if you are struggling, halve the roe and scoop out the roe from the skin.

I find that the intensity of the cod's roe can vary significantly from roe to roe, so always taste your taramasalata while making it. If the cod's roe is lightly smoked, you might not need to add all the oil. If the cod's roe is super strong, you may need more oil than the recipe calls for, as the oil softens the smokiness.

ASPARAGUS WITH CAMBRIDGE SAUCE OR AJO BLANCO

When English asparagus comes into season you will see them on our menu every day. To me, they signify something special and as the season is so short, we need to pay homage to them. I often serve them with Cambridge sauce or ajo blanco, gribiche, romesco, trapanese, dukkah and feta or Parmesan shavings with butter and lemon.

I always remember calling Cambridge sauce, sauce gribiche, but Rosie Sykes corrected me – technically a sauce gribiche does not contain anchovies whereas a Cambridge sauce does. I love Rosie for her knowledge of the history of dishes. She has an encyclopaedic brain when it comes to all dishes old and new.

Ajo blanco is most commonly eaten as a chilled soup in Andalusia. In summer, I will serve it in little glasses, drizzled with olive oil and scattered with cherries or melon over the top. At Towpath I also serve it thicker, as a sauce to pour over asparagus. Ajo means garlic but the real flavour comes from the almonds. It is important to use a good-quality almond when making this sauce – Marcona almonds are fatter and wetter, more delicate than your average almond.

I've given recipes for both sauces here so you can choose the one you like the sound of best or make both.

Serves 4

For the asparagus
28 (500g/1lb 2oz) very fresh
    asparagus
salt and pepper

For the Cambridge sauce
6 eggs, boiled for 7 minutes,
    cooled and peeled, yolks and
    whites separated
2 teaspoons Dijon mustard
4 anchovy fillets, finely chopped
2 teaspoons red wine vinegar
300ml/10fl oz sunflower oil
4 sprigs parsley, leaves only,
    chopped
4 sprigs tarragon, leaves only,
    chopped
2 tablespoons capers, drained
    and chopped
2 tablespoons cornichons, drained
    and finely diced

Cut or snap off the woody bottoms of the asparagus and discard. Wash the remaining spears well to remove any grit from the tips.

Boil the spears in salted water for 3–5 minutes, depending on the thickness – they should still have a bit of crunch. Drain but do not rinse under cold water.

Lay on individual plates, spoon over your chosen sauce, season and serve with bread to soak up the delicious sauce.

To make the Cambridge sauce, blend the egg yolks, mustard, anchovies and vinegar in a Magimix or blender until smooth. Continue blending, slowly pouring in the oil until a smooth, creamy mixture forms.

Finely dice the egg whites and add them along with the herbs, capers and cornichons to the egg-yolk mixture. Stir and season.

Notes
There will be more Cambridge sauce than you need, but since the eggs are cooked it will last up to a week in the fridge and it is delicious served with poached leeks or any other robust green vegetable, roast chicken or to dress a potato salad.

OR

For the ajo blanco

200g/7oz blanched Marcona
    almonds
180ml/6¼fl oz water
2 tablespoons sherry vinegar
1 large or 2 small cloves garlic,
    minced
150ml/5fl oz olive oil

Notes

To make ajo blanco for a soup,
just whisk more water into the
sauce until you have a soup-like
consistency. You may need to
add more sherry vinegar to get
the proportions right. This soup
is incredibly rich so I only serve
it in small glasses and it is lovely
with a beetroot salad or tossed
through monk's beard. It's also
delicious with beef, lamb or fish.

Preheat the oven to 160°C fan/350°F/gas mark 4.

Lightly toast the almonds on a tray in the oven for
10 minutes. They will start to release their natural oil,
but you don't want them to colour. Transfer the
almonds to a Magimix or liquidiser and blitz to form a
smooth paste – this will take about 8–10 minutes as it
takes some time for the oils to release and loosen up.
You will have to stop and scrape down the sides and
bottom of the container regularly with a spatula. Please
be patient as this stage can be very frustrating, but it is
very important to get a smooth sauce. If you add water
immediately, you will end up with a coarse texture and
you want this to be silky smooth.

Once you have a smooth paste, add a dash of
water, a little at a time, so it is fully incorporated. It
will take a few minutes for the water to be absorbed.
Once you have the consistency of double cream (you
may not need all the water), add the vinegar and
garlic, season and blitz. Slowly pour in the olive oil
until the mixture takes on the consistency of thick
yoghurt. The sauce will thicken as it sits, so you
might need to add a dash more water before serving.

BEETROOT BORANI

This is our version of a recipe that I love from Morito restaurant. Traditionally, it's served as a dip with flatbread, but I serve it with a spoon, to be eaten like chilled soup. I love this as a starter as the colours are so vibrant that it brightens up any table.

Serves 4

For the borani

8 medium beetroot, washed and scrubbed, boiled until tender, peeled then returned to their cooking water
1 clove garlic, minced
2 teaspoons ground cumin
1 tablespoon merlot red wine vinegar (or a red wine vinegar with a pinch of sugar added)
2 pinches of sugar (if the beetroot is not that sweet)
200ml/7fl oz Greek or natural yoghurt
75ml/3fl oz olive oil
salt and pepper

160g/5¾oz feta
80g/3oz walnuts, toasted
8 sprigs dill, leaves picked
best olive oil, to drizzle

Chop the beetroot into chunky dice. Place in a liquidiser with a ladleful of its cooking liquid. Blitz until thick and smooth – you may need to add in a bit more liquid if it is thicker than the thickest of yoghurts.

Add all the remaining ingredients and blitz until smooth – you are aiming for the consistency of thick yoghurt. Season to taste.

To serve, ladle the borani into a bowl, crumble the feta over the top, scatter with toasted walnuts and sprigs of dill and drizzle with olive oil.

Sprinkle with salt and pepper and serve with flatbread or sourdough bread.

MOZZARELLA, PICKLED RADICCHIO AND PANGRATTATO

Another of my all-time favourites, this dish appears on the menu all the time and I love it so much that when Alex and I got married we served it at our wedding lunch at Towpath. Even thinking about the bitterness of the radicchio with the richness of the mozzarella, paired with the crunchy pangrattato breadcrumbs, makes me want to eat it right now!

Serves 4

1 x 250g/9oz ball of good-quality mozzarella (take out of the fridge and drain in a sieve at least an hour before using)
240g/8¾oz Pickled Radicchio, drained (see recipe overleaf)
25g/1oz Pangrattato (see recipe overleaf)
best olive oil, for drizzling
salt and pepper

Break up the mozzarella into nice chunks, place on a plate and season.

Roughly chop the pickled radicchio and scatter over the top of the mozzarella, but make sure that you can still see the mozzarella underneath.

Sprinkle the pangrattato over and drizzle with olive oil.

PICKLED RADICCHIO

I just love anything pickled. It fills me with absolute happiness and I could quite easily put a pickle on almost anything or just nibble on them on their own.

Pickling is also something I love to do as it is a great way to use up leftover vegetables and fruit, especially on a rainy weekend. Almost anything can be pickled – at Towpath, we pickle kohlrabi, radishes, cauliflower, cucumbers, carrots, fennel, beetroot, chicory, cherries, apricots, plums, melon, elderberries, gooseberries, blackberries. My theory is if you can eat it raw you can pickle it!

Makes a 1 litre/1¾ pint jar

500ml/18fl oz white wine vinegar
250g/9oz caster sugar
4 heads radicchio
1½ tablespoons salt

Place the vinegar and sugar in a saucepan and bring to the boil so that the sugar melts. Leave to cool. With some pickles, you pour the liquid over when hot but for something like radicchio or cucumber, which have a high water content, the liquid should be cool.

(If I am in a rush, I will just use enough vinegar to cover the sugar and bring to the boil. I then add the rest of the vinegar which, as it is at room temperature, speeds up the cooling process.)

While the pickling liquid is cooling, prepare the radicchio. Remove any outer leaves that look a bit sad. Cut into quarters, remove the core and separate the leaves.

Place in a colander either in a sink or with a bowl underneath and sprinkle some salt over each layer of radicchio. Give it a gentle toss and leave for a good hour. Sometimes very little liquid comes out.

Now take a sterilised container and place the radicchio in it. I don't rinse the salt off because I find this makes everything much wetter and harder to dry the radicchio.

Pour over the cold pickling liquid. Make sure the liquid completely covers the radicchio. To ensure this, cut out a piece of greaseproof paper to cover the top of the container. Place it on top of the radicchio and weigh the paper down with a plate or a lid. This will prevent the radicchio from floating to the top and coming out of the liquid.

Leave for a week in the fridge before using, but a minimum of 2 days if you are desperate to eat it.

Serve this pickle with any type of cheese, on the side of smoked fish, beef or chicken, or tossed through lentils or a raw radicchio salad with anchovy dressing. It is incredibly versatile and complements lots of dishes.

PANGRATTATO

At Towpath we always have lots of bread ends because we make so many cheese sandwiches. Pangrattato is a great way to use them up and lasts for a long time if kept in an airtight container. It is so versatile, as everyone loves a crunch to their dish, so I often liberally sprinkle pangrattato over everything.

Makes 385g/13¼oz

250g/9oz stale or old bread, crusts on
3 cloves garlic, minced
4 sprigs thyme
2½ tablespoons olive oil
½ lemon, juiced
½ teaspoon chilli flakes
2 tablespoons white wine
¼ teaspoon black pepper

Notes
Toss through a simple garlic and olive oil pasta to add some crunch.

Crumble over all kinds of salads or stews or braised greens with aioli.

Sprinkle on top of gratins or use for breading when you deep-fry courgettes or aubergines.

Preheat the oven to 160°C fan/350°F/gas mark 4.

Line a big oven tray or several baking trays with greaseproof paper.

Cut the bread into chunky pieces (about 4cm/1½in square) leaving the crusts on. Put the bread on the tray(s) with all the other ingredients and mix everything together thoroughly. Spread them out so that they are not too crowded – you want the bread to crisp up rather than sweat.

Place in the oven and bake until golden brown – about 25–35 minutes.

Leave to cool for 5 minutes and then blitz in batches. If you don't have a Magimix, you could try crumbling it in a pestle and mortar, although it might be quite a laborious task.

Cool and store in an airtight container.

Canal Life

I was in India a couple of winters ago with friends and, while four of us were haring around the Mysore market like unruly children, my partner Rob leaned up against a stall selling temple paraphernalia and quietly watched it all go by. 'It's like the Great Barrier Reef,' he said. 'Why swim around trying to see everything? I just drop to the bottom and stay until I need to come up for air.'

Our perch at Towpath feels something like that – a fixed point in a kaleidoscope of water, sun, (duckweed!), rain, wind, ice, (snow!), coots, swans, geese, (terrapins!), pike, (eels!), narrowboats, kayaks, (coal barges!), walkers, runners, (police divers!), cyclists, dogs, (foxes!).

Oh the things you see if you stay in one place long enough with your eyes open. People falling into the drink, for example. Which we are often asked about. This happens much less frequently than you might imagine – and mostly to cyclists. There is a curious lack of commonsense etiquette regarding the communal use of a pathway once intended only for slow, plodding horses.

The most memorable kerfuffle took place just this year. It was early afternoon when we heard a great splash under the bridge, followed by the wailing of an infant, the howling of her two young brothers and the raised voices of the many adults who rushed to the scene to find a sopping wet baby, her mother and their bicycle all in the canal, forced off the path by a now-hangdog and profusely contrite oncoming cyclist who seemed to have thought that repeatedly ringing his bell gave him some sort of right of way under the bridge. Mother and child were whisked across the canal and into a warm shower, then wrapped in borrowed clothes and blankets. The boys revived themselves at Towpath with hot chocolate and olive oil cake.

On most days, though, there's a curiously bucolic air to our particular bit of the canal, surprising for something both man made and situated three minutes from a dizzying stretch of the Kingsland Road. I've spent many an hour looking out at it from behind the bar, pondering what particular combination of elements gives this little patch of water and land its vague sense of countryside.

There is the way the canal curves just as it meets the bridge, whose Georgian brickwork arches low and wide over the water. On one side is a stand of fluttering silver birches. On the other, an elder (from whose blossoms we make elderflower cordial) and a grand old sycamore with gnarled, sprawling limbs. In midsummer, the late setting sun streams golden light through the underside of the bridge. I am not waxing lyrical – it is a beautiful sight.

On summer nights, the place can feel like a bayou. The city dissolves into darkness, the water an inky black, broken only by the slow passing of a boat or the skittering of waterbirds. We have yet to tire of the moment when we turn off the last light and see the liquid, wavy reflection of water appear on our tiled walls, like stars in the night.

We have our share of urban Huckleberry Finns. Boys trailing fishing rods with all the time in the world to cast their lines, sit patiently and wait. One of them, a shy, lanky teenager named Henry, brought us photos of his prize catch – a glittering pike as long as his outstretched arms.

Then there are the birds. Waterfowl, mostly, whose complex class structure we've come to understand over the years. Slate-black coots, our favourites, are the

lowliest – which is not as bad as it sounds. They're the canal jesters, squawking and haring about the water until they're chased back to their higgledy piggledy nests. The geese fly in neat formation, aiming straight for the bridge until the very last moment when, who knows why, they choose to swoop under it or soar above. The swans rarely fly at all but, when they do, it is with a great whooshing of wings. They are bossy and imperious, prone to hissing at dogs or children

who get too close, and generally behave as if they think they should be living in Regent's Park. But they charmed us last year – a family of eight signets, riding, four at a time, on their parents' backs. Little grey balls of fluff, they were a marvel to see and they knew it. All year long they stopped traffic as they grew and grew, gliding across the water, stretching their wings, until by the end of the Towpath year all but two had fledged. The gulls are not a part of this community except as occasional violent and terrible villains – mostly in springtime, when they dive-bomb the coots' nests to steal away the little chicks. We despise them. Herons are more rare and always solitary. Only yesterday we watched one swallow a whole, live eel. And not in one swift gulp. There's always a pair of binoculars on hand for the curious.

Finally, there is the water itself, reflecting back London's moody skies, sparkling in sunshine, pattered with rain, rippled by wind, hosting its parade of birds and boats. . . and sometimes alas, the rubbish, which seems to gather and travel across the water like some distant cousin of the Great Pacific Garbage Patch. We are, after all, in what was once the grittiest part of the largest city in Europe. Which means that some days the canal feels like Varanasi on the Ganges, with its funeral pyres, ablutions, clothes washing and prayer offerings all happening at once. A collision of the sacred and the profane. Open your eyes to any of it and you get, as Zorba the Greek called it, 'the full catastrophe'. This is a good thing, though not always an easy one. Unless you're totally blinkered, it is hard to ignore.

We could argue until the cows come home about whose responsibility it is to make things better. The council can't keep up with the rubbish, which piles up every weekend beside the one lonely bin next to the bridge. The Canal & River Trust has the task of caring for miles of an increasingly busy waterway as an underfunded charity. The infrastructure is insufficient to the tasks required of it. It's a familiar tune. Maybe the whole world is going to pot and we really *are* doomed. And so? Meanwhile, rubbish begets rubbish.

Luckily the opposite is true.

There are two little green spaces on either side of our bridge. When we first opened Towpath, the far one was occupied by two large dead trees and the near one by overgrown shrubs and decades of accumulated debris. With the help of our friend Kevin, master tree surgeon and accordion player, we dug up the trees and replaced them with a ramshackle raised garden. This year, thanks to Rob's green thumb, there are sunflowers, cistus, orange cosmos and hollyhocks. The shrubs made way for bike hoops, a raised woodchip bed we call 'the beach' and a wall of climbing roses, wisteria, hops and clematis. Neither garden is ever as tended as we'd like it to be. And there is still litter, though not nearly as much.

The canal seems to attract the sort of people who not only go out of their way to follow its watery path through the neighbourhood, but are willing to roll up their sleeves and help take care of it. This year the Wildlife Gardeners of Haggerston raised money for floating reed beds and planted them with rushes and sedges, which will act as a natural water filter and purifier, and provide a living habitat for fish, birds and butterflies. To our great good fortune, they've anchored one of their floating sanctuaries right across from the Towpath.

Cleaning up the neighbourhood is not an event, it's an approach. Which with any luck becomes a habit. Like brushing your teeth. It's good for you and it feels better than ignoring the whole mess. And we've noticed something – help is all around. All you have to do is ask.

We carry out our little beautification projects in the low-tech manner with which we do most things. Whoever has the best handwriting will chalk up a plea for volunteer gardeners on a blackboard and lean it up on the table with the water jugs and glasses. And they come, bless them, even in rain, even if they know nothing about gardening and even if there's nothing to do but weed, water and pick up rubbish. The past couple of years we've collaborated with the Canal & River Trust on canal clean-ups. We supply the men, women and children. They turn up with kayaks, canoes, litter-pickers, grappling hooks and the services of one of their long, flat barges to collect our haul. It is by necessity a wholly collaborative effort. One person paddles or steers while the others try to grab whatever's been spotted in the water. It's hilarious good fun that happens to do a bit of good. And there are few sights as lovely as that of a bunch of seven year olds in high-vis lifejackets marching up and down the canal brandishing litter pickers or sitting in a rowboat scanning the water for treasures. Then wanting to know when they can come back and do it again.

BRAISED CUTTLEFISH WITH PEAS, JERSEY ROYALS, ROCKET AND AIOLI

Of all the recipes featured in the book, this is the most time consuming, but the end result is worth it – this recipe personifies spring and it's like giving yourself a hug all over.

Serves 6

3.5kg/7lb 10oz cuttlefish, unprepped (the larger the cuttlefish the easier to prep)
6 tablespoons olive oil
4 spring onions, sliced on a slight angle in 2cm/¾in batons
6 cloves garlic, minced
2 teaspoons chilli flakes
250g/9oz Jersey Royal potatoes, washed and scrubbed, left whole if small or cut into 3cm/1¼in pieces
250g/9oz podded peas
250g/9oz podded broad beans
2 lemons, peel and juice
4 bay leaves
500ml/18fl oz white wine
bunch of rocket
salt and pepper
150g/5½oz aioli (see page 60)

Notes
I like cooking everything together so that all of the flavours develop, but this means it is not the brightest or most vibrant braise as the peas and broad beans lose their colour and shape. If you want everything to look fresh, cook the peas and broad beans separately and stir through at the end, but I insist on cooking the potatoes from the start as they act as a vessel for soaking up all the deliciousness in the pan.

Start by prepping the cuttlefish. Pull the head away from the body, remove the cuttlefish bone and discard. Separate the tentacles from the body and get rid of the ink sac (in other recipes, for example cuttlefish ink risotto, you want the ink sac to be intact). Discard the guts.

Gently pull the wings away from the sides, being careful to keep the body whole. This should also remove the light pink membrane with it. Prepare the tentacles by cutting them just above the eyes and mouth (discard the eyes and mouth). The tentacles should come away together. Cut the tentacles into a few pieces. Save the wings to put in the stew.

Score the body on the inside and cut into large 4cm/1½in different-shaped pieces.

Heat the olive oil in a medium saucepan over a medium heat. Add the spring onions, garlic and chilli flakes. Cook for a few minutes to soften.

Turn the heat up and add the tentacles, body and wings. Cook for a few minutes to colour the fish.

Add the potatoes, peas, broad beans, lemon peel and juice, bay leaves, white wine and season. Bring to the boil and add just enough water to cover.

Turn down the heat to a simmer, cover with a piece of greaseproof paper cut to the size of the saucepan and then the lid and cook on a very low heat. You can do this either on the stove or in a low oven (130°C fan/300°F/gas mark 2), which I often find more convenient and the heat easier to control. Cook until incredibly tender, about 1½–2 hours – you want the cuttlefish to melt in your mouth, so check after 1 hour. Check the seasoning and acidity.

Serve with a handful of rocket, a generous drizzle of best olive oil and a big bowl of aioli. And have some bread to hand as you won't want to waste all the delicious juices left in the bowl.

HUNGARIAN SAUSAGE, SAUERKRAUT, POTATO SALAD AND MUSTARD

I remember going for dinner at the Canton Arms, owned by chef Trish Hilferty, with a group of friends. We looked at the menu – everything sounded delicious. Let's share everything we thought. Our waitress then came and told us about the special. It was a smoked Hungarian sausage with Russian salad and gherkin – every single one of us ordered it. No sharing. I still remember it so vividly. It was perfect in every way. This is my version of it.

The sausages come from Swaledale and are a smoked chorizo recipe with lots of paprika. I often make it at home using Polish sausages as there is a great Polish deli near me, but anything smoky and salty will work well here.

Serves 4

For the potato salad
800g/1¾lb salad potatoes, such as Charlotte, Jersey Royals or Cornish new
1 tablespoon white wine vinegar
2 spring onions, thinly sliced
handful of parsley, chopped
handful of tarragon, chopped
200g/7oz mayonnaise
4 tablespoons small capers, drained
salt and pepper

4 smoked sausages
300g/10½oz sauerkraut (see opposite)
Dijon mustard

Wash the potatoes. If the potatoes vary in size, cut them to the same size for even cooking.

Put the potatoes in a pan and cover with water. Bring to the boil and salt. Turn down to a gentle boil and cook until the potatoes are soft, but still holding their shape – about 15–20 minutes.

Drain and, while hot, cut the potatoes into bite-sized pieces and pour over the vinegar, giving them a good toss.

Let cool for a bit, so the mayonnaise doesn't split when added, then add all the rest of the ingredients and mix well.

Check the seasoning and set aside. As the salad sits, the flavour will get better and better.

Now bring a pan of water to the boil. Add the sausages and simmer for 8 minutes. Remove and drain.

To serve, place a sausage on each plate with a pile of potato salad, a handful of sauerkraut and a generous spoonful of Dijon mustard.

Notes
I make many variations of potato salads, with mayonnaise, a mustard dressing or with crème fraîche. Some as simply as that, or I may add cornichons, red onions, mint, dill. The combinations are endless but, for this potato salad, you want it to be creamy, rich and simple. The sausages are the star of the show and the potatoes a worthy complement.

Other pickles will work well with the smoky salty sausage and creamy potato salad, so substitute the sauerkraut for pickled red cabbage, gherkins or any other pickle you might have in the fridge.

SAUERKRAUT

At the beginning of Towpath's season, when it's still quite miserable and cold, I make seasonal pickles and jams, and every year I get out the fermenting pot and ferment a big batch of sauerkraut.

Makes 2 x 1 litre/1¾ pints

1½ tablespoons coarse sea salt
2kg/4½lb green cabbage, outer
   leaves removed (save this
   for covering the shredded
   cabbage), cored and shredded,
   but don't slice it too thin,
   3mm/⅛in is good, as salting
   the cabbage will draw out the
   moisture and the slices become
   more delicate
2 bay leaves
1½ teaspoons caraway seeds
1½ teaspoons black peppercorns

Before you start, make sure your hands are meticulously clean as are the fermenting pot or jar and lid and the bowl for macerating the cabbage. The best way to do this is to boil water and rinse your equipment, and then use a clean tea towel to dry them.

Sprinkle the salt over the cabbage and massage the cabbage for 5 minutes to really macerate it. Leave for 5 minutes and repeat again. Leave for another 5 minutes and repeat again.

Now mix in the bay leaves, caraway seeds and peppercorns.

Place the cabbage in the sterilised fermenting pot or jar with a tightly fitted lid. Cover the surface with the outer cabbage leaves, using them like clingfilm, pressing out any air gaps underneath. Place weights, plates or tins on the cabbage so that the brine covers the cabbage and cover with the lid.

Over time, the cabbage will reduce in volume and brine, or liquid, will form, but I find that for the first few days you might not have enough liquid to cover all the cabbage, so massage the cabbage every few days. As the cabbage starts to ferment, more liquid will collect and cover the cabbage completely.

Leave in a dark, cool place for at least 4–6 weeks, giving it a stir every few days and removing any scum that forms on the top.

Once it has reached the sourness you want, place in sterilised kilner jars in either a dark, cool room or the fridge. It will last for months unopened. Once opened, keep in the fridge and eat within 2 months.

CRISPY LAMB WITH HUMMUS, CARAMELISED ONIONS, PINE NUTS AND PARSLEY

This is a lovely dish to use with any leftover lamb shoulder. I often braise lamb shoulders when we host private dinners and since I serve the shoulder whole on a platter, there are invariably leftovers. This is the perfect way to use up all those pieces of lamb that people are too polite to really dig into at the dinner party.

If you want to make this dish and don't have any braised lamb shoulder, you can substitute with some minced lamb. Of course, you can also cook a lamb shoulder from scratch (see page 220).

At Towpath I always make a big batch of caramelised onions at the beginning of the week – they seem to come in useful in so many different ways and you can store them in the fridge for up to 10 days.

Serves 4

For the caramelised onions
6 brown or red onions, thinly
    sliced
3 tablespoons olive oil
salt and pepper

For the lamb
2 tablespoons olive oil
600g/1lb 5oz lamb shoulder, torn
    into big shreds, or minced lamb
1 tablespoon ground cinnamon
100g/3½oz caramelised onions
    (see above)
50g/2oz unsalted butter
200g/7oz hummus (see page 96)
40g/1½oz pine nuts, toasted
2 handfuls of chopped parsley

On a high heat, cook the onions in the olive oil until they start to brown. Turn the heat down to medium and cook until softened, sweet and fully brown. This should take about 20 minutes. Season with salt at the end. Remember to keep stirring the onions as they often catch. If they do, pour in a little bit of water as that unsticks all the yummy caramelisation on the bottom of the pan.

Heat the oil in a large saucepan and when it's smoking hot, add the lamb. Let the meat get super crispy and brown before turning over.

Season with salt and pepper and add the cinnamon.

The lamb shoulder will only need to crisp and warm up as the meat is already cooked. This should only take about 3 minutes on each side. The minced lamb will take a bit longer to cook – turn after 4–5 minutes and cook for another 4–5 minutes. If the meat is too crowded, cook in batches as you don't want the meat to steam.

When the meat is almost cooked, add the caramelised onions and stir to mix well. Check the seasoning, turn off the heat and add the butter. Let it melt and give it a good mix.

On a platter, first spread the hummus, then the lamb and onions. Scatter over the toasted pine nuts and the parsley. Drizzle over the melted butter from the saucepan to create delicious juices.

Serve immediately with bread or flatbread.

HUMMUS

I am currently cooking in my parents' kitchen in sunny Sydney, listening to the sound of the waves crashing on the beach just below us. This is where I come for my quiet time, my peace, every year when Towpath closes and I prepare dinner and test bits and bobs from recipes in the book. Every night before dinner, my dad loves to have a little nibble with either a beer or glass of wine. His favourite is hummus – a perfect opportunity to test my hummus recipe.

Serves 8 as a pre-dinner nibble,
  4 as a main course

200g/7oz cooked chickpeas,
  reserving the cooking liquid
  (see page 128)
3 cloves garlic, minced
1 lemon, juiced
1½ tablespoons tahini
45ml/2fl oz delicious olive oil
salt and pepper

If the chickpeas haven't been cooked fresh, warm in a saucepan with the liquid. Blitz the drained chickpeas (but save the liquid) in a Magimix or with a pestle and mortar until you have a smooth consistency. Add a few tablespoons of the liquid if the chickpeas need loosening.

Add the garlic, lemon juice, tahini and a pinch of salt and pepper. Mix well.

Now add the olive oil in a slow stream. Check the seasoning and consistency. If it's too thick, add more liquid – the hummus should be runnier than you would think because it thickens as it sits. Aim for the consistency of Greek yoghurt.

ELDERFLOWER CORDIAL

I first made elderflower cordial when I was working in Chassignolles in the centre of France. From the end of May to mid June, the elder trees were in full bloom. I loved going out in the early mornings to pick the flowers, then making the cordial to drink a few days later. Having grown up in London and definitely not from a family that would go foraging, let alone go camping, I had never cooked with my own foraged blossoms. Chassignolles opened my mind to this concept and when I returned to London, I suddenly noticed all these things around me, right in the centre of the city, that I could pick and use in my food. There are elder trees everywhere, but I now have my secret patches around London. Sadly, when I returned to my favourite spot last year the whole area was being demolished because of Crossrail. I will have to find a replacement!

Makes 3 litres/5¼ pints cordial

10 large elderflower heads,
    picked in the early morning
900g/2lbs sugar
2 lemons, sliced
25g/1oz cream of tartar
2.3 litres/4 pints boiling water

Place all the ingredients in a bowl. Cover and leave for 48 hours, stirring occasionally. Strain through muslin and refrigerate.

Serve with still or sparkling water (one-third cordial to two-thirds water) or with prosecco.

Note

There is an old wives' tale that says if you don't pick your elderflower early in the morning it will smell and taste like cat's wee. I have definitely smelt that so I urge you to pick them early in the morning!!!

CHOCOLATE CHIP, WALNUT AND OAT COOKIES

We have been making these since day one and they are always on the counter. Weirdly, each batch comes out differently, but they are definitely a crunchy, crispy choc chip cookie, rather than a gooey one. This recipe comes from Sean Moran's *Let It Simmer*. Before Towpath opened, my sister lived in Sydney for many years. When I finished my first cooking job I took two months off to visit her. I had heard amazing things about Sean's restaurant, Panorama, which overlooks Bondi Beach. It's been around for years and the simplicity of Sean's cooking shines through with all the incredible produce he mostly grows on his farm in the Blue Mountains. I would say it is the equivalent of the River Cafe. When I went to eat there, I loved it so much that I bought the cookbook and I made these cookies the next day.

Makes about 24 cookies

145g/5¼ oz unsalted butter, softened
2 tablespoons caster sugar
150g/5½oz brown sugar
1 egg
1 tablespoon full-fat milk
½ teaspoon salt
95g/3½oz plain flour
1 teaspoon baking powder
125g/4½oz walnut halves
100g/3½oz jumbo oats
190g/6¾oz dark chocolate chips

Cream the butter and both sugars with an electric hand whisk or food mixer until light and fluffy. Sometimes if it is very cold and impossible to soften the butter, I start by creaming the butter on its own for a while to soften, then I add both the sugars and continue to cream.

Whisk the egg and milk together and pour into the butter-sugar mixture slowly, with the machine at a high speed. This is to prevent the mixture from splitting, so make sure you add the liquid very slowly, combining properly between each pour.

Add the remaining ingredients and fold in very gently until just combined.

It is much easier to roll the cookies when the dough is cold, so chill in the fridge for 30 minutes before rolling out. Since this makes a large mix, you could either shape the cookies and put them in the freezer or the dough will be happy in the fridge for up to a week. In the restaurant, we refrigerate the dough and bake a fresh batch of cookies every morning.

Preheat the oven to 160°C fan/350°F/gas mark 4. Line a baking tray with greaseproof paper.

We roll the cookies to 36g/1¼oz so that they are exactly the same, but at home I just measure by eye. They just need to be quickly shaped in a ball as they spread out on the tray.

Spread the cookies out so that there is a gap between them the size of the cookie – they really spread. Bake for 18 minutes till they hold their shape. Let cool on the tray for 5 minutes and serve.

June

Towpath Family

If we had a penny for every time a customer told us we were 'living the life' out on the canal doing what we do, we could stop working altogether. On a midsummer's day, when the sun sparkles on the water and everything is cast in a warm yellow glow, Towpath can inspire a kind of dreaminess. Oh to trade in the desk job for days devoted to trafficking in deliciousness. If only that was all there was to it.

It's like the fantasy of owning a horse or a sailboat... before you've thought it all through. Mucking out stalls and sweeping the decks is not for everyone. Nor are the thousand dishes that once washed will soon want washing again. Chores. Even the word sits awkwardly on the tongue, like something to spit out. And yet there's a grounding quality to the daily, necessary tasks of our work and our lives. On a good day they focus our attention while somehow setting our minds free to wander. Hands in warm, soapy water. The making of order out of chaos. It's satisfying. In an ordinary, unremarkable sort of way.

There's no getting around the fact that you have to enjoy a certain kind of physical labour, unglamorous daily discipline and wholehearted collaboration to be happy spending your days at Towpath. And though ours are mostly spent doing what we're each best at, there's no strict hierarchy of labour. We are deckhands and farmhands, all doing whatever's needed, asking a lot of a little place that demands as much from us in return.

Laura and I had woefully little experience running a business or a kitchen when we first opened Towpath. My first real turn as an employer was in hiring her and Amanda Thompson, both of whom had just returned to London after finishing a season at Harry Lester's Auberge de Chassignolles in the Auvergne – Laura cooking

and Amanda running the front of house. We all agreed to give our little experiment three months before deciding whether it had legs, wings even, and seeing who wanted to stay.

The early days were wildly exhila-rating. The neighbourhood seemed genuinely delighted that someone was doing something on the canal, however inexpertly. It didn't take very long before we realised we needed help, which materialised in the form of those nearest and dearest to us: my daughter Micky, Jason's daughter Rae, Jason's assistant Joe (who for a while would become Micky's boyfriend, Joe), Micky's best friend Aida (my best friend Heather's daughter), Rae's cousin Sam. Everyone was either in school or simultaneously working another job. These helpers (except for Joe who had done time as a cook) were uniformly inexperienced. But willing. It was, as they say, a steep learning curve.

When she wasn't standing out in the cold with me making coffees and selling whatever Laura dreamed up from the confines of Jason and my home kitchen, Amanda tried to put systems into place and teach me everything she knew about the bureaucracy of restaurant life – an education for which I remain eternally

grateful. It wasn't a huge surprise when three months in she thanked us and said she wasn't sure Towpath life was for her. She went on to get a degree in winemaking, then left the big city for an off-grid permaculture farm in the Loire.

Laura, on the other hand, declared that there was no place she'd rather be than cooking at Towpath. Thus began a de facto partnership, which a few years ago was formalised into a legal one. Like a good marriage, both of us all in, for better and for worse, warts and all. And like a marriage, we are uniquely aware of each other's skills and weaknesses. We look to each other to bounce ideas off. We laugh at our random similarities that have nothing to do with Towpath but surely explain something about the natural chemistry between two left-handed, hard-working, family-loving Jewish girls who are both allergic to cats. And at the end

of every year it's almost a ritual for us to state the obvious: 'I wouldn't want to do this without you. And I probably couldn't.' We adore each other. We respect each other. And luckily, we complement each other.

Towpath would close in five minutes if I took over the kitchen and Laura the bar. Our skill sets don't run that way. Although she swears her gifts don't come naturally, Laura's genuine love of feeding people is like a vocation, to which she brings enormous energy and a superb palate. She hates being watched when she's cooking, but she's a sight to behold: rolling out puff pastry, deep in concentration, rhythmically working

the wooden rolling pin, leaning in with her whole body, turning the dough, folding it, transforming a lumpen ball of flour and water into something soft, elastic and delicious. Or doing something as simple as filling a bowl with soup – dipping the ladle into a steaming pot, lifting it in such a way that not a drop falls on its way to the plate, then tipping it out with a quiet, focused attention.

Laura does not delight in engaging with the great wide world in the way that standing behind the counter asks you to. She is fierce, steady, passionate, harder working than anyone I've ever met, loyal beyond measure and a perfectionist. Her intensity has been known to be intimidating to some. She doesn't mean it to be. If she asks you to chop celery, she'll cut you a little sample piece and say, 'about this size'. Ten minutes later she'll come to see how you're doing and most likely say, 'Where's your sample piece? Look at these! They're all different sizes!' And she is so much harder on herself. She wears her emotions on her face and shows her love on the plate. You cannot but notice if she is frustrated or displeased. But if you truly find joy in feeding people, there is no one you would rather be trained by. She knows how to show you what she wants and she's an exacting and generous teacher. Once you've learned the ropes, her kitchen is a happy home indeed.

I'm more interested in people. In the possibility that we can make them happy with the most simple, ordinary things, while not giving them exactly what they think they need. They might be looking for wifi or a decaf almond latte to go, when what might actually delight them is to share a table with someone they don't know, look out at the canal and eat something delicious.

From a practical standpoint, my discerning palate and respectable cooking skills don't translate in a professional kitchen, where I have proven myself to be too slow, shambolic and unmethodical to be anything more than a potential liability. In a pinch, I run food and do dishes. I love shucking peas and picking herbs. But in front of a long row of orders, I'd lose my mind. I'm not particularly good at explaining things. Probably because, especially in the beginning, I hardly knew what I was doing myself. My survival skills run more along the lines of peacekeeping and curiosity. If the kitchen is like the army, front of house is the diplomatic corps. When we're at our best it doesn't look like we're working at all. Which must be annoying for the kitchen. I try to lead with a smile and a question, though if I'm truly rubbed the wrong way, my inner dragon emerges and I'm ferocious. Frightening, even to myself. Laura is never as upset by these moments as I am. They reset the balance. Any good cop/bad cop illusion our differing work styles might have created dissolves as I fall on my own barbed sword.

We like to think we've learned something about being good employers over the years. We had loads of fun in the early days, but I wouldn't necessarily want to have been employed by us. Jason and I were like hippy parents. There were late-night rosé-fuelled swims in the canal (which almost everyone but Laura and I indulged in). A trip to my house in Tuscany where we cooked in the wood-fired oven, ate at our favourite restaurants and two of our number (without naming names) jumped naked on the big trampoline out in the garden. The following year we hired a van and drove across France, stopping to feast in Paris before continuing on to the Auberge in Chassignolles where Harry taught us how to butcher a pig and we made sausages to take back to London.

Our escapades made a very happy tribe of us, but on a day-to-day basis, Towpath life was barely controlled mayhem. We were too busy too quickly, doing far too much within a very awkward set-up. Thrilling, absolutely. Sustainable, not really. What began as almost a lark became our livelihood and our sustenance. When it became clear that Laura and I were in it for the long game, we had to figure out how not to exhaust ourselves or the people who worked with us. Laura needed to learn how to delegate. I needed to learn how to translate our ethos into the practicality required to run a small business.

I've always found it a bit cringeworthy when someone tells me with a vaguely pious, self-satisfied half-smile that they're 'blessed' about this or that. But here I sit at my desk thinking back over the years about all the people who've worked with us, who've come and gone, and sometimes even come back again, and the only phrase that keeps popping into my head is that we've been blessed. So forgive me. But we get to spend our days with the most talented, funny, quirky, kind, caring, willing group of people. And if that's not a blessing, then what is?

There's no particular type of person who works at Towpath. We're a bundle of vastly different talents and temperaments. Take, for example, Toby, the first person we hired from

outside our little circle of friends and family. You will never meet anyone more wickedly charming. Or so thoroughly untrainable. He was forever rearranging the tables into new configurations and dreaming up ways we could rig up wing mirrors so that the kitchen and bar could see each other. His coffees were never as good as his chat at the bar, which was so laced with playful innuendo that no one cared. Luckily we have also had people like Alex, whose mad scientist approach to coffee-making helped the rest of us up our game.

Then there was Lucie, a friend of James (who ran his bike shop out of the fourth kiosk in those first two years). She arrived several hours late for her first shift looking like she'd come straight from a rave. But she had a directness that was intriguing and so we gave her a chance – and watched her become one of our most beloved collaborators and the inspiring mother of Ruben and Bel.

We've had chefs like Rachel and Rosie who delight in coming up with new recipes, and ones like Mark who are genius at giving Laura exactly what she wants. There have been 'recovering chefs' like Davo, who'd run high-powered kitchens and came to Towpath looking for the simple pleasure of cooking in a room with a view. Fledgling chefs like Casey, Polly, Rosie M. and the two Sara(h)s who arrived with more enthusiasm than experience, and quickly made themselves indispensable. And transient chefs in between projects or just helping out like Anna (whose Café Deco will have opened in London by the time this book hits the press), Johnny (who now has his own amazing restaurant in Tasmania) and Sam who cooks at Leila's. We've hit gold with random good fortune or with our own customers – Ebony, Rose, Bill, Patricia and Kika, who asked if we needed help and suddenly found themselves with aprons tied around their waists and as much work as they wanted. We've had big personalities – Siobhan, earth-mother goddess, bestower of the world's best hugs. My own inimitable brother Steve.

But don't for one minute think that we haven't had our share of mismatches – like some sort of bad online date that can't be over fast enough. People who looked good on paper but were of the 'every man for himself' school of life or didn't have the flexibility to help make gallons of jam on a rainy day.

Praise be those unsung heroes who wash dishes, run food and provide general bar and kitchen helpfulness. They are the oil that keep the wheels turning. Queen of that crew (which has included Naya, Haak, Brian, Emily, Charlotte, Avi, Yaz and Eva, superstars all) is Lindy, love and kindness incarnate, who has been with us since nearly the beginning. Her way in the world invites us to be our best selves. And she can dance like nobody's business.

Last but not least are the teenagers (usually the children of friends or customers) looking to get their first work experience. They are as we mostly all were at that age: charming, hormonally challenged, and not particularly interested in getting up early or having anyone rely on them. Hannah and Beatrice were the exception to that rule. We're hoping their sister Matilda will want to spend some time with us when she's old enough.

Finding all those marvellously talented individuals, each with their own particular skills, ineptitudes (because we all have those too), personalities and temperaments, is one thing. Then there is the making of a team. Every combination of people has a chemistry all its own. I can be lured into working an evening if it means that Sami and I can put on that playlist only we love and talk about life.

At our best we are like a family. Laura and I aren't of the 'leave your personal life at home' philosophy of employment. We're happy for everyone to bring their whole selves to work. It connects us. I think even our customers can feel it. So we're never just the person making coffee, the person buying it, employee or boss. We also get to see each other in all our complicated humanity, 'trailing clouds of glory' (thank you Wordsworth), which is so much more interesting.

Towpath has the added peculiarity of closing for winter, so that every November feels a bit like the end of a school year. However brilliant the class, not everyone will be back. We struggled with this at the beginning, wanting to hold on to people we love working with. But it's a losing strategy – they're still going to leave when something else calls them. Better to want for them what they want for themselves and trust that some new face will appear with all its bright, fresh energy and talent. Besides, you never know what's going to happen. Take Mike, for example. He came to Towpath in the early days, having worked with Laura in Chassignolles. He was steady and reliable, lovely to be around and made excellent coffees. He eventually left Towpath to help his sister and brother-in-law get the wonderful Black Axe Mangal up and running. A couple of years later he returned. The same lovely Mike but grown up somehow. Ready to take on more responsibility. Now he's my right hand behind the bar. And we try not to let ourselves hope he'll never leave.

TURKISH EGGS

The first time I had Turkish eggs was probably 15 years ago at Peter Gordon's restaurant The Providores and Tapa Room in Marylebone. It was literally the most delicious breakfast I had ever eaten. Something about the combination of the creamy yoghurt, caramelised butter, gooey poached eggs and fresh dill worked wonders together. When I researched it, it turned out that Peter's inspiration for this dish had come from a restaurant in Istanbul. It's always hard to know what the etiquette is of putting someone else's dish on your menu. I always think one should be flattered and I have added my little take on it.

Serves 2

1 tablespoon colourless vinegar
100g/3½oz Greek yoghurt
1 clove garlic, minced
50g/2oz unsalted butter
4 eggs, as fresh as possible
4 sprigs dill, picked
salt and pepper

Fill a medium saucepan with water and add the vinegar.

While the water is boiling, mix the yoghurt with the garlic and season with salt and pepper.

In a small saucepan, melt the butter over a low heat until it starts to caramelise but don't let it burn. Sieve to get rid of any scum and set aside in a warm place.

The water should now be ready to poach the eggs, so turn the heat down and, using a spoon, make a whirlpool in the centre of the pan. Crack an egg into the water as close as you can to the surface. Repeat with all the other eggs as quickly as possible. After a couple of minutes, check the eggs as you want the yolk still to be gooey – they should take about 4 minutes. Use a spider or slotted spoon to remove the eggs and place on a piece of kitchen paper or tea cloth to get rid of excess water.

Split the yoghurt mixture between two bowls. Place two eggs in each bowl, on the yoghurt. Generously drizzle the butter over the top and season the eggs with salt and pepper. Put the dill over the top and serve with toast.

SOFT LITTLE BUNS

In the early years, before we seriously committed to opening for dinners, if it was a lovely evening we would often decide during the day whether we should stay open. I laugh thinking about this as it really wasn't a very clever idea. Since we wouldn't have enough food for substantial meals, we thought about what snacks we could offer with a glass of wine. Although I'm embarrassed to say I've never been to Venice, these buns that Lori and many others told me about, are a typical Venetian snack. I loved the idea of a soft, fluffy bun with a variety of fillings, and the truffle paste and Parmesan has become our signature bun. An incredible little bar in Florence called Procacci serves them this way. These buns are best served fresh out of the oven.

Makes 30 buns

30g/1¼oz unsalted butter
185ml/6¼fl oz full-fat milk
450g/1lb plain flour, plus extra
    for dusting
1 tablespoon caster sugar
2 teaspoons fast, instant yeast
2 generous pinches of salt
olive oil, for greasing

Notes
At Towpath I always make the dough at the end of the day and leave to prove overnight in the fridge – I find it much easier to roll the balls when cold. It also means that you can shape the balls first thing in the morning, leave to prove and then bake.

Fillings include: truffle paste; Parmesan shavings with a squeeze of lemon; Cured Wild Sea Trout (see page 12), Pickled Cucumbers (see page 152) and crème fraîche; roast beef, horseradish cream and watercress; braised mutton and redcurrant jelly; anchovy paste and butter; egg mayonnaise and watercress.

Melt the butter into the milk over a low heat. Remove the pan from the heat and stir in 135ml/4½fl oz water. Set the mixture aside until it cools to lukewarm.

In a bowl, combine the flour, sugar, yeast and salt. Make a well in the centre of the dry ingredients. Pour the lukewarm milk mixture into the bowl and use a wooden spoon in a circular motion to slowly incorporate the dry ingredients until a smooth dough is formed.

Turn the dough out onto a floured work surface. The dough will be quite wet, so lightly oil your hands to keep the dough from sticking. Knead until a smooth, soft dough is formed – this should only take a minute or two. Add a bit of flour if the dough is overly sticky.

Place the dough into an oiled bowl. Cover with a damp tea towel and leave to rest in a warm place until doubled in size – about 1 hour. Knock the dough back and knead for a minute to form a smooth dough.

Preheat the oven to 160°C fan/350°F/gas mark 4 and line a baking tray with greaseproof paper.

Divide and shape the dough into 28g/1oz balls. Place on the tray, leaving a finger's width between each ball so that they will touch each other once they rise. Cover with a slightly damp tea towel and leave to prove in a warm place until doubled in size, about 30 minutes.

Bake in the oven for 10–12 minutes. They should be golden on top and soft in the centre. Leave to cool with a damp tea towel over the top.

This dough is also perfect for baps, so you can roll the dough into 80g/3oz balls for a larger bun.

FRIGGITELLI PEPPERS, SMOKED ANCHOVIES AND CHOPPED EGG

When the weather starts to warm up and evening service begins at Towpath, this is a perfect evening bar snack or starter to have with some delicious wine or sherry. The inspiration for this dish comes from the famous Spanish dish of Little Gem lettuce, chopped shallots, anchovies and sherry vinegar – the combination of textures, acidity and saltiness makes it so perfect on a balmy evening. Friggitelli peppers are a sweet Italian chilli pepper, but sweet in the sense that they have no heat rather than because they are sweet. Their size makes them perfect to cook whole and you don't have to remove their seeds.

Serves 4

For the friggitelli peppers
2 tablespoons olive oil
32 medium-sized (800g/1¾lb) friggitelli peppers
4 tablespoons sherry vinegar
2 tablespoons best olive oil, if needed
salt and pepper

3 hard-boiled eggs, grated
8 smoked anchovies, cut into small pieces

At Towpath we deep fry the peppers in a fryer as it is quick and easy, but you can fry them in a pan. Start by heating the oil in a large frying pan on a high heat. You don't want the peppers to be squashed, so depending on the size of your frying pan, you might have to cook them in batches. When the oil is hot, add the peppers in and let them sizzle. Be wary – the peppers can cause the oil to spit. Turn the heat down and cook for a few minutes. Turn the peppers over once brown and turn the heat up high to brown the other side. Cover with a lid, turn the heat down low and cook until the peppers are soft – about 5–10 minutes.

Once the peppers have browned, you could also put them in a roasting pan, cover with foil and put in a low oven – 140°C fan/325°F/gas mark 3. This will also allow you to start cooking the remaining batches.

Once cooked, pour the sherry vinegar over the peppers immediately so that the peppers absorb the vinegar. The vinegar will also deglaze the pan, picking up all those flavours. Put in a bowl, the good olive oil if needed and season.

Pile up on a plate. Scatter the grated eggs all over the top and the anchovy pieces over the egg. Pour the leftover dressing from the bowl over the top and serve.

Notes
I also serve this dish with crumbled feta and chopped herbs instead of eggs and anchovies. You can also replace the smoked anchovy with plain anchovies.

Vino

Towpath has always been a work in progress. We applied for an alcohol licence when we opened, not because we wanted to make the tiny spot a watering hole but because, in the European style, the idea of really good food without delicious wine was inconceivable.

Our first year at Towpath we had one white and one rosé. That's all. But then those were the days when we were still cooking from home. Now at any one time our list has about 25 wines on it, any of which we will open and serve by the glass, the carafe or the bottle. In practice, this means that once we have, let's say, four different whites open, we pour glasses from those until one is finished and someone asks for something else. It also means that people tend to drink all sorts of things they wouldn't necessarily try if it meant they had to commit to a mysterious and not inexpensive bottle they'd only read a few words about.

We like to think that if we made wine instead of doing what we do, we would make the kinds of wine we serve at Towpath. We are drawn to small wineries whose winemakers spend more time among the grapevines and in the cellar than promoting their wines. Who are passionate and idiosyncratic. Whose wines have a homemade feel. Wine is in large part, of course, an agricultural product. Whatever ideas the winemaker has, whatever he or she does in the cellar, there are also the elements to contend with – and in this sense too we feel a camaraderie with our winemaker friends, tied as we all are to the whims of the weather gods.

Many, many people have tried to sell us wine over the years, but the ones we love to work with are Raef and Kit Hodgson of Gergovie Wines (and the wonderful 40 Maltby St restaurant), Carlo Luperi of Caves de Pyrene, and Alex Whyte and Damiano Fiamma of Tutto Wines. They share an old-world generosity in the way they introduce wines to us and an uncontrived enthusiasm at the prospect of whiling away an evening at Towpath, eating and drinking, talking and tasting. You'd think that's the way everyone works, but I promise you, it's not.

We tasted summer wines last night with Carlo. It was a Thursday evening in May, the very first night we were staying open for dinner (which we do from Thursday through Sunday from sometime in May until sometime in September). The weather was finally warming up after an abysmal early spring and the days were beginning to feel beautifully and endlessly long, the sun gentle but still high in the sky at six in the evening.

Carlo had sent two boxes of assorted wines to Towpath that morning. We'd chilled the whites and sparkles and lined the reds up on the counter. Like it or not, the first approach to a wine is what it looks like on the outside. True you shouldn't judge a book by its cover, but the label, the cork, the shape of the bottle, even the colour of the glass, can't help but tell you something about the sensibility and the particular aesthetic of the people behind the wine, about their playfulness or their sense of tradition. The bottle itself is a sort of calling card.

Carlo hands us each a sheet of paper with a list of the wines we'll be tasting. Bread and little bowls of salted almonds and green olives are brought to the table along with an old enamel jug to use as a spittoon.

We begin with the sparkling. We already have one from Caves de Pyrene that everyone loves, but we've been serving it for a year and it feels like it's time to try something new. We pour ourselves each an inch or so from the bottle into little glass tumblers. It is delicious. Biscuity smelling and bubbly, but not overly so. Dry. Easy to imagine drinking with food or as an aperitif with one of Laura's cordials.

Now the whites come out. Carlo tells us about the wineries. Not so much in technical terms (although that too), but in human terms: this winemaker's wife just ran off with a neighbour; that one's finally managed to buy a plot of land the family had been renting to grow grapes on for years. We'd choose a story over a technical sheet any day. There are about eight of us around the table and we take turns bringing the bottles to everyone in the kitchen and bar to taste before they all join us when service is over to try them properly. It's a tame little scene at this point. Like good schoolchildren, we make neat annotations next to each wine on our sheets – what it tastes like to us or the others, its scent, how it lingers in the mouth. The reds have been chosen with a nod to the fact that a meal at Towpath is essentially an outdoor experience. And that however fine the wine, it will always be served out of Duralex tumblers. On we go, tasting each wine, then comparing it to the others, going back to a wine we liked or thought we liked. More food is coming from the kitchen now. Taramasalata with radishes and toast. Peas in their pods and Ticklemore cheese. Asparagus with ajo blanco. Cauliflower and cheese croquettes. We are tasting attentively, using the spittoon (although admittedly less and less as the night wears on), but we are also tasting as we would drink in real life. In company. In conversation. With food.

There is some, but by no means unanimous, agreement about each wine and no shortage of strong opinion. We've each starred certain wines on our lists. Underlined or put smiley faces next to some. And occasionally a little frown or something along the lines of 'not for me' next to others. We've had conversations about whether we can have a wine on our list that makes some of us swoon and others think of offal and barnyards. Yes is the answer. We don't all have to love everything on the menu or on the winelist to be able to understand that it has its place. It is a democracy of the passionate. I don't want a wine list that only has things on it that I love. Laura makes things in the kitchen that she never eats herself.

A tasting like this lodges in the psyche like a memorable visit to a winery. Huge fun in and of itself, but important also. Our feeling is this: if you want the people you work with to be able to speak about the food and drink they are serving, they need to know in their own bodies what it tastes like. Otherwise every description sounds like a recitation of lines. And how much fun is that? For anyone?

By the end of the evening, our wine-and-food-stained notes look like they've been through a monsoon. We all help put away tables and chairs, sweep and mop and put Towpath to bed for the night. I cycle home a little bit tipsy. Happy to be part of the merry band we are. Grateful for Carlo's generosity of spirit, which will come back to him tenfold, as generosity tends to do.

JUNE

GLOBE ARTICHOKES WITH A MUSTARDY VINAIGRETTE

I have such fond memories of eating whole globe artichokes as a kid. I vividly remember mum cooking them on special occasions – I would get so excited when she did. I loved the ritual of pulling off the leaves, dipping them in a delicious vinaigrette and getting to the treasure at the end... the heart. Whenever I cook artichokes at Towpath I always put a big bowl of them on the counter in the kitchen. It's amazing how many people walk by, point and exclaim at them. A real crowdstopper! They really are beautiful and they taste even better. Perfect on a hot summer's day. I'm always amazed how many hearts are uneaten on the customers' plates and Lori and I are always telling our staff to go back and politely tell them that they've left the best bit. It's a bit of a tricky one to explain to the customer, but I just feel so upset for them that they've missed it!!!!!

Serves 4

For the artichokes
4 very fresh globe artichokes,
    stalks cut or twisted off,
    washed
1 head of garlic, cut in half
    horizontally
4 bay leaves
2 lemons, sliced
1 tablespoon black peppercorns
1 tablespoon fennel seeds
1 tablespoon coriander seeds
3 sprigs thyme
3 sprigs rosemary
100ml/3½fl oz white wine
salt and pepper

For the vinaigrette
2 tablespoons Dijon mustard
2 tablespoons red wine vinegar
1 clove garlic, minced
175ml/6fl oz sunflower, vegetable
    or a neutral oil

Place all the ingredients for the artichokes in a pot. Cover with water and salt generously. The artichokes will want to float to the top. Keep this from happening by covering the pot with a cartouche – a layer of greaseproof paper – and weighing it down with a lid or plate. Bring to a boil, reduce the heat and simmer gently for 30 minutes. Check to see if they are done by trying to pull off one of the lower leaves. If the leaf does not pull away easily, continue to simmer for 10 minutes, then check at 5-minute intervals until cooked. You can also check by inserting a knife into the core of the stem – if it goes in easily, it is cooked. Use a slotted spoon to remove each artichoke, turning them on their heads to drain the water. Leave to cool for 30 minutes before serving or serve at room temperature.

To make the vinaigrette, whisk the Dijon mustard with the red wine vinegar, the minced garlic, 50ml/2fl oz water and some salt and pepper. Slowly pour in the oil. Whisk continuously. You may need to loosen the dressing with a bit of water as you go along.

Notes
Before we serve our artichokes, we remove the hairs. This is very simple to do. Gently spread out the outer leaves to expose the inner softer leaves. Remove these smaller softer leaves. Using a small spoon, scrape out the fuzzy hairs as these are not edible. If the artichoke is properly cooked, the hairs should be easy to remove. Push back the outer leaves so that it resembles the original artichoke.

CURED WILD SEA TROUT WITH SWEET MUSTARD DRESSING

I'm always excited when wild sea trout comes into season. They have a fairly short season that varies from year to year. For me, wild sea trout is far superior than salmon. It is so buttery, rich and soft and I love poaching it whole. It makes an excellent dish when cured. If you can't find wild sea trout, wild salmon is lovely as well. This is delicious served with crème fraîche (as photographed) or the mustard dressing below and any type of pickle, and also great with scrambled eggs for breakfast or chopped up and put in a savoury tart.

Serves 8

1½ bunches of dill, plus extra for
   serving
400g/14oz table salt
260g/9½oz sugar
2 teaspoons black peppercorns
2 teaspoons coriander seeds
2 teaspoons fennel seeds
1 small side of wild sea trout or
   wild salmon (750g/1lb 10oz),
   pinboned, skin on. All white
   sinew removed from down
   the centre

Start by making the curing salt. Chop through the dill and stalks a couple of times, then place in a food processor and blitz till finely chopped. Add in the salt and sugar and blitz till well combined and bright green.

Place in a bowl, add the peppercorns, coriander seeds and fennel seeds, and mix well with your hands.

Line a rimmed baking tray with clingfilm – the clingfilm should be longer than the fish so you can wrap the fish up tightly. Spread half the curing mix all over the clingfilm and place the fish down on it, flat and skin-side down. Spread the rest of the mix over the sides and the top of the fish, making sure that the fish is completely covered. Wrap very tightly with several more layers of cling film – you will be surprised at how much liquid leaks out. Refrigerate for 24 hours.

Remove the fish from the cure and rinse well to remove the cure. Pat dry and thinly slice starting from the tail end. Serve with Sweet Mustard Dressing (see below), Pickled Cucumbers (see page 152) and dill.

SWEET MUSTARD DRESSING

Makes 500ml/18fl oz

1 egg yolk
50g/2oz Dijon mustard
90g/3¼oz wholegrain mustard
10g/¼oz salt
30g/1¼oz caster sugar
pinch of black pepper
1 tbsp merlot red wine vinegar
375ml/13fl oz veg or sunflower oil

Place the egg yolk, mustards, salt, sugar, pepper, vinegar and 50ml/2fl oz water in a food processor or a bowl, and mix well. Slowly add the oil, mixing all the time, until you have a thick, emulsified dressing. You may need a bit of water to loosen it up along the way.

This will last in the fridge for up to a week and is delicious over a lovely green salad or potato salad, or over poached leeks or with asparagus and grated egg.

RICOTTA GNUDI

This recipe is inspired by Lori's *Beaneaters & Bread Soup* book. In our second year, when we finally had the kitchen on site, we started occasionally hosting communal dinners. One of them had a Tuscan theme and these fresh, light, fluffy balls proved to be really popular. Ever since then they have appeared regularly on the menu, much to one of our regular customers, Susanne's happiness. She could eat them every day – and let me tell you she does come every day!

Serves 4

500g/1lb 2oz ricotta
170g/6oz Parmesan, grated, plus
   extra to serve
2 eggs, lightly beaten
5 tablespoons fine breadcrumbs
2 pinches of freshly grated
   nutmeg
plain flour, for dusting
250g/9oz unsalted butter
bunch of sage, picked
salt and pepper

Notes
Every time I make gnudi, they come out slightly differently. Until you feel confident, I suggest cooking one ball as a tester to see how it turns out. If it's still wet, add some more breadcrumbs. Ideally you want as little flour on the outside as possible. However, if the gnudi are falling apart, add a bit more.

The gnudi are also delicious served with a rich ragu or some roast pumpkin or squash.

Start by placing the ricotta in a fine sieve and leave to drain for at least 40 minutes to remove any excess liquid – if it's too liquidy, the gnudi will fall apart during the poaching. The longer you can leave the ricotta to drain, the better.

Tip the ricotta, Parmesan, eggs and breadcrumbs into a bowl. Add the nutmeg and season with salt and pepper. Using a wooden spoon, very gently mix everything together until well combined, but do not overmix. The less you mix, the lighter your gnudi will be. The mixture should be thick, so if it seems at all wet, add some more breadcrumbs. Leave to rest in fridge for about 20 minutes.

At Towpath I weigh the balls at 22g/¾oz but you can roll them by eye – they should be the size of a walnut in its shell and you are aiming for 30 balls. If the gnudi mix is a bit sticky, lightly flour your hands, but use as little flour as possible.

Once shaped, rest again in the fridge for 20 minutes.

Melt the butter and sage on a low heat until the sage goes crispy and the butter starts to caramelise. Turn off the heat and keep in a warm place.

Boil a medium saucepan of water and add salt. Using a slotted spoon, carefully lower the gnudi into the water. You may need to do this in batches as you don't want to overcrowd the pan. Turn the heat down and wait until the gnudi floats – about 3 minutes. Scoop out with a slotted spoon, making sure to drain all excess water and put each portion into a (warmed) bowl. Drizzle over the sage butter, sprinkle with Parmesan and finish with a grind of pepper.

Serve immediately.

Laura's Love Letter to Lori

I asked Lori if I could write something about her. Her response was that she explained everything about herself in one of the stories. It wasn't necessary. She interviewed me when we were shooting in Italy and wrote a little story. I just had to write something about her, from my perspective. Sorry Lori!

Lori and I have worked together since day one or since we acquired the kiosks. For the last six years we have been official partners in the business. Initially Lori and Jason asked if I wanted to be involved as a partner, but firstly I didn't have any money and secondly I hardly knew them. It could have gone either way: a complete disaster or the best thing I've ever done. I feel so lucky as I sit here writing this, a week before we start year 11 that it was the latter.

Lori, this may sound cheesy, but seriously I couldn't imagine doing this with anyone else. I love how easy it is to work together and how much you support me. We express our work ethic completely differently, but somehow it works perfectly and our views and thoughts of how we want to run the place are similar. In all my uptight, controlling analness, you are a breath of fresh air. Your aesthetic qualities, your innate ability to strike up a conversation with every customer and make them feel like you are old friends is incredible. My initial thought is how can you be bothered, why are you so interested? But this is what I love about you. I often laugh when I think about Lori and I switching positions for the day. Put me behind the bar and her in the kitchen. We joke on unbearably busy days that we should do that. As a way of turning people away. Not because Lori is a bad cook, in fact she is an amazing cook – just not a restaurant cook. But more because of me. My tolerance levels are pretty low. I think I would probably offend one out of every two customers – especially if someone asked for a substitution, complained about the cost of something or that we didn't offer a certain type of food or drink… Which is why I love to hide in the kitchen and express my feelings through my cooking. This dynamic therefore works perfectly.

I also want to thank you for helping me adapt to situations the way I do now. When Towpath first opened it was a massive challenge for me. I had never run my own kitchen before and never been in charge of other staff. It was exciting but also incredibly overwhelming and stressful. Every day there is always an issue. The gas stops working mid lunch, at least one delivery a day is wrong, something might be missing or been mixed up with another order. The dishwasher may start leaking. The oven may stop working. The toaster explodes. I could go on and on. I love the way Lori has taught me to adapt to these situations. To realise that getting stressed and worked up benefits no one. To stay calm and figure out what we can do with the given situation, even if we have loads of orders on and we have to tell all the customers that their hot stew will now become a salad. The way that we are human, things happen and customers always understand. This is all thanks to you.

I love how you have always respected me since day one. Even before I was a partner, there was never any sense that you didn't like what I was putting on the menu. That you didn't involve me in everything. You always left the menu up to me, allowed my creative freedom. Of course I speak to you about menu ideas but never once did you say you must do this or make this. That sense of freedom is so rare so I thank you for that and for your endless support.

I love how you always put fresh flowers on the counter for me every day. I love how you sit with customers and have a long breakfast while I'm running around like a headless chicken trying to get lunch organised. I giggle how you are able to come into the kitchen on the busiest weekends and start helping yourself to whatever is around while I'm trying to plate up 20 or more dishes at once. The way you have created a family within Towpath, an incredible community, is all down to you. I'm so lucky to have you as my best friend and my business partner. I love you very much.

COD, TURMERIC AND COCONUT CURRY

Most years after Towpath closes, I help friends out in their kitchens as it's the busiest time of year for other restaurants and it's a great time for me to learn and be in a new, different environment. After Christmas I hibernate in Australia. My parents conveniently emigrated there the year after Towpath opened. What a perfect opportunity to escape winter and flee to the summer sun and sea of beautiful Australia. My mother saves me recipes and books that she thinks I will be interested in and this recipe has been adapted from one of these. It has a Sri-Lankan influence and it is now a regular in my mum's repertoire. I'm always a little bit hesitant putting on Asian-inspired dishes because of my lack of experience in that area, but this dish is definitely a winner at Towpath.

Serves 4–6

750g/1lb 10oz cod (or any other white meaty fish – monkfish, haddock, pollock), filleted and skinned
¾–1½ tablespoons fine salt, for lightly curing
2 tablespoons sunflower, vegetable or a neutral oil, plus a little extra
2 red onions, sliced
2 sticks lemongrass, bruised
4 hot red chillies, bruised
6 sprigs curry leaves
20g/¾oz ginger, sliced
200g/7oz datterini or cherry tomatoes, quartered (or tomatoes you have to hand)
800ml/1 pint 7fl oz coconut milk, tin rinsed out with water
4 teaspoons ground turmeric
2 teaspoons salt
1–2 teaspoons sugar
2 limes, juiced
1 tablespoon fish sauce (optional)

Notes
The curry base can be made in advance and warmed up when ready, but cook the fish fresh.

Cut the fish into 4cm/1½in pieces and toss lightly in the fine salt. Make sure it is lightly salted as this will contribute to the seasoning of the curry. Put back into the fridge until ready to use. Salting the fish first also helps the fish keep its shape and not crumble into a million pieces when cooking. This stage can be done hours before – the longer it sits salted the better it will hold its shape.

On a medium heat, warm the oil in a large saucepan. Add the red onions, lemongrass, chillies, 4 sprigs of curry leaves and the ginger. Cook for about 20 minutes until all the flavours have taken on and the onions have softened.

Add the tomatoes and cook for 15 minutes on a medium heat. Once the tomatoes have softened, add the coconut milk. Gently rinse the tin with water to capture all the remnants of the milk – add this water to the saucepan. Add the turmeric and stir well, then bring to the boil and lower to a simmer. Cook for about 30–45 minutes to allow the flavours to mature. The liquid should reduce and concentrate. When the milk is the consistency of double cream, add in the fish (you don't need to wash off the salt as this will be the seasoning). Poach for about 6–8 minutes.

Take the rest of the curry leaves and fry in a little bit of oil (or butter) to crisp up. Drain on kitchen paper.

When the fish is cooked, taste the curry and adjust the seasoning using the salt, sugar, lime juice and fish sauce, if using. You may not need to use all of it.

Serve with steamed basmati, brown or jasmine rice, the Red Onion, Coriander and Chilli Salsa (see opposite) and the crispy curry leaves.

RED ONION, CORIANDER AND CHILLI SALSA

As you may have realised by now, I am a lover of the condiment. This salsa is extremely versatile – delicious with fried eggs, on top of some avocado and/or tortilla chips and lovely with any type of curry or on the side of fish. If you make a larger amount than you need, it will last in the fridge for a few days. Just remember to bring it up to room temperature before serving.

Serves 4–6

1½ red onions, diced
½ bunch of coriander, including
   stalks, chopped
1½ jalapeños or red chillies, diced,
   seeds left in
1 lime, juiced
1 tablespoon best olive oil
salt and pepper

Mix the onions, coriander and jalapeños or chillies together. Season with salt and pepper and stir in the lime juice and olive oil. Leave for about 30 minutes and check the seasoning just before serving.

ROAST LAMB CHOPS, CAMONE TOMATOES, CHICKPEAS, CUMIN AND YOGHURT

I had never used camone or marinda tomatoes before I started working at Towpath, when our Italian fruit and veg suppliers introduced them to me – they were not readily available in the UK until seven or eight years ago, but now you see them everywhere on menus. They are what we call a winter tomato: camone are grown in Sardinia and marinda come from Sicily. They are both grown close to the sea and the salty soil produces a unique flavour that is both savoury and meaty. Their texture is firm and crisp so I always feel the need to serve them raw. The camone are smaller and rounder, whereas the marinda are larger and ribbed, but they are interchangeable.

Serves 6

1 x 400g/14oz tin chickpeas or
  250g/9oz cooked chickpeas
12 camone tomatoes, eyes
  removed, cut into wedges
3 spring onions, sliced thinly on
  a slight diagonal
bunch of coriander, roughly
chopped with stalks, some
leaves saved for garnish
1½ tablespoons cumin seeds,
  toasted and ground
2 cloves garlic, minced
3 tablespoons lemon juice
3 tablespoons best olive oil
1 tablespoon sunflower, vegetable
  or a neutral oil
6 lamb loin chops (if you choose
  rib, you'll need 2 chops per
  person)
100g/3½oz Greek yoghurt or
  natural yoghurt
salt and pepper

Notes
A word of warning. Lamb fat can spit like mad, so please be careful when browning the lamb chops.

In a small saucepan, gently warm the chickpeas in their liquid until hot. Drain in a colander and reserve the liquid for soups, broths, etc (if using tinned chickpeas, discard the liquid).

Put the chickpeas, tomatoes, spring onions, coriander, cumin, garlic, half the lemon juice and half the olive oil in a big bowl and mix well. Season. Leave for at least 30 minutes before serving and, just before serving, mix well and check the seasoning,

Preheat the oven to 150°C fan/340°F/gas mark 3½.

About 20 minutes before you want to eat, heat a large frying pan over a high heat and add the vegetable oil. Put the lamb chops in straightaway, fat-side down. Using a pair of tongs, hold the chops to render down the fat. They will emit a lot of fat which will turn crispy. Once brown and crispy, turn the chops on to one side. Season and cook for about 3 minutes until browned. Repeat on the other side. When both sides are brown, put in the oven on a baking tray and cook for about 5 minutes. Take out of the oven, place the chops, fat-side down, and leave to rest for at least 5 minutes. It should read 52°C/126°F on a thermometer before resting, which will give a medium-rare chop. Or touch the fattest part of the chop – it should feel like (or have the same amount of give) as the fleshy part of your palm beneath your thumb.

While the lamb is resting, sprinkle the remaining coriander over the top of the salad.

Serve the lamb chops with the juices drizzled over the top, with the salad and a bowl of yoghurt.

LEMON BARS

A weekend staple for us. People go crazy for sweets on the counter at the weekend, so on a Friday multiple bars, cakes and cookies are prepared for the weekend onslaught.

This is normally lovingly prepared by the talented Elaine Murzi. Elaine and I go way back to when I first worked at Melrose and Morgan and she's helped us in the kitchen at Towpath since we first opened, though there was a big gap in the middle where she took time off to have Bonnie and Orla, her beautiful twin girls. The past few years she's been in charge of the sweets section – Elaine has an incredibly light touch. She usually dashes off around 2.30pm on a Friday to pick up the girls from school. Once lunch service is over at 4pm, I find her cakes, slices and tarts scattered all over the room, tucked into high places so they won't get ruined. I'm always surprised to find them and wonder how she gets up there as she is not much taller than me and I can hardly reach anything!

The lemon bar is a recipe developed from a New Zealand Women's Institute recipe book. It was given to me by the immensely talented and inspiring Rosie Sykes, who has been cooking up a storm at Towpath on and off for years. She was my very first head chef at Melrose and Morgan and to be able to cook with her now is such a privilege.

Makes 16 bars

For the base
260g/9½oz plain flour
40g/1½oz icing sugar, sifted
225g/8oz unsalted butter, melted,
    plus extra for greasing

For the topping
1 lemon, zested
120ml/4fl oz lemon juice
440g/15½oz caster sugar
½ teaspoon baking powder
4 tablespoons plain flour
4 eggs, beaten

To make the base, mix the flour, sugar and melted butter together in a bowl until a smooth ball forms.

Take a 23 x 23cm/9 x 9in baking tin and line with greaseproof paper. Grease the tin and fit the paper inside, folding and overlapping it to form a neat edge.

Lay the pastry in the tin and flatten it using your hands. To form a smooth and even layer, place a piece of greaseproof paper over the top and use a jar or glass to roll over it. The paper prevents the pastry from sticking to the glass. Remove the paper when ready and fork holes in the pastry. Put in the fridge to rest. Leave for at least 1 hour. You can make the base the day before and leave in the fridge until needed.

Preheat the oven to 150°C fan/340°F/gas mark 3½.

Once rested, bake the base slowly for 20–25 minutes. You do not want any colour on the base and it doesn't need to be fully cooked as it will be cooked again with the topping. If you cook the base for too long at this point, it becomes too crumbly and can be a nightmare to cut neatly.

While the base is cooking, make the topping. Mix everything together in a big bowl and give it a good whisk until you have a smooth mixture.

Pour on top of the cooked base (which doesn't need to have cooled). I find it easiest to pour the mixture into a jug and then pour it over the base while the base is still in the oven, otherwise it can be a nightmare to carry to the oven as the mixture is extremely liquid. Turn the heat up to 160°C/350°F/ gas mark 4 and cook till it sets but has a tiny wobble – it will continue cooking as it cools down. You might need to turn the tin a few times while in the oven. It should take around 30–45 minutes.

Let it cool properly in the tin before slicing.

Notes

I make the bars the day before so they have plenty of time to set up and cool overnight in the fridge. This makes it extremely easy to cut and serve the next day. The bars will also last in the fridge for up to 4 days.

July

Two Things

There are two elements in the daily Towpath equation I simply cannot do without. You may think their purpose is to lure in passers-by. Window dressing to get people to stop and see what we're up to. And they may indeed have a bit of a bees-to-blossoms effect. But they are there in the first place because they make me happy. Because I cannot imagine spending my days in a space no bigger than a horsebox without them.

One of them is music, the other flowers.

In the very beginning, we made playlists from what at the time felt like an extensive home CD collection. Amanda, who started with Laura, took this on and gave them names like Beauty, Worldly Soulful, Love Lust Abandon, Weird but Good and Sunday Morning. Beauty had Neil Young and Jose Gonzales on it. Weird but Good had Moondog and Bonnie Prince Billie. Then along came Spotify and we all got into the game. I started a running playlist of music I loved. First track: James Taylor, 'You've Got a Friend'. (I know. What can I say? Music from the first album I ever owned.) Third: Rolling Stones, 'Stray Cat Blues' (a teenage favourite). Eighth: Keith Jarrett, 'the Köln Concert'. Tenth: Ali Farka Touré, 'Ruby'. It was all over the place. Which is how it remains, though I've added many more playlists to this beginner's folly. And so has everyone else.

Few things in life delight me more than being alone behind the bar in the morning while we're setting up. Every day we recreate ourselves. Unfolding like reverse origami, putting out tables and chairs, hanging up blackboards,

constructing our outdoor space for the day. In the meantime, bicycles whizz past and kids trundle off to school. Pale morning light skims the water. Even the birds act like they're shaking off sleep. If ever there was a scene that begged for a soundtrack…

Alone is best because I can indulge my musical proclivities without too much embarrassment. We're not open yet so no one's waiting at the bar. Whoever's working with me is on table and chair duty. I can play my current morning favourite a few times in a row without hearing my son's voice in my ear accusing me of trying to kill it. Last year I was stuck on something called 'C'est Aujourd'hui Grand Fete' by Keith Murphy for a few weeks. Then 'Nightingale' by Nora Jones. Sometimes

it's a rambling Indian morning raga. Or a bit of Irish fiddle. Weekends are different. Van Morrison's 'Astral Weeks'. Aretha Franklin on a Sunday.

Once we're open there's more of a democracy around what we listen to. Depending on the combination of people working, our general mood, the weather, how busy we are, whether it's morning, noon or night, and a thousand other factors, our musical accompaniment can veer off in any direction. None of this involves the kitchen, which is entirely independent of the bar, musically speaking. We occasionally take our cue from what they're listening to, like an echo chamber. But mostly we sound like we're on different planets. Occasionally we all opt for silence. Which is its own music if you're really listening.

Our Towpath playlists are like time capsules. And every bit as potent as Proust's madeleines for stirring up emotion and capturing the past. José Feliciano's 'California Dreaming' will forever conjure up the memory of my brother Steve. 'If I Ain't Got You' is bound up in the gorgeous spectacle of Lindy belting it out into a wooden spoon. 'A Lover's Holiday'? That's the sound of the entire Towpath family crowded behind the bar dancing after our 2018 fireworks.

I think the all-importance of flowers is tied to my years in Tuscany. Our little house is perched on a hill, surrounded by fields and woods where all manner of wild things grow in every season. Yellow broom, mallow, sweet peas, hellebore, milk thistle, buttercups, cow parsley, spikey shrubs with small, dark berries, golden grasses, wild fennel, mint, chives and borage. On walks, I'd make little posies to bring home and mix with the lilacs, old roses and 'proper' flowers from the garden.

Perhaps as a result, I am not a fan of hothouse blooms. Or of operatic arrangements you'd never see in nature. Cellophane-wrapped, Crayola-coloured bunches of closed tulips evoke as much feeling in me as a perfunctory box of

Valentine's chocolates picked up last minute from the supermarket. But give me something that looks like a tiny meadow in a jam jar and my heart will leap. Have you ever noticed the simple beauty of a forget-me-not – the way the pale blue petals surround its tiny yellow heart? Picked a single papery blossom off a hollyhock and put it in a vase? Grown sunflowers from seed? Towpath lets me do all these things and this is good medicine to help balance out its more prosaic demands.

The universe is winking and waving at us all day long, even when we're too busy to notice. I'm drawn to anything that slows me down and rewards me for my attention. Whoever works behind the bar has learned by now that putting flowers out on tables in the morning is anything but a rote activity. A tired, wilted vase is so much worse than no flowers at all. They also know that, whether the task provokes in them terror or delight, they will eventually be sent to the garden with secateurs and asked to bring back something lovely. There are naturals at this sort of thing. And those who have something to learn. I try to give a bit of direction and the promise that they can't go wrong. It's all an exercise in seeing.

Over the years we've planted herbs and flowers outside the kitchen, along the woodchip area by the big sycamore tree and in the raised garden we built on the far side of the bridge. Cyclamen, wisteria, rock roses, climbing roses, nasturtiums, geum, hollyhocks, geraniums, hops, cosmos, verbena and the occasional tomato have all put their roots in the soil. Woe to the person who plonks their backpack on top of the flowers growing outside the kitchen. 'They don't like it,' I find myself saying in a horrifyingly schoolmarmy way to the offender. Try as we might, there's always a higgledy-piggledy air to our garden. But it is so much better than what was there before we came.

We've amassed a motley collection of enamel jugs, glass jars and stoneware pots in which to house cut flowers. When not in use, they live in the fourth kiosk,

which was once home to our friend James' bike shop, and now acts as a sort of open pantry (which I am known to have as much fun arranging as I do the flowers). James still repaints our shutters every year, reclaiming his painstakingly drawn lettering and the gaggle of painted coots we inevitably lose to graffiti.

Every so often on a Sunday I sneak off to the Columbia Road flower market and come back with an armful of lovely things I know can survive out on the canal. Pale pink and white wax flowers, pussy willow, yarrow, feverfew, ranunculi and long, thin stems of vaguely extraterrestrial-looking yellow flower balls that somehow fit into the mix.

But even this is not the horticultural moment of our week. That belongs to my friend Hilary, who regularly pedals up on her bicycle looking every bit the English

rose she is, bearing a gorgeous basketful of flowers fresh from her garden. You would think this garden is enormous, so plentiful, varied and frequent are her offerings. But really it's her generosity that is. She comes with cabbage roses like something out of a fairy tale, smelling deeply, properly, of themselves. Intoxicating sprays of lily of the valley. Grape hyacinth, daffodils and honey-scented euphorbia. Towpath would not be the same without her.

One of Tuesday's rituals is what we call the 'Flower Hospital'. Instead of putting our little floral compositions all over the place as per usual, we gather them on a big wooden table outside the bar to give them a close look. Only rarely do we chuck out all our old blooms and start fresh with a whole new lot. We take more of a sourdough bread/sherry-making approach, always holding back a bit of the old to enhance the new. So we give the flowers fresh water, trim their stems, retire the ones that look unhappy, add a few new cuttings if we have them and refashion what's left into fresh arrangements that end up looking like an echo of something that would naturally appear in nature. I make little floral offerings to a kitchen that feeds me with a thoughtfulness I can never properly return.

While this is all happening, the table is a riot of petals, leaves, water and decay. Somehow this is always an irresistible magnet to customers who love nothing better than to sit down in the middle of it all.

I think my not-so-secret agenda at Towpath is to get whoever I can – customers, staff, my own self – to slow down and look at the beauty all around us. If this sounds more hippy than hipster, so be it. But I think we're more likely to be our best selves in this world when we love it.

MILLIE'S SPECIAL

This recipe is named after Lori's mum, who's made it for as long as she can remember. Avocados are nowhere near as plentiful and reliably delicious as they are in California where she grew up. But we hand-pick a box every Friday to get us through the weekend. I know some of the front-of-house staff members get a little tired of having to explain what Millie's special is, but Lori loves seeing her mum's name on the menu and getting to tell people about a favourite dish she grew up eating. So we indulge her!

Serves 4

8 eggs, hard-boiled for 9 minutes
2 avocados
½ red onion, diced
2 limes, juiced
4 sprigs coriander, leaves picked
1 jalapeño, halved and thinly sliced
salt and pepper
sourdough, to serve

Peel the eggs and mash them up in a bowl. Add the avocados and mash up altogether.

Mix in the red onion and half the lime juice. Season. Taste and add more lime juice if necessary. This mixture acts like a sponge and will soak up some of the lime juice and seasoning, so if you are not serving straightaway, always check the lime and seasoning again just before serving.

Serve on some delicious sourdough bread. As much as I am a butter fiend and am outraged when I order a sandwich and it comes without butter, I think the richness of the avocado allows it to be eaten without.

Sprinkle the coriander and jalapeño over the top. Enjoy, Millie!

GAZPACHO

Anyone who comes to Towpath will know that it is a place that is totally dependent on the weather. On a rainy, miserable day, all will be quiet and calm. On a hot, balmy summer's day, the queue will be never-ending from the minute we open to the minute we close. Since there is very little indoor seating, the weather really determines the type of food that I cook. On a cold, rainy day, you will always see a hearty stew or soup, pies or gratins. On a hot day, fresh light salads and cured, pickled or smoked fish. At the height of summer, a refreshingly cold soup is always a winner. Gazpacho is a favourite – for me, a clear sign that it is summer. If you can, prepare the vegetables at least the day before. This will make a large batch but it lasts up to a week in the fridge.

Serves 10–12

2kg/4½lb San Marzano tomatoes, or any other ripe tomatoes, chopped – you want the most delicious tomatoes you can get hold of
2 cucumbers, lightly peeled and chopped
2 red peppers, deseeded and chopped
2 red onions, chopped
4 cloves garlic, chopped
bunch of basil, stalks only, chopped
250g/9oz slightly stale bread, torn into pieces
6 tablespoons sherry vinegar
300ml/10fl oz olive oil, plus extra to drizzle of the good stuff
salt and pepper
3 eggs, hard-boiled, grated, to serve

Place the tomatoes, cucumbers, red peppers, red onions, garlic, basil stalks, bread, vinegar and olive oil in a big bowl and season. The vegetables can be cut quite chunky as they will all be blended in a food processor. Give it a good mix and leave to marinate in the fridge, ideally for a day in advance.

When ready to serve, blitz in batches. I like the soup to be a little bit chunky. If it seems too thick, add a bit of water or more vinegar to taste.

Serve in chilled bowls with a drizzle of olive oil, grated hard-boiled eggs and a grind of black pepper.

Notes

If you want a super silky, smooth soup, then strain it through a sieve once blitzed. I don't like to do this as you end up losing quite a bit of the soup and it's extremely time consuming.

There are so many garnishes you could use. Put basil leaves on the top of the soup or add tiny croutons, diced cucumber, tomatoes, olives, red onion or all of the above.

RUNNER BEANS AND TRAPANESE

Over the years I've had some pretty inspiring and exceptional chefs come through the door and I have learnt such invaluable things from all of them. They have been my inspiration, and one very special person who has cooked here for over three seasons is Rachel O'Sullivan. Even when not at Towpath, we still chat and get excited about food, and she tells me about a delicious new dish she has made and how it would be a great one to put on at Towpath. She is so generous – I always want to be learning from her. The dish below is one of Rachy rach's (as we call her).

Serves 4
Makes 500g/1lb 2oz of trapanese

1 punnet or 250g/9oz datterini
   tomatoes, stalks removed
150g/5o½oz salted Marcona
   almonds, lightly toasted
75g/3oz Parmesan, grated
1 teaspoon dried oregano
2 cloves garlic, minced
2 tablespoons red wine vinegar
5 tablespoons olive oil
600g/1lb 5oz runner beans,
   each topped, tailed and cut into
   3 pieces on a slight angle
2 tablespoons lemon juice
salt and pepper

Place the tomatoes in a blender or Magimix and blend well.

Now add the almonds, Parmesan, oregano, garlic and red wine vinegar. Season.

Blitz well until it forms a smooth but still slightly chunky paste.

Slowly pour in 4 tablespoons of olive oil with the motor running so the oil amalgamates.

Leave the trapanese to sit and then check the seasoning after about 20 minutes.

When ready to serve, bring a pan of water to the boil. Salt the water and throw in the beans. Cook for about 8 minutes until they are soft but not mushy – I personally don't like my runner beans al dente and have a nostalgia about them being soft and almost mushy.

Drain and toss in the lemon juice, the remaining tablespoon of olive oil and season.

Place on individual plates or one big platter. Dollop a generous amount of trapanese on top and drizzle over the leftover dressing from the bowl on top.

Notes
Trapanese originates from the Trapani region in West Sicily, where tomatoes and almonds are abundant. The texture of it reminds me of a pesto and it is truly delicious. This recipe will make plenty, so keep it in the fridge to serve with pasta, fish, lamb, chicken, crispy potatoes or really any other veg.

SPINACH, FETA AND PINE NUT FILO PARCELS (SPANAKOPITA)

When I worked at Rochelle Canteen back in the day, my incredible head chef at the time, James Ferguson, used to make many Greek dishes. His granny, Elektra, was Greek and was an incredible cook, and his parents had a restaurant in Yorkshire, so James was taught to cook some amazing Greek dishes. This one is inspired by him. The great thing about this dish is that it can be served as a proper meal with a salad, as a canapé or I often serve it in the evening as a bar snack.

Makes 32 parcels

2kg/4½lb fresh spinach, stalks picked off and washed thoroughly, or 1.2kg/2lb 10oz cooked spinach
6 spring onions, thinly sliced
3 cloves garlic, minced
350g/12oz feta, crumbled
75g/3oz Parmesan, grated
¼ bunch of dill, finely chopped
¼ bunch of mint, finely chopped
¼ bunch of parsley, finely chopped
50g/2oz pine nuts, toasted
1 packet (400g/14oz) filo pastry
250g/9oz unsalted butter, melted
salt and pepper

Notes
This recipe makes a large quantity. The mix can live in the fridge for up to a week. The parcels will keep in the fridge for 3 days before cooking or can be frozen.

If your spinach is quite stalky (but not woody) don't throw away the stalks but finely chop and sweat them down in some olive oil and salt and pepper until softened. Drain over a colander and add as part of the spinach weight.

Take a large saucepan with a tight-fitting lid and heat until it starts to smoke. You can test the heat of the pan by pouring in a few drops of water – they should evaporate as soon as they hit the pan.

When the pan is super hot, pour in a tablespoon of water and add the spinach. Place the lid on tightly and allow the spinach to steam. This method means that not too much water is absorbed as spinach is incredibly watery. You may need to do this in a few batches. Once cooked, place in a colander and leave to cool.

Take small amounts of the spinach and really wring out all the excess water. Chop up the spinach.

Combine the spinach, spring onions, garlic, feta, Parmesan, dill, mint, parsley and pine nuts in a mixing bowl. Season with salt and pepper and give the mixture a really good mix. Check the seasoning.

Divide and roll the mixture into 32 similar-sized shapes and place on a lined baking tray. At Towpath I measure each ball out at 38g/1⅓oz, but you can do it by eye. Put the tray of balls to the side.

Take a pastry brush, a damp tea towel, the melted butter and a large knife to cut the filo pastry.

Take a sheet of pastry and place it flat on the work surface, so the longer edge is horizontal. (Place a damp tea towel on top of the unused filo pastry to prevent it from drying out.) Lightly butter the whole surface of the filo and place another piece of filo on top of the original piece. Butter the surface and repeat. You should end up with 3 sheets of buttered filo. Now cut the sheets in half vertically and into half horizontally, then cut each horizontal into half again. This should give you 8 strips.

Place a ball of spinach in the bottom left-hand corner of each strip. Now fold the bottom left-hand corner upwards to form a triangle. Continue to fold along the strip in a triangular shape until you reach the end. This should take three folds.

You might need to add more butter as the pastry dries up very quickly. Make sure there are no gaps in the pastry. You will need to work quite quickly with the filo as it dries up easily, but you can ask someone to help or add a bit more butter to wet the filo.

Repeat until the mixture is used up and you have 32 parcels. Place on a lined baking tray in the fridge. They will stick to each other if placed too close. Leave for 30 minutes or more to cool the pastry before cooking.

Preheat the oven to 210°C fan/450°F/gas mark 8.

When ready, brush the parcels with melted butter and place in the oven. Bake for about 12–15 minutes until the parcels have gone crispy and brown. Turn the parcels over halfway through.

Take out of the oven and leave to cool on kitchen paper to remove any excess grease. Serve as is or with a salad. Also delicious served at room temperature.

JULY

RICE AND PEAS (RISI E BISI)

I first read about this in Simon Hopkinson's *Gammon and Spinach* cookbook. I remember having almost a whole box of peas leftover from the week before. The weather had taken a turn for the worse so putting peas in their pods and Ticklemore on the menu wasn't really working. I needed something more comforting and I had these beautiful sweet Italian peas.

It is definitely a dish that doesn't need much messing about. He follows the recipe in Marcella Hazan's *Classic Italian Cookbook* and I follow mine from him and therefore hers, with a few small changes. I love the idea of recipes being passed down from one chef to another.

I also find it funny that writing a dish in a certain way on the menu can cause the dish to sell or not sell. Whenever I used to put this dish on as 'risi e bisi', hardly anyone ordered it. It's a loose risotto, so I called it rice and peas – it flew off the menu.

Serves 4

2 onions, diced
75g/3oz unsalted butter
300g/10½oz podded fresh peas
    (or frozen – I often make this
    dish in the winter)
1 litre/1¾ pints chicken stock
    (or veggie – you can also make
    a stock using the pea pods, see
    Notes)
200g/7oz arborio rice
100g/3½oz Parmesan,
    freshly grated
2 tablespoons chopped parsley
½ lemon, juiced
salt and pepper

Sweat the onions and butter in a wide saucepan over a medium-low heat. Cook gently until they are soft and sweet and not too coloured – around 15 minutes.

Add the peas and season with salt. Mix well, cook for a few minutes, then add the stock and rice and bring to the boil. Cover and turn the heat down to a simmer. Cook for 15 minutes, then turn the heat off. Take the lid off, place a tea towel tightly over the pan and cover tightly with the lid. Leave for 10 more minutes. Add in half the Parmesan and the parsley. Stir well, check the seasoning and add the lemon juice. You want this to be quite wet.

Sprinkle the rest of the Parmesan over the top and serve with a generous grind of pepper.

Notes
You can use the fresh pea pods to make a stock, so you don't waste them. Place the pods in a saucepan and cover with water. Cook for 30 minutes until the pods have softened and then blitz in a food processor and strain. If you have a super powerful food processor like a NutriBullet or Vitamix, you could put the pods in the machine with water and process them directly.

SMOKED AUBERGINE, PIQUILLO PEPPERS, YOGHURT AND CARAMELISED BUTTER

One of my favourite places to eat in London is a Turkish café called Mangal in Dalston. We often go there after work or for Towpath outings – it is our special place. I remember the first time I went I ate this very simple and delicious smoky aubergine dish with lots of butter and yoghurt called *patlican salata*. Every time I go I order this dish and, in fact, I dream about it, so a couple of years ago I decided to create my own version of it. The exact description of their dish is lightly grilled aubergine, peppers, parsley and garlic, chopped and topped with yoghurt and butter sauce. I've tweaked mine a bit. I'm happy with the outcome but it will never taste as good as theirs.

Serves 4

1.6kg/3½lb large purple
   aubergines
2 cloves garlic, minced
3½ tablespoons lemon juice
3 tablespoons olive oil
100g/3½oz unsalted butter
250g/9oz Greek or natural yoghurt
150g/5½oz piquillo pepper strips
   or whole, cut into 1cm/½in strips
6 sprigs coriander, leaves picked
salt and pepper

Notes
This dish is also delicious served with lamb chops or any roast lamb. If you can't find piquillo peppers or have a surplus of red peppers, roast, peel and deseed them and use instead. Parsley or dill could be used in place of coriander.

Start by smoking the aubergines. If you have a gas hob, the best way to blister the skin and cook them is over an open flame. You will have to watch them constantly and may only be able to do one at a time. You can also do this on a barbecue. At Towpath, I use a large griddle pan to cook them. Every 5 or so minutes, check the aubergines – you want each side to blacken and the flesh to soften and be completely cooked through. Alternatively, you can place the aubergine in a super, super hot oven and roast until the same thing happens, which should take about 45–60 minutes.

As soon as each aubergine is cooked, place in a heatproof bowl and cover immediately. This allows the aubergines to steam, making it easier to peel. Leave to steam for about 20 minutes.

Take one aubergine out at a time and place on a chopping board. You can either peel the aubergine whole or cut the aubergine in half lengthways and scoop out the flesh. I keep a bowl of cold water nearby to dip my fingers into as the blistered skin always stays attached to my hands. The blistered skin tastes burnt so you really don't want to have very much of it in with the flesh.

Once peeled, roughly chop the aubergine flesh so it almost looks mashed but still has the definition of pieces. Place in a bowl with the garlic, lemon juice, olive oil and season with salt and pepper – it should be punchy and fresh.

Heat the butter in a small saucepan on a medium heat and cook until it caramelises – I like to serve it a light brown colour. Sieve the butter and keep in a warm place.

To assemble, place the chopped aubergine on a platter or on four individual plates. Thickly spoon the yoghurt over half the aubergine. Generously scatter the piquillo pepper strips all over the aubergine and yoghurt. Season. Scatter the coriander leaves over the top, so you can see every element of the dish.

Drizzle over the caramelised butter and serve with lots of bread. The Yoghurt Flatbread (see page 204) would be particularly delicious with this.

Summertime

People love to talk about the rain in this country as if it were its defining meteorological event. Like sunshine in Southern California. Only not as nice. But ten years on the canal watching the world go by has taught us something: it's not so much the rain (or lack thereof) that's the barometer of our happiness, it is the light.

You have to have lived through a London winter to fully appreciate the delirium that summer can bring. True, winters here are not so endlessly dark as to be mythical, as they are in Norway with its polar bears and northern lights. They are simply dreary. Interminably so.

Summer is another story altogether. The transformative effect of long days of sunshine plus temperatures that invite us to peel off the many layers needed to get through the endless parade of cold, dull Tupperware sky days is impossible to overstate. You know those silhouettes of the evolution of man – early hominoids dragging their knuckles on the floor gradually morphing into striding homo sapiens? Well, from our vantage point behind the bar, that's what the transition into summer looks like.

From a strictly practical standpoint, this requires Laura and I to follow the weather forecast with an obsessiveness most people reserve for social media. All week long (and often many times during the course of a single day) we compare notes and quibble about which source the other is getting their information from. The sight of a row of bright yellow suns on my iPhone weather app (which Laura totally discounts) is the Towpath equivalent of a tsunami warning.

The sunshine effect is evident even in spring, especially if, as is sometimes the case, it's already mid-April, the trees have yet to blossom and we're all still wearing sour-smelling puffer jackets and taking vitamin D supplements. And it comes as a shock to new employees.

We tend to open well before the weather is hospitable enough to do what we do out in the open air. This gives us time to find our stride and train newcomers. 'It can get quite busy,' we tell them, as we struggle to get through the cold, quiet days. We even start to doubt ourselves. 'Maybe people are over Towpath. They've found someplace nice and cosy over winter and they're not coming back.'

Maybe one day this will happen. We hope not.

As the days get longer, people get up earlier (at least the runners and the ones with dogs and small children do). They turn up before we've woken up the coffee machine or written up the board. If we're still putting out tables and chairs, some of them offer to help. In the early days, we'd start making coffees while still setting up, then spend the rest of the morning trying to catch up. If there is a downside to being exposed to the world in the way that we are, it's that getting ourselves ready in the morning feels a bit like doing one's ablutions in public. What a luxury it would be to simply fling open the doors when we're ready.

Properly long, warm beautiful days are cause for elation in our neck of the woods. Anyone with an ounce of control over their schedule seems to declare

themselves a personal holiday. More people than you can imagine show up for breakfast and end up staying the entire day. It can be exhausting. But it's also the best kind of work. There's a giddy sort of happiness in the air. Everyone wants to be outside. We're like squirrels storing nuts for winter, making the most of the light because even though the sun is shining mediterraneanly, we all know what tomorrow may bring.

In the early years, we found ourselves freestyling on bright, balmy days. Who had the heart to deny anyone a glass of rosé when the late afternoon sun was so lovely? Glasses turned into bottles and, while we were at it, a few salted almonds and little bowls of green olives and pickled guindilla peppers. The kitchen began to dream up delicious snacks from whatever was at hand. A potato and onion tortilla for the counter. Little truffle paste and Parmesan buns. When the sun finally set, we lit candles and lanterns. The city dissolved into the night and it felt like we could be anywhere.

These impromptu evenings were undeniably lovely and so different from the days – even if our tables were filled with the very same people. They were different too from the dinners we'd hosted over the years. Those were occasions. One-off causes for delight, but not exactly relaxing. Now there was a spaciousness that the rush of days rarely allowed for. A slowing down. As if a simple glass of wine and something delicious were reward enough for having made it through the day.

We never at this point officially declared a change in our opening hours. There just came to be an unspoken expectation on both sides of the counter that if the evening was truly glorious, we'd keep on pedalling.

But exuberance can only take you so far. There is a particular pleasure in the long haul and the strange mixture of euphoria and exhaustion it leaves in its wake – though try not to make a habit of it. Among other things, it puts you at risk of

coming to loathe the very work you once loved. We soon tired of spontaneous 15-hour shifts, even though they mostly still felt like a bit of a party. But we didn't know how to commit to staying regularly, properly, reliably open in a country where summer never entirely allows you to put away your jumpers and raincoats. Still, we ourselves found evenings on the towpath so beguiling that every year we inched the boat out a little more. Snacks became more substantial and intentional. We *sort of* planned for the weather and rota'd on extra people to help at night. But our approach remained haphazard.

A few years ago, we finally asked ourselves, 'Do we really want to do this?' Tell everyone we'll be open for dinner and really mean it? So that customers can do more than look up at the sky and try to intuit whether we'll be there. And staff can stop proving how loyal and hardcore they are by working insane hours. We wanted to try. And so, from Thursday through Sunday, from sometime in May until sometime in September (each particular year's weather helps us decide precisely when), we cook dinner. Rain or shine. Whatever the temperature. No bookings – just turn up.

We announced our summer evenings on the blackboard. Added beautiful new wines to our list. Hired more lovely people – enough so that we could bring in a fresh crew for the evenings and let the day folks go home. Everyone is happier.

There are still times when dinner feels like the one-too-many-things we've taken on at Towpath. Especially after too many days of rain. Or crazy days of sun and heat. But when the light is low and golden and everyone seems to be leaning into each other, laughing and talking, sharing food and wine, there's no place we'd rather be. And no better antidote for the long, dark nights of winter ahead.

POTTED SHRIMP AND PICKLED CUCUMBERS

Potted shrimp is a quintessentially British dish. It originates from Lancashire and the tiny sweet shrimps come specifically from and around Morecambe Bay. Traditionally they would have first been boiled in seawater and then peeled before eating. The dish was invented as a form of preservation, mixing a spiced, clarified butter through the shrimp and pouring a layer on top to form a barrier. In a similar manner, pickling cucumber is also a form of preservation and great to cut through the richness of the shrimp. Most recipes call for a spiced melted butter mix, but I love making a hollandaise for mine – it just makes the dish seem lighter and fluffier!

Serves 4

For the reduction
150ml/5fl oz white wine vinegar
150ml/5fl oz white wine
2 shallots, roughly chopped
5 peppercorns
3 bay leaves
5 sprigs tarragon
7 blades mace
2 allspice berries

For the hollandaise
200g/7oz unsalted butter
1 egg, plus 1 yolk
1–2 tablespoons of the reduction

For the potted shrimp
250g/9oz brown shrimps, cooked
    and peeled
¼ teaspoon freshly grated nutmeg
2 pinches of cayenne pepper
⅛ teaspoon ground allspice
10 chives, finely chopped
6 sprigs dill, finely chopped
salt and pepper

Start by making the reduction. Place all the ingredients in a saucepan and reduce until you are left with 2 tablespoons of liquid. Strain and cool.

While the reduction is cooling, put the butter in a saucepan on a low heat and gently melt. Make sure the butter is not too hot when it's time to add to the eggs or the hollandaise will split.

Using a bain-marie, whisk the egg, egg yolk and 1 tablespoon of the reduction over a low heat until it becomes light and fluffy. Keep stirring as you do not want the eggs to curdle. Occasionally you may have to take the bowl off the bain marie to cool down the mix. Remove from the heat when ready.

Remove 50g/2oz of the melted butter for topping the shrimp. Slowly whisk the remaining butter into the egg mixture until it forms a glossy, thick hollandaise. Check the seasoning and, if necessary, add the other tablespoon of reduction.

In another bowl, put in the brown shrimps, nutmeg, cayenne, allspice, chopped chives and dill. Mix well and then gently coat the shrimps with the hollandaise.

Check the seasoning. Place the potted shrimp into 4 x 90ml/3¼fl oz glasses. You can also place in a container and scoop out when ready to use. Top with the remaining butter and refrigerate.

When ready to serve, remove the potted shrimp from the fridge. Place in an oven heated to 160°C fan/350°F/gas mark 4 for a few minutes to warm them briefly. Turn each potted shrimp over onto a plate, removing the glass. Serve with Pickled Cucumbers (see opposite) and toast.

PICKLED CUCUMBERS

Makes 1 litre/1¾ pints

300ml/10fl oz white wine vinegar
150g/5½oz caster sugar
5 large cucumbers (about
    1kg/2¼lb)
2 tablespoons salt

Notes
There are endless flavourings you
could add to the pickling liquid –
dill, coriander or mustard seeds.

I like to make big batches,
using up to 20 cucumbers. Just
multiply the liquid and sugar
from the start. It's a great way to
use up cucumbers.

Heat the vinegar and sugar in a saucepan and bring
to a boil. Stir to dissolve the sugar, then turn off the
heat. Cool completely.

While the liquid is cooling, wash and stripe-peel the
cucumbers. Slice the cucumbers into rounds using a
mandoline or knife to a 3mm/⅛in thickness.

In a colander with a bowl underneath, place a layer
of sliced cucumber and sprinkle over some salt. Toss
well and keep repeating until all the cucumber has
been salted, but add only enough salt for seasoning.
Leave for a good hour, then pat dry the cucumbers.
They should taste a bit salty but not too salty.

When the pickling liquid is completely cool, immerse
the cucumbers in the liquid. Put in a sterilised, airtight
container and leave for 24 hours or more. These
pickles will last for years if unopened. Once open,
keep refrigerated – they will last for a few months.

BRAISED LENTILS, BEETROOT AND RICOTTA

This is a ridiculously flexible dish and one that you will see appear at Towpath all year round. It is a great hot vegetarian option and can be adapted for any season. The lentils can be made well in advance and you can even make a much bigger quantity and use as and when you need to. A great way to use bits and bobs up in your fridge. They will last in the fridge for a good week.

Serves 6–8

250g/9oz Puy lentils
2 tablespoons olive oil, plus extra
   to serve
2 onions, sliced
4 cloves garlic, minced
4 bay leaves
2 sprigs rosemary
2 sprigs thyme
2 carrots, thinly sliced
½ head fennel, sliced on an angle
2 inner celery stalks, sliced on
   an angle
½ leek, sliced on an angle
4 tablespoons vinegar, preferably
   merlot red wine vinegar or
   sherry vinegar
salt and pepper

To serve
350g/12oz beetroot, cooked,
   peeled and sliced into bite-
   sized wedges
250g/9oz ricotta
2 tablespoons chopped parsley
   leaves

Place the lentils in a medium saucepan. Cover with water and bring to the boil.

While the lentils are coming to the boil, prep all your vegetables.

Turn the heat off the lentils as soon as they come to the boil and drain. Rinse the lentils thoroughly with cold water to get rid of any scum.

On a medium heat, take the same pan and add the olive oil and onions. Sweat down so the onions soften and start to brown a little. Add the garlic, bay, rosemary, thyme, carrots, fennel, celery, leek and season. Cook for about 15 minutes so the vegetables soften.

Add the lentils, mix thoroughly with the vegetables and cover with cold water – the water should be at least 3cm/1¼in above the top of the lentils.

Bring to the boil slowly and turn down to a very, very gentle simmer. You want the lentils to cook slowly so that they keep their shape and don't fall to pieces. When the lentils feel as if they are almost cooked, turn the heat off as they will continue to cook in the residual heat. This should take about 30–40 minutes.

Add the vinegar and check the seasoning. You will always need to add more vinegar to the lentils just before serving.

To serve, warm up the lentils and add the beetroot wedges. Check the seasoning and acidity. Serve in bowls or plates, adding a blob of ricotta on top of the lentils and sprinkling over chopped parsley, a drizzle of olive oil and some salt and pepper.

Notes
At Towpath I also serve the lentils with mozzarella and basil sauce, wild garlic sauce or Pickled Radicchio (see page 84). Pumpkin or squash in autumn, rainbow chard and anchovies in spring. They're delicious with sausages, cotechino or on the breakfast menu with anchovies and a soft-boiled egg.

WHOLE PLAICE, PANZANELLA AND AIOLI

As the sea temperature starts to warm up in spring, the brown or dusky green flat fish with their incredible bright red spots move from the cold, deep waters, where they have spent the winter months spawning, to the shallower waters to feed. Plaice are caught in the UK generally between May and September. Initially, when the plaice arrive, they are skinny and used mostly as bait. Come July, they have had plenty of time to feed and fatten up. I love plaice and I think it is an incredibly handsome and luxurious thing served whole. Its meat is sweet and tender and when roasted in a super-hot oven, the skin crisps up and is delicious.

Serves 4

For the salad
750g/1lb 10oz heritage tomatoes, ripe
100g/3½oz stale bread, cut or torn into approximately 3cm/1¼in squares
1 clove garlic, minced
6 tablespoons best olive oil
4 teaspoons sherry vinegar
4 teaspoons merlot red wine vinegar or red wine vinegar with a pinch of sugar added
½ bunch of basil, leaves picked
salt and pepper

For the fish
4 whole plaice, scales, fins and guts removed
160g/5¾oz unsalted butter, softened
150ml/5fl oz white wine
1 lemon, cut into wedges
aioli (see page 60), to serve

Notes
The fish could be served with chopped salad, runner beans and trapanese, potato salad or crispy potatoes and romesco.

To make the salad gluten free, replace the bread with red onion, shallot or spring onion.

Preheat the oven to as hot as it can go. At Towpath I turn it up to 230°C fan/475°F/gas mark 9.

Now prepare the salad. Do this about an hour in advance so the bread has time to soak up all the juices from the tomatoes and the dressing.

Wash the tomatoes and take out the eyes. Slice each into 8 wedges.

Place in a bowl with the bread, garlic, 4 tablespoons of the olive oil, the sherry vinegar, merlot vinegar and season. Leave to marinate for 1 hour.

When ready to serve, mix through the rest of the olive oil as the bread will soak up a lot of the oil while it is sitting. Add the basil leaves.

Place the fish on a large baking tray/s. Divide the butter into 8 blobs and place a blob on the underneath and topside of each plaice. Season both sides with salt and pepper and distribute the wine evenly between the four plaice.

Place in oven for 12–16 minutes until the plaice is crisp and cooked. The fish is cooked when a toothpick inserted right next to the spine on the thickest part and thickest side (brown side) of the fish comes away easily. Remove from the oven and baste the juices over the fish.

Make sure all the delicious juices are served over the fish, alongside some lemon wedges, the panzanella salad and lots of aioli.

COURGETTE, SAFFRON AND WHITE BEAN STEW WITH CREME FRAICHE AND MINT

This is a regular dish on the Towpath menu and I am always amazed by how popular it is even in the height of summer. This stew is a great vegetarian option and is also vegan if you omit the crème fraîche.

Serves 6–8

For the beans

250g/9oz dried white beans, such as arrocina (which I use), cannellini or butter, soaked overnight
1 head garlic, cut in half horizontally
3 bay leaves
2 sprigs rosemary
2 sprigs thyme
handful of black peppercorns
2 red chillies, whole
2 tablespoons olive oil
salt and pepper

For the stew

150ml/5fl oz olive oil
4 onions, thinly sliced
1kg/2¼lb courgettes (once topped and tailed), washed and cut into 1cm/½in-thick rounds
2 bay leaves
4 cloves garlic, minced
½ teaspoon saffron strands
150ml/5oz boiling water
2 tablespoons lemon juice
salt and pepper

To serve

100g/3½oz crème fraîche
4 sprigs mint, picked and roughly chopped
best olive oil

Take the soaked beans and drain in a colander. Place in a saucepan and cover with 1.5 litres/2½ pints water. Bring to the boil and remove all the scum that forms on the top.

Turn the heat down to a simmer and add the garlic, bay, rosemary, thyme, peppercorns, chillies and olive oil.

Cook very slowly until the beans are soft, but have kept their shape and are not falling apart – about 45–90 minutes. Remember the beans will be cooked again with the courgette base. Once cooked, add plenty of salt.

While the beans are cooking you can start with the courgette stew. Start by heating the oil in a large saucepan over a medium heat. Add the sliced onions and cook until soft and sweet with a little bit of colour – this should take about 20 minutes. Season.

Now add the courgettes, bay leaves and garlic and turn the heat up. You want to get some colour on the courgettes, so keep an eye and stir from time to time. After about 10 minutes, turn the heat down to medium and cook for a minimum of 45 minutes. This is the most important stage as you want to cook the courgettes for as long as possible so they become sweet and mushy. I've been known to cook them for as long as 2 hours. Season.

While the courgettes are cooking, soak the saffron in the boiling water and leave for at least 10 minutes to infuse. Add in the saffron and its infused water and stir well. Saffron is incredibly expensive so make sure you get every last morsel out of the jug. Use the liquid to scrape all the deliciousness that has stuck to the bottom of the pan. Cook for another 10 minutes so the courgettes take on the colour of the saffron.

Now add in all the cooked white beans and their stock, removing the garlic, bay, rosemary, thyme, peppercorns and chillies. Cook for another 30 minutes at a simmer so all the flavours get to know one another and the liquid thickens. Stir from time to time as the beans can catch and burn quite easily.

Check for seasoning and add the lemon juice. Start with half the juice and taste. Add more accordingly.

Serve with a generous dollop of crème fraîche, the chopped mint and a generous drizzle of delicious olive oil.

Notes

A lovely thing to do is to use the base for the courgette stew and omit the saffron, but add red chillies, anchovies and lemon juice instead. Cook until it becomes incredibly mushy and then serve either with pasta or on toast with mozzarella. Drizzle some lemon juice over the top. It is truly delicious and something I put on the menu.

DAWNY'S CHICKEN OR CHICKEN MARBELLA

Although my mother will insist otherwise, I have such strong memories of her delicious cooking. Like mine, her food is simple but tasty. To this day, I love to cook all her dishes, although she always says that they are nothing special. I think they are.

My parents are Jewish South African and moved to London in the early 70s to escape the political situation. I always remember big long lunches with many of their friends, who also moved to London. I've adapted this recipe from the iconic *Silver Palate Cookbook,* which was a must-have for all of them in the early 80s. I always brown the meat off first to crisp up the skin, but my mother would never do that – far too messy and smelly for her immaculate kitchen! She would also use water rather than chicken stock, but I always have chicken stock in the kitchen and think it adds more flavour. It is still delicious with just water.

This is one of my fondest memories of my mum's cooking.

Serves 4–6

8 organic or free-range chicken thighs, skin on, but edges trimmed
8 cloves garlic, thickly sliced
2 tablespoons dried oregano
6 bay leaves
420g/15oz prunes, pitted
340g/11¾oz green olives, pitted or not
220g/8oz capers in brine, with a bit of their juice in
160ml/5½ fl oz red wine vinegar – I use a slightly sweet merlot vinegar
135ml/4½ fl oz olive oil
2 tablespoons sunflower, vegetable or a neutral oil
100ml/3½fl oz white wine
100ml/3½fl oz chicken stock or water
40g/1½oz muscovado sugar
salt and pepper

Place the chicken, garlic, dried oregano, bay leaves, prunes, green olives, capers (and a bit of their juice), red wine vinegar and olive oil in a container and mix really well. Cover, place in the fridge and marinate overnight (48 hours if possible).

Preheat the oven to 135°C fan/300°F/gas mark 2.

When ready to cook, heat an ovenproof frying pan and add the vegetable or sunflower oil. While the pan is heating up, remove the chicken from the container, leaving everything else behind.

Once smoking hot, add the chicken, skin-side down. Season with salt and pepper. Cook until the skin is brown and crispy. Turn on to the other side, season and cook until coloured. The second side will be much quicker – you just want a bit of colour. If your pan is too small for all the chicken thighs, cook them in batches as overcrowding the pan will cause them to sweat rather than brown.

Once the chicken has been browned, remove from the pan and set aside. Add the white wine to the pan to deglaze the pan and get all the deliciousness off the bottom of the pan. Place the chicken back in and add either the stock or water. Bring to the boil.

Add all the remaining ingredients from the marinade, including all the liquid, and bring to the boil. Turn the heat off. Make sure the chicken thighs are skin-side up and sprinkle over the skin with the sugar.

Cook for about 20–30 minutes in the oven, until the chicken is cooked through. Serve with rice or Barley Couscous (see page 246).

Sideshows

Something about the open-to-the-world configuration of our set-up invites experimentation. Over the years, Towpath has been a makeshift stage for the things we love, other people's talents and all manner of invention and celebration. Occasionally, we take our show on the road. It's good for us. Our daily rhythms are grounding, but our forays off-piste wake us up.

We'd only been open for a month when we invited everyone we knew to a *calçotada*, something that usually happens in Spain, in springtime, when the delicate alliums, which taste like something between an onion and a leek only sweeter and juicier, are harvested and grilled, then wrapped in a bit of newspaper to be eaten with romesco sauce, bread and lots of red wine. If you've never heard of calçots it's probably because you don't live in Spain. When our promised supply fell through (beware of these sort of promises), we did the only thing we could think of – bought a ticket to London for the Barcelona-based brother of a customer and invited him to come to Towpath with a suitcase full of them. This more-or-less set the tone for our approach to disaster management.

We've taken Towpath to a frescoed villa deep in the Lazio countryside to cook a wedding feast for 200, and across the canal to our friend Dan's studio to celebrate the Day of the Dead. We've brought the Extremadura to Towpath, thanks to Paul and Nacho who farm off-grid on a *finca* there. They set up a *bodega* in the fourth kiosk with olive oil, *pimentón,* wines, cheeses and cured meats, and we had a night of tasting, listening and learning about the culinary ways of old Spain.

We've had friends from Tuscany – Dario, who brought recipes, a trumpet and strains of Dante's Inferno from his famed *maccelleria* in Panzano. Guido who grows olives, ancient grains and makes what he calls 'archaeological wines' using old Tuscan grape varieties and traditional, non-intrusive farming practices. Back when we were the only ones on our stretch of canal, we served a community dinner for more than 100 people at one long table. For a while, we had a lopsided old barge outfitted with a few benches, kept it moored across the canal and paddled it over on sunny weekends. There was also an equally ancient Citroen horsebox we drove around town to events.

But it's not always about food. One summer night a string quartet played from the middle kiosk. We've danced jigs to Kevin and his band's accordion, fiddle and guitar. Sold our friend Ann's handmade linen dresses on a couple of Mondays (otherwise our day of rest). Hosted screenings of *The Lion King* and *Othello* during the Shakespeare in Shoreditch Festival with the films projected

onto a screen rigged up under the birch trees across the canal, their mirror image reflected in the rippling water. Moviegoers watched from the beach wearing glowing blue wireless headphones. Meanwhile, cyclists pedalled by. Dogs and their owners went past on their evening constitutionals. It was surreal. Dreamlike.

And then there are Tuesdays. The start of our Towpath week is a very roll-up-your-sleeves kind of day. The fridges are empty. 'There's nothing left to eat,' is Laura's most frequent lament. There are always lots of big deliveries. Wine orders to make. A well-spent Tuesday makes for a happy rest of the week, but it can be tiring. So when our friend Rachel (whom we hardly knew almost ten years ago when she approached us with the idea), asked if she could give Thai shoulder and foot massages at Towpath, we thought, 'Well, that could be a reason to want to come to work on Tuesdays.'

Rachel sets up home in the fourth kiosk just before lunchtime, rolling out mats, arranging stools and cushions, potions and oils. 'What'll it be?' she asks, when it's your turn. 'Shoulders or feet? A little bit of both?' You sit down and let your eyes wander over the canal or you close them and drift off while she works on you. The only downside, if there could possibly be one, is figuring out how to get your spaced-out self off the cushion and back to work when she's done.

We've been the site of much revelry over the years – birthdays, weddings, anything really that's cause for celebration. The setting up for these occasions seems to be an advertisement in itself. The location is still very much Towpath, but it's Towpath dressed up for a party. Cloth napkins, old French china, wildflower posies, bunting, candles, lanterns. Half the people coming upon the scene try to sit right down at the table and order dinner. Or book Towpath for their own gathering – but we only do them for the friends of Towpath. People who know us, and what we do. It's somehow more of a real celebration that way.

ROAST PORK TENDERLOIN AND FRIGGITELLI PEPPERS

I'm not a massive lover of pork though I do love bacon and all cured meats. Lori is also quite specific about what she likes and doesn't like. She tends to go for lighter, cleaner options and very rarely has meat at lunch. But occasionally when I go to ask her what she wants for lunch she will say I'm just dying to have the pork. I'm always quite shocked when she says that but it also puts a smile on my face. Marinating the pork for a few days makes it so tender. I love the crunchiness of the peppers with the softness of the pork mixed in with the vinegary, cumin, fennel, smoky flavours. So does Lori. The marinade comes from the Moro cookbook.

Serves 4–6

For the pork marinade

2 pork tenderloins or
   1.5kg/3lb 5oz pork tenderloin
1 tablespoon coriander seeds
1 tablespoon cumin seeds
1 tablespoon fennel seeds
1 tablespoon sweet smoked
   paprika
6 cloves garlic, minced
3 pinches of saffron strands,
   infused in 6 tablespoons boiling
   water
2 tablespoons dried oregano
3 bay leaves, crumbled
90ml/3¼fl oz merlot red wine
   vinegar or red wine vinegar
   with a pinch of sugar added
90ml/3¼fl oz olive oil
salt and pepper

For the frigitelli peppers

800g/1¾lb friggitelli peppers,
   cooked as per the recipe on
   page 113
3 sprigs coriander, leaves picked
3 sprigs mint, leaves picked
3 sprigs parsley, leaves picked

If you can, marinate the pork 1–2 days before you want to use it – it will really help it to tenderise. Prepare the pork by removing any sinewy bits and portion the meat into 6 pieces. One whole tenderloin should give you three portions.

Toast the coriander, cumin and fennel seeds in a dry pan till fragrant and then grind finely together.

In a container that neatly fits the meat and marinade, put the coriander, cumin, fennel, smoked paprika, garlic, saffron and its water, oregano, bay leaves, vinegar and olive oil. Mix well. Add the pork and give it a good mix so it's fully coated. Cover, place in the fridge and leave until ready to use.

Preheat the oven to 160°C fan/350°F/gas mark 4. Take an ovenproof saucepan large enough to fit all the pork and heat on high. Remove the pork from the marinade and season all over, reserving the marinade.

Place the pork in the smoking hot pan and cook for about 2–3 minutes until the side has browned. The first side may take a bit longer than the other sides. Rotate until each side has browned.

Turn off the heat and add half the marinade to the pan. This helps deglaze the pan and get all the caramelised flavours off the bottom of the pan.

Place in the oven and cook for about 8 minutes. Turn the pork over and add more marinade if the pan looks dry. Place back the in oven and cook for another 6–8 minutes. The pork is done when a skewer inserted into the thickest part comes out hot or if a thermometer reaches 62°C/144°F. Remove from the oven and if the pan is dry, add more marinade immediately while the pan is still hot. Give it a good stir with a wooden spoon. Leave to rest for at least 5–10 minutes.

While the pork is resting, cook the peppers as per the recipe on page 113. Toss the fresh herbs through.

To serve, slice the pork on the angle in 0.5cm/¼in-thick slices. I place the pork on top of the peppers and then pour the pork juices over.

Make sure you have lots of bread handy to soak up the delicious juices.

RASPBERRY AND FRANGIPANE TART

I love making pastry and I love making tarts. This dessert always seems to me like an elegant and refined way to finish off a meal. It's light and rich at the same time and I find there is always room for a slice, no matter how full you are. It's a great tart to have in your repertoire as the variations of fruit are endless. My favourite combination is raspberry due to its tartness. But as you go through the seasons, use fruit accordingly. Rhubarb, quince, cherries, apricots, peaches, figs, blackberries and gooseberries are all delicious. It's also a great way to use up fruit that might be turning. Poach the fruit and use the fruit for a tart and the liquid for cordial.

Serves 8

For the pastry

225g/8oz plain flour, chilled, plus extra for dusting
140g/5oz unsalted butter, diced and chilled
60g/2¼oz caster sugar
1 egg, plus 1 yolk, whisked

For the frangipane

350g/12oz unsalted butter, softened
250g/9oz caster sugar
4 eggs
100g/3½oz ground almonds
250g/9oz almonds in their skins, blitzed finely or finely chopped
50g/2oz plain flour

3 x 125g/4½oz punnets of raspberries
crème fraîche, to serve

Start with the pastry. Make sure all the components are very cold as this will result in a crumbly pastry. In a Magimix, Kitchen Aid or bowl, rub the flour and butter together to form coarse breadcrumbs. Add in the sugar and mix gently. Slowly incorporate the egg and yolk, adding a little bit at a time to form a dough. Be patient, as I am always surprised at how easily the dough forms with very little liquid and you might not need all of it. Make sure you have a smooth dough and roll into a flat ball. Wrap and rest in the fridge for at least 30 minutes.

Remove from the fridge and, when the dough is pliable, (don't try to do this stage if the dough is too cold), roll out on a floured surface into a big circle 4cm/1½in larger than the base of a 28cm/11in tart tin that has a removable base. The easiest way to do this is by drawing around the base. The dough should be 3mm/⅛in thick. If you have too much pastry, set the excess to one side for another use.

Line the tart tin with the pastry, pressing in gently to make sure that the pastry hangs slightly over the top of the tin. Rest in the fridge for at least 30 minutes.

Preheat the oven to 140°C fan/325°F/gas mark 3.

While the pastry is resting, make the frangipane.

Cream the butter and caster sugar together until super, super light and fluffy. If the butter is soft, this should take about 5 minutes. Slowly add in the eggs, whisking briskly to prevent the mixture from splitting. If it begins to split, whisk in a small amount of flour until the mixture comes back together. Gently fold in the almonds and the plain flour. Don't overmix. Place in the fridge until ready to use.

Take the tin out of the fridge, line the pastry case with greaseproof paper and then baking beans. Bake for 30 minutes – you want the pastry to cook but not become too browned. Remove the baking beans and greaseproof paper. If the base is still a bit undercooked, place back in the oven for 5 more minutes.

Now spoon in the frangipane (you might not need all of it) and place in the oven for 5 minutes to soften the frangipane. Remove from the oven and smooth the frangipane so that it is even and has spread out to the edges. At this stage you might need to add a bit more.

Top evenly with the raspberries, making sure they are all presentation-side up.

Place on a baking tray as the frangipane might overflow slightly and put in the oven.

Cook for 30 minutes. Turn up the heat to 160°C fan/350°F/gas mark 4 and cook for another 15 minutes to firm up the tart and brown the top a little. You want almost no wobble when you remove it from the oven.

Let cool for 10 minutes, then remove the tart from its tin. Leave to cool on a wire rack for another 10 minutes and serve with a blob of crème fraîche.

CHOCOLATE SALTED RYE COOKIES

These cookies appear every weekend and we refer to them as 'crack' cookies. I first tasted this cookie when a customer brought one in insisting that I must try it and that it was the best thing ever. It came from e5 Bakehouse and, after speaking to Ben from e5, he told me that the recipe came from *Tartine Book No. 3* by Elisabeth Prueitt and Chad Robertson, who own the amazing Tartine Bakery in San Francisco (they now have several branches). Now every Saturday and Sunday morning when we are baking them, an 'accidental' few are always cooked off so the kitchen can indulge in their hot molten gooiness. We look forward to them on every weekend.

Makes 14 cookies

230g/8oz dark chocolate
30g/1¼oz unsalted butter
2 eggs
160g/5¾oz muscovado sugar
45g/1¾oz wholegrain dark rye
  flour
½ teaspoon baking powder
¼ teaspoon salt
¾ tablespoon vanilla extract
coarse, flaked sea salt, for serving

Melt the chocolate and butter in a bain marie. Remove from the heat and let cool slightly.

Whisk the eggs and add in the sugar slowly until the mix has tripled in volume. This should take around 8–10 minutes.

In a separate bowl, mix the flour, baking powder and salt.

Slowly add the chocolate-butter and the vanilla extract to the eggs and sugar.

Fold in the dry ingredients by hand. Put in the fridge to firm up for about 1 hour or so – the dough will be very soft.

Preheat the oven to 180°C/400°F/gas mark 6.

Roll the mixture into round balls, each weighing 36g/1¼oz or the size of a ping-pong ball. Place on a lined baking tray, leaving space between each one.

Sprinkle a little salt over the top of each cookie.

Bake for 12 minutes exactly. You want the cookies to be soft and gooey in the middle. Let cool.

August

The Patron Saint of Towpath

Ideas live one way in our imagination and quite another when they come into the world. Children are like that too, of course, and opening a small business is a bit like having one. And if you do take the plunge, one of the first things you'll notice is that your little creation has a personality all its own.

We weren't sure what to expect when we opened in 2010. Our stretch of the canal was still a sleepy place. Many of the buildings surrounding it were derelict. It was peaceful, mostly. A little sad and neglected, but in a nicely melancholic way. I pictured myself with lots of time to let my mind wander, looking out on the water, listening to music, maybe writing a bit after I'd sliced a piece of olive oil cake and laid it on a little square of cotton for the odd customer. In my imagination, and I can conjure it still, there would be a pile of homemade cloth napkins in various faded patterns – gingham, plaid, Liberty, paisley – sitting under a smooth stone on the counter. It was all going to be very slow and dreamy.

Which is not at all the way things turned out. For one thing, there were a lot more people around than we thought there would be. But also, our relationship to them was different than we'd imagined. We'd spent so much time thinking about what we could do with our little space to delight people, we hadn't foreseen all the ways in which they'd delight us back.

Our first customers were unfailingly patient with us. The ground outside the kiosks was still unpaved in those early days and when the wind blew, dust would swirl around alarmingly before depositing itself in a fine layer over everything. It was awkward. And surreal, since everyone just smiled and pretended it wasn't happening. Which would have seemed *so English* except that instead of fleeing in horror, people kept coming back for more. Which made us try even harder to make them happy – and created a kind of snowball effect of goodwill.

Some wise person once said that it's best to be hospitable to everyone you meet as you just might be in the presence of an angel. One rolled up to our counter on a bright red mobility scooter during Towpath's first year. His name was Colin Major. Seventy-something, dapper, hard-living and exceedingly polite and wry at the same time. His cockney accent was so strong I needed a translator at the beginning, but we were charmed by him. He came every day. Always ordered a tea with milk and refused anything else. He lunched at the Salvation Army and came to Towpath in the afternoon. Every day like clockwork. Until one day he didn't. A few days passed and we were convinced something had happened to him. However presumptuous that sounds, we were certain he would not have just stopped coming. So we did the thing you hope never to have to do and called around the hospitals trying to find him.

He was at Homerton. We packed a little bag with cookies, cake and Yorkshire tea and found him in his jammies sneaking a fag in the garden. Friendship has its own mysterious alchemy and this little moment transformed him into Towpath's patron saint. From then on he plied us with gifts. Hilarious charity shop cookbooks for Laura. All manner of knick-knackery for the rest of us. And always flowers.

'Nicked 'em from the cemetery,' he'd say winking. He let us have a turn up and down the towpath on his shiny new scooter, taught toddlers to beep its tinny horn and always volunteered to nip over to Hoxton Street for anything we needed.

Sometimes Colin brought his grandson Wiggles with him. He didn't seem to think much of us at first, eyeing us silently while picking at his cheese sandwich. But he warmed up and, by the time he was a teenager, we'd tied an apron around him and put him to work. No matter how much we told him to pretend he was running to catch a train, he could only move with the I-have-all-the-time-in-the-world gait particular to just about every young person who's ever done work experience with us. But he liked us. And we liked him back.

It was Wiggles who showed up in tears one summer day and told us Colin had died in the night. He brought us a note from his dad. 'Thank you for being a friend to Colin. He always spoke about his little gang down the canal.' Just like that, our angel had flown.

A great sea of humanity streams past us every day. Some people stop, some don't. Some pass us a hundred times before they finally do. Not everyone finds engaging with strangers they'd probably never otherwise cross paths with interesting, but it's what I like best about what we do. Because people really are endlessly fascinating. And we flower under each other's attention.

Something about the seat-of-our-pants way Towpath exists in the big city is a great facilitator of friendship and of community. For all its bells and whistles, its raggle-taggle mix of humanity, its genius, London can be an alienating place. Some of us look for ways to pretend we're living in a village, with familiar faces and gentler rhythms. So maybe we go to the same place every day for a coffee. Like a kid hanging around the playground with a ball. And sooner or later we get to talking with whoever else is around. Which might actually be the real reason we've gone out for that coffee anyway. Just to catch glimpses of each other, bobbing around in the deep ocean, trying to dodge the waves. Because somehow this is comforting. The world has its ten thousand joys and ten thousand sorrows and it's nicer to feel like we're in it together, watching the coots and eating cheese sandwiches.

The arrows of friendship fly in all directions – across the bar, between customers (countless friendships have been born at our tables) – wherever that little spark of connection ignites. We begin conversations that beg to be continued and make appointments to see each other without the counter between us. Enrico, one of my favourite people on the planet, came into my life this way. If he were all I was ever to get from Towpath, it would be enough. The bar's set-up is more immediately conducive to the making of friends than the kitchen's. At its best, ours is a delightful little fan dance of deliciousness and conversation. If it looks like we're having fun, it's because we are. The kitchen's choreography is all fire, knives and speed. Laura shows her affection on the plate and when she's in the middle of a busy lunch, only a fool would dare disturb her. But it's another story at the end of service when she steps out of the kitchen, wipes her hands on her apron and takes a look around to see who's there.

Who *is* there? Well. You never know. But there are a few people we can count on no matter what. They are the ones who make us want to come to work even when it's pissing down rain for the tenth day in a row. To them we will never be able to say a big enough THANK YOU:

For making it feel like there's nothing you'd rather do than hold off on breakfast and run to the market to fetch us whatever it is we've suddenly discovered we need.

For bringing great basketfuls of flowers from your own garden and arranging them in gorgeous little posies over a breakfast you insist upon paying for.

For giving our ramshackle Towpath garden so much love and for doing dishes all afternoon when you thought you were coming for lunch.

For coming every single day as sure as the sun rises because you feel at home, because your dog does.

For helping us set up tables and chairs in the morning just because you showed up early.

For standing in our kitchen and eating lunch when the canal is frozen over, when anyone with a speck of good sense is tucked up somewhere warm and cosy.

For bringing us gifts. Fingerless gloves for the bar. Bitter greens, quinces and wild garlic for the kitchen.

For standing at the counter and talking to us about more than what's on the menu.

For being so talented, interested, interesting and willing.

Some of our friends are four legged: Jodie. Stanley. Florence. Alva. Oscar. They're the ones who act like they own the place.

Many of our friends are children: Bluebell, Ruben, Bel, Irah, Romy, Maya, Echo, Locker, River, Wren, Kalind, Elijah, Marlowe, Dexter, Ilia, Synnove, Sigrid, Atlas, Tundra, Tiger Lily, Zeni, Ruby, Torben… They sit on the stoop outside the bar and eat ice cream. Bring us drawings to put up on the wall. Cry crocodile tears when we tell them we're closing for winter. They are small people of great substance – as happy to clean-up the canal or dig in the garden as to gobble up a piece of cake. And they give us hope that the world is in better shape than it sometimes seems.

FRIED EGGS WITH CARAMELISED SAGE AND CHILLI BUTTER

We always have fried eggs on the menu. My take on fried eggs is that they should be super crispy on the bottom and the yolk should be runny and gooey. For the first few years, the fried eggs were served simply on toast with butter. As we got busier and started experimenting with how a fried egg could evolve we came up with different toppings. The caramelised chilli sage butter is by far the most popular.

When Rachel O'Sullivan, chef extraordinare, joined the team a few years ago, she came up with this recipe, but I also want you to know about some of the chefs who have had to cook this dish millions of times. Sarah, Sara, Rosie, Polly, Micky, Eleni, Ella, Casey and Leah. My brigade, without all of whom I could not do this. A lot of them started with very little experience and to see how dedicated they are and how hard they work is truly amazing. Breakfast can be the busiest service of the day and they often do it on their own. They are so important to me and for the functioning of the kitchen – it is a small space, it gets busy and stressful, but as a team we do it, some days elated, some days deflated. They are just as important as I am in the kitchen and this is my ode to them.

Serves 4

For the sage and chilli butter
bunch of sage
150g/5½oz butter, cut into pieces
½ lemon, juiced
2 cloves garlic, minced
½–1 teaspoon chilli flakes
salt and pepper

sunflower, olive or a neutral oil,
    for frying
8 fresh eggs
4 slices sourdough bread, toasted

Notes
The sage butter will make more than you need. It is delicious tossed through pasta, on top of gnudi, roast veg or a veggie stew.

If left in the fridge overnight, gently warm it up when you want to use it. The sage will lose its crispiness as it sits, but will still taste delicious up to 2 days later.

Pick the sage, saving the stalks for a stock.

In a medium-sized frying pan, place the butter in the pan with the sage leaves.

Melt over a medium-low heat. Continue cooking until the sage leaves start crisping. Turn the heat to low to prevent the butter and sage from burning.

Once the leaves are crispy, turn off the heat. Add the lemon juice to prevent the sage and butter from cooking further. It will sizzle loudly! Add the garlic and chilli flakes. Stir well and season to taste. Pour into an appropriate container and leave in a warm place until needed.

Warm another frying pan over a high heat. Pour in the oil so you have a generous coating on the bottom. Wait until the pan starts smoking, then crack in your eggs – you may need to do this in batches so you don't overcrowd the pan, which will prevent the eggs from crisping. Cook the eggs until the edges go crispy – about a couple of minutes. Turn down the heat to finish cooking the eggs. This should take another couple of minutes. Use the oil in the pan to baste the centre of the whites if they are still quite raw.

Serve with buttered, toasted sourdough bread and the sage and chilli butter over the top.

FIG LEAF CORDIAL

As the seasons change, so obviously do the fruits and vegetables. At Towpath there is always a seasonal cordial on offer. Our bar is so small and our ethos is to make everything we can ourselves. We didn't want fizzy drinks, packaged fruit juices or bottled water (that said, we do have a soda stream to fizz up London's finest tap water). By making seasonal cordials ourselves there are a multitude of choices, and it is a no-brainer for me, as making a cordial is generally a by-product of something else or the perfect way to use up fruit that is looking a bit sad, but still tastes delicious.

We first started making this cordial a few years ago when Rach brought in an overflowing bag of freshly picked fig leaves. The sugar in the cordial means that it will last for weeks in the fridge without going off, so why not make a good amount to last a while?

Makes 20 glasses

10 (or around 70g/2½oz)
   fig leaves, washed
180g/6¼oz caster sugar
2 lemons, peel and juice

This is probably the easiest cordial to make as you literally put all the ingredients in a large saucepan with 2 litres/3½ pints water, bring to the boil and reduce by half. This should take about 25–40 minutes.

Leave to cool and in an ideal world wait a couple of days before using to allow the flavours to intensify. Storing in the fridge with the leaves in the cordial will add more flavour, but strain when ready to drink. Serve with still or fizzy water or add a splash of cordial to some prosecco.

Notes
We also use the fig leaves to make ice cream. In a similar way to the cordial, we infuse the leaves in milk and add eggs and sugar. It produces a delicious figgy tobacco flavour and it has become one of our favourite flavours.

CORNBREAD, ROASTED RED PEPPERS AND CREME FRAICHE

I remember in our first year, Lori's sister Val and husband Ross came to visit from Connecticut. At the time, Ross was running a bakery and he baked some of his breads – I was blown away by his cornbread. Sadly I lost the original recipe, though I feel like it must be hiding somewhere in one of my many recipe books or scribbles. Every year though when sweetcorn comes into season I ask Lori to email Ross for the recipe, hoping to find the original. This year though I felt that I succeeded in amalgamating two of his recipes to produce that original cornbread.

I often serve this as a canapé for a catering party or in the evening as a bar snack.

Makes 9 pieces

For the cornbread
235g/8¼oz polenta
170g/6oz plain flour
145g/5¼oz caster sugar
20g/¾oz baking powder
13g/½oz salt
170ml/5¾fl oz sunflower,
    vegetable or a neutral oil
150g/5½oz sour cream or
    crème fraîche
2 eggs, whisked
150ml/5fl oz full-fat milk
65g/2½oz Cheddar, grated
½ red pepper, deseeded and
    diced
kernels from 1 corn-on-the-cob
    or 140g/5oz tinned sweetcorn
    (drained weight)
1 jalapeño, diced

To serve
60g/2¼oz salted butter
100g/3½oz crème fraîche
2 red peppers, roasted and
    cut into strips
6 coriander sprigs, leaves picked

Preheat the oven to 180°C fan/400°F/gas mark 6.

Line a 23 x 23cm/9 x 9in baking tin with greaseproof paper.

To a large mixing bowl, add the polenta, flour, sugar, baking powder and salt. Give it a good stir.

Pour in the oil, sour cream or crème fraîche, eggs and milk. Using a wooden spoon, stir gently until well combined. Add in the cheese, pepper, corn and jalapeño. Pour into the tin and place in the oven. Bake for about 35–45 minutes, but check after 20 minutes. If the bread is browning too quickly, turn the oven down to 160°C fan/350°F/gas mark 4.

To test whether it's cooked, insert a skewer into the centre of the bread and if it comes out clean, it's done. Leave to cool in the tin for 10 minutes. Turn out of the tin and cool for another 10 minutes on a wire rack.

I love eating this cornbread warmish, when fresh, with generous amounts of butter on top so it melts. Add a dollop of crème fraîche, followed by the roasted red pepper strips. Garnish with a few coriander leaves.

ROAST CHERRY TOMATOES, SPINACH AND GOAT'S CURD TART

Weekends can get extraordinarily busy. We have a 30-minute changeover between breakfast and lunch, during which many hungry customers arrive, so we needed to come up with some food options for this gap. Delicious savoury things that are happy to sit on the counter and are quick and easy to serve. This savoury tart is one of them and as we move through the seasons so the fillings of the tart change. The key to this tart is to make the pastry as crumbly as possible. It comes from Simon Hopkinson's Beef Wellington recipe in *The Prawn Cocktail Years* and he describes it as a quick flaky pastry. Keeping all the ingredients for the pastry as cold as possible along with not overmixing will produce a light, rich, buttery and crumbly pastry.

Serves 6–8

For the pastry
(this will make 2 tart cases)
250g/9oz plain flour, kept in
   fridge
150ml/5fl oz ice-cold water
200g/7oz unsalted butter, chilled
   in the freezer

For the filling
280g/10oz cherry tomatoes
2 tablespoons olive oil
4 eggs
250ml/9fl oz double cream
250ml/9fl oz full-fat milk
200g/7oz Caramelised Onions,
   (see page 94)
2 bunches of spinach, stalks
   removed, cooked, squeezed dry
   and chopped through
150g/5½oz goat's curd
50g/2oz Parmesan, finely grated
salt and pepper

Put the flour and water in the fridge and the butter in the freezer at least 2 hours before using and ideally the night before.

Preheat the oven to 200°C fan/425°F/gas mark 7.

Toss the cherry tomatoes in the olive oil and season. Roast for 12 minutes until the skins start to blister.

Place the flour in a mixing bowl and season. Grate the butter into the mixing bowl. From time to time, lightly dip the butter in the flour to prevent the butter getting too soft and greasy to grate. Mix by hand or in a Magimix to form a breadcrumb consistency. Add 1 tablespoon of water at a time until a dough forms. If you take the time to mix the liquid in slowly so that it is properly incorporated, you will find that the dough forms quite quickly and you most likely won't use all the water, which will make for a crumbly, short pastry.

Once you have a smooth dough, form into a flat circle, wrap in clingfilm and place in the fridge to rest for at least 30 minutes. When rested, remove from the fridge, divide into two balls and roll one into a 32cm/13in circle, with a thickness of 3mm/⅛in. If you have two tart tins, you could roll the other one out and freeze or just freeze the other ball.

Press the dough neatly into a 25cm/10in-round and 4cm/1½in-deep tart tin with a removable base and let the pastry hang a bit above the top of the case as it will shrink a bit when cooking. Rest in the fridge for at least another 30 minutes.

Preheat the oven to 150°C fan/340°F/gas mark 3½.

Once the dough has rested, remove from the fridge. Line the tin with greaseproof paper and weigh down

Notes

This tart can have a multitude of fillings. I tend to use caramelised onions on the base, but if you don't have onions you could always sweat down some leeks. Other tart fillings include pea, broad bean, asparagus and ricotta; courgette, feta and mint; roast fennel and parmesan; and roast crown prince squash, cavolo nero and blue cheese. The list goes on...

with baking beans. Bake for about 30 minutes – you want the pastry to cook but not brown too much as it will be cooked again. Remove the beans and the paper. Leave to cool for 5 minutes.

Turn the oven up to 180°C fan/400°F/gas mark 6.

Whisk the eggs, cream, milk and salt and pepper together until you form a savoury custard. Set aside.

Put the caramelised onions in the base of the pastry case to form a layer. Dot the roasted cherry tomatoes and spinach on top and then add the goat's curd. Pour in half the custard, put the tart in the oven and then pour in the rest to prevent the custard from overflowing when moving it. You might not need all the custard. Sprinkle the Parmesan on top.

Bake until the custard has just set and the top is lovely and caramelised – about 35–45 minutes. Test by gently wobbling the tart. If the tart is browning too fast, turn the heat down. Remove from the oven, let cool for 10 minutes and then remove from the tart tin.

DEVILLED CRAB IN LITTLE GEM

Along with the truffle paste buns, this is one of our signature Towpath canapés. Over the years we have catered birthday parties, weddings and other celebrations and these are always a winner. This dish reminds me of Lori, which is another reason why I love it. She absolutely loves it and whenever I have it on the menu at Towpath, in the heat of lunch service, I'll see this spoon float up from behind me. If I'm super on the ball, I will send her a plate of devilled crab in Little Gem, before she has the chance to come in. This normally results in a note being passed back to the kitchen by a random customer handing in their food order, with my name on it. Inside it is always a little word or drawing of gratitude. I know this may sound corny but I love how even though we are separated by a concrete wall and can go most of the day without seeing each other, we can still do little acts to look after one another.

Serves 5
(3 Little Gem with crab per portion)

200g/7oz white crab meat,
 picked through for broken shells
100g/3½oz brown crab meat,
 picked through for broken shells
¼ bunch of coriander, finely
 chopped, stalks and leaves
4cm/1½in piece ginger, peeled
 and minced
4 spring onions, finely sliced
1½ red chillies, finely chopped
90g/3¼oz mayonnaise
1 lime, juiced
3 heads Little Gem lettuce
salt and pepper

Mix all the ingredients except for the lime juice and Little Gem in a bowl. Slowly add in some of the lime juice, tasting for flavour. Leave to sit for 10 minutes, stir well, check the seasoning and lime juice and adjust if needed.

Now prepare the Little Gem. Cut the bottom off each head and peel off the leaves. Remove the big outer leaves and the tiny inner leaves and set aside. These can be used in a salad another time.

Keep the middle leaves. You should get around 6–8 per head. Wash and dry.

When ready to serve, blob a generous amount of devilled crab towards the top of the leaf. This is to allow you to pick up the Little Gem without getting your fingers covered in the crab mix. Squeeze a drop more lime on top, if desired. Eat immediately!

Notes
The devilled crab mix also makes a delicious omelette for a great lunch or even breakfast, served with some buttery toast.

Caffè Sospeso

Man walks into a bar (which is what they call a café in Naples) and orders a coffee (well, two coffees actually), saying, '*Uno per me, uno per quello che viene.*' A coffee for me and one for whoever's coming. He's served one coffee, which he drinks, and then he pays for two (because in a working-class bar in Italy you'd always drink first and pay after). The second coffee is *sospeso*, or 'suspended' and will hang in the air until just the right down-on-their-luck person comes in looking in need of a coffee.

A few years ago, my friend Martino (Italian yes, but from Bergamo, which is about as far from Naples as you can get) asked me if I'd heard of this old tradition. I had. It had been described to me by a Neapolitan friend who lived in Florence where this sort of behaviour is unlikely. *Un amico*, a colleague, or your butcher might pay for your coffee if he sees you standing at the bar. But buy one for some unknown, future stranger? No. That isn't going to happen.

And it hadn't happened at Towpath, where we'd given away many a coffee, but it was always us doing the giving. The more Martino and I talked about it, the more it sounded like the perfect Towpath social experiment. How to go about it though? It's a bit of a long story to explain to random people who might not be interested in hearing it. And to the cynical, 'We'd like you to think of buying coffees for more than only yourself,' it risks sounding more self-reverent than community spirited. When we heard that Starbucks was selling suspended coffees as part of a UK charity appeal, we thought, 'What, we're going to do what Starbucks is doing?' This was swiftly followed by the next thought, which was, 'Would it be the worst thing if generosity to strangers went mainstream?'

So here's how we do it at Towpath. There's a little blackboard by the coffee machine that lists all the drinks we have. Espresso, milky coffees, apple juice and so forth. At the very bottom of the list we simply added 'caffè sospeso' and priced it the same as a coffee. In the top-right corner of the board is a little number, circled. It's the number of coffees hanging in the air. Martino, of course, bought the first one.

And then we waited. Who reads the board anyway? Who would see it listed there, wonder and then ask? Who would buy one? Or ask to have one? Who would we decide to give one to? In case you've ever wondered, these are the ways we amuse ourselves behind the bar.

It's been interesting. For one thing, very few people seem to read the blackboard. We can go a week without anyone noticing the *sospeso* up there or wondering what the little circled number is about. Sometimes someone does ask and, since everyone at the bar seems to be listening to everyone else, this can result in a flurry of *sospeso*-related conversation and activity. Occasionally, the *sospeso* story elicits a blank 'oh' and the ordering of a cheese sandwich. This is balanced out by a number of people who act as if you'd offered *them* a gift, so delighted are they by the idea of it. There are those who make a habit of paying for a *sospeso*, our friend William first among them. He's got some very good karma in the bank.

Who ends up drinking all these suspended coffees? All sorts of people. Anyone who looks like they're having a hard day, while still managing to be nice to us. People who have forgotten their wallets, so long as not intentionally. Someone whose card isn't working. We get to be fairy godpeople for a moment, bestowing a lovely little surprise on the unsuspecting.

Who won't we give them to? Well, once a girl asked if she and her boyfriend could please use 'two sospesos for one hot chocolate and one piece of cake.' I wish I could have replied with a dying laughing emoji. Instead we just said (possibly a tad self-reverentially), 'Sorry, no. It doesn't work that way.'

CHICKEN CAESAR SALAD

This recipe is adapted from my aunt. As a young kid, I would spend weeks every summer with my aunt Avrille and uncle Harold and my cousins. They became my second family and I always remember eating certain dishes during this time. My aunt would always make this one and I always looked forward to eating it. Even today, when I visit I look forward to her Caesar salad. This recipe is not the traditional way of making a Caesar salad, but it's just as delicious, if not more, and it brings back so many childhood memories for me.

Serves 4

For the dressing (makes 700g/1lb 9oz)

1 x 47.5g/1¾oz tin of anchovies (I use Ortiz)
2 tablespoons Worcestershire sauce
2 cloves garlic, minced
4 generous dashes of Tabasco
100g/3½oz Parmesan, grated
½ lemon, juiced
6 tablespoons red wine vinegar
1½ tablespoons Dijon mustard
450ml/16fl oz sunflower or vegetable oil

For the rest of the salad

175g/6oz roast or poached chicken meat, picked
4 handfuls croutons
4 heads Little Gem lettuce, leaves separated
75g/3oz Parmesan, grated
pepper

Start by making the dressing. In a blender or liquidiser, put in the anchovies, Worcestershire sauce, garlic, Tabasco, Parmesan, lemon juice, red wine vinegar and Dijon mustard. Blitz until smooth.

In a slow stream and with the motor running, pour in the oil. As the dressing thickens, you may need to add a dash of water to loosen it because if it gets too thick and you continue adding the oil it may split the dressing, so keep a glass of water close by and add as much as you need. If the sauce does split, hard-boil one egg, peel and chop coarsely. Remove the dressing from the blender and add the chopped egg with 100ml/3½fl oz of the dressing. Blitz to combine and then slowly pour in the rest of the dressing. This should bring it back together. The consistency of the dressing should be like double cream.

In a bowl, mix the chicken, croutons, Little Gem and 50g/2oz of the Parmesan. Generously pour over the dressing and give it a really good mix. Normally with salads I err on the side of caution when dressing, but with this you want to coat everything thickly. This is all about the dressing! Scatter the rest of the Parmesan over the top and grind over some black pepper. Serve.

Notes

This recipe will leave you with plenty of extra dressing. It will keep in the fridge for up to 2 weeks (1 week if you added an egg).

If you are roasting a chicken from scratch for this one, please, please place the croutons in the chicken juices when the chicken is resting. This will change your world as the croutons will absorb the amazing chicken gravy. Do this as soon as the chicken comes out of the oven so it has enough soaking time – at least 30 minutes.

GRILLED SARDINES, CHOPPED SALAD AND YOGHURT

On a hot summer's day at Towpath, grilled sardines with a fresh salad is just perfect. The sardines I use come from our local fish supplier, Ben's Fish based down in Colchester. I always get excited about the start of the season, which usually starts towards the end of July/beginning of August. When the boxes of fish come in, I am always mesmerised by how fresh they are. Silver, shiny, glossy, rigid bodies, they glisten even on a miserable day. They are also bountiful in the sea, sustainable, local and, as a result, are really reasonably priced. I love how a sardine tastes with a squeeze of lemon, so serving the grilled sardines with a tangy lemony salad works a treat.

Serves 4

For the salad

2 cucumbers, stripe-peeled, seeds removed, chopped
16 datterini tomatoes, quartered
1 red onion, diced
1 red pepper, deseeded and chopped
1 red chilli, deseeded and diced
1 head Little Gem lettuce, ends removed, quartered lengthways and chopped through
¼ bunch of coriander, roughly chopped
¼ bunch of parsley, picked and roughly chopped
¼ bunch of mint, picked and roughly chopped
¼ bunch of dill, picked and roughly chopped
1 lemon, juiced
4 tablespoons olive oil

12 medium sardines, scaled and gutted
2 tablespoons olive oil
45g/1¾oz Greek or natural yoghurt
1 tablespoon nigella seeds (optional)

Start by making the salad. Grab a big mixing bowl and add the cucumbers, tomatoes, red onion, red pepper, red chilli, Little Gem, coriander, parsley, mint and dill. Season with salt and pepper. Add half the lemon juice and half the olive oil, toss through and taste.

Leave to marinate for 15 minutes and, just before serving, taste the salad. Add more lemon juice, olive oil and seasoning if needed. Things always mellow when they sit for a while.

Heat a griddle pan on the highest heat so it starts to smoke.

While the pan is heating, place the sardines in a tray and lightly coat with the olive oil – if you add too much oil the pan will smoke and create havoc.

Place the fish in the pan so the griddle lines sit across the width of the fish. Sprinkle with salt (coarse sea salt is ideal for this). Leave for about 3 minutes until the skin goes crispy and the eyes become opaque. Turn over and repeat. Season and leave for another 3 minutes, until cooked.

Serve the sardines with the salad on the side. Drizzle the yoghurt over the top of the salad and sprinkle the nigella seeds over, if you wish.

Notes

There are no rules for a chopped salad. Often I put in florets of cauliflower, radishes, asparagus, peas and broad beans when they are in season. You could remove the Little Gem. Ultimately, you want it to be fresh, crispy, raw and zingy.

AUGUST

AUBERGINE AND OLIVE STEW, YOGHURT AND CORIANDER

A favourite of our vegetarian options and great for vegans too as it can be served without yoghurt. This dish deserves to made at least 24 hours in advance so all the flavours really get to know one another.

Serves 6–8

250ml/9fl oz sunflower, vegetable or a neutral oil
4 large (1.2kg/2lb 10oz) aubergines, halved, then quartered lengthways and cut into 6cm/2½in pieces
6 tablespoons cumin seeds, toasted and finely ground
3 tablespoons sweet smoked paprika
1 tablespoon hot smoked paprika
100ml/3½fl oz olive oil
6 red onions, cut into wedges
4 cloves garlic, minced
4 tablespoons coriander seeds, toasted and finely ground
600g/1lb 5oz tinned whole tomatoes, mashed or blitzed, tin rinsed with hot water
½ bunch of coriander, leaves picked, stalks finely chopped
200g/7oz green olives
2 tablespoons lemon juice
150g/5½oz Greek or natural yoghurt
salt and pepper

Preheat the oven to 180°C fan/400°F/gas mark 6.

Generously coat the bottom of your largest pan with oil and heat over a high heat. When it's hot, add the aubergine so it covers the base but is not too crowded (you might have to do this stage in several batches). This is to prevent the aubergine from steaming as you want it to brown. Start turning the aubergine individually when brown and slightly softened – this should take 4–5 minutes each side. Keep topping up the oil as the aubergine will soak it up.

When brown all over, remove the aubergine with a slotted spoon and place in a roasting tray. Toss the aubergine with half the ground cumin, 2 tablespoons of the sweet smoked paprika, the hot smoked paprika and season. Place in the oven and roast until the aubergine is completely soft – about 25 minutes.

While the aubergine is cooking, cook the base for the stew. Using the saucepan you browned the aubergine in, warm on a medium heat. Add the olive oil, red onions and garlic, the rest of the ground cumin and sweet smoked paprika as well as the ground coriander. Cook till soft and sweet – about 20–30 minutes.

Add the tinned tomatoes and the water from the tin. Cook over a medium heat for another 20 minutes until reduced. Add the aubergine to the base, making sure you scrape all the goodness off the roasting tray. Mix well.

Cook for another 30 minutes and then check the seasoning, adding in the coriander stalks and the green olives too.

Just before serving, add the lemon juice to cut through the richness.

Ladle into bowls and serve with generous blobs of yoghurt and the coriander leaves sprinkled on top.

STEAMED CLAMS, CHORIZO AND SHERRY

This is probably the easiest recipe in the book and I love it for its simplicity. It is a regular on the dinner menu as it's perfect on a hot sunny, evening. The flavours are strong, salty and punchy but it's the saltiness I find you crave on a hot day. To make this dish a bit more substantial, I sometimes add in cooked white beans or chickpeas at the same time as the clams and the sherry.

Serves 4

1.6kg/3½lb palourde clams, cleaned
2 tablespoons olive oil
6 chorizo piccante or 250g/9oz chorizo, chopped
100ml/3½fl oz manzanilla sherry or any other dry sherry
½ bunch coriander, leaves picked
salt

Notes

There is no need to add salt here as the chorizo, clams and sherry are all naturally salty.

If you don't have any sherry at home (or you don't like the flavour) you can use white wine instead.

Start by cleaning the clams. The best way to do this is to give the clams a good rinse with cold water in a bowl. Always remove the clams from the bowl rather than pouring the water out so the sand stays at the bottom of the bowl and is not just poured back onto the clams. Rinse for a few minutes.

Submerge in extremely salty water – the water should taste like seawater. If you have time, leave overnight in the fridge to soak or at least for a few hours – the last thing you want is a gritty clam. Take about a quarter of the clams out of the water and put them in a small container, then gently shake and repeat and then put them in a bowl of fresh, unsalted water.

This is important as any open clams that don't close will be dead. Occasionally you will get a dud clam, which is entirely full of sand, but shaking the clams will open any duds. Discard all dead and duds.

Soak the clams for 15 more minutes to de-salt.

Heat a saucepan that has a tight-fitting lid on a high heat. Add the oil and the chorizo pieces. Let the chorizo brown and become crispy – this should take about 4 minutes and a lot of delicious chorizo fat will leak out. Once crispy, add the clams and pour in the sherry. Immediately cover and leave to steam. This should take a matter of minutes – check after 2 minutes to see if any of the clams have opened.

Cook until they have all opened, which should take about 5 minutes at most. Turn the heat off and pour into a bowl, together with all the delicious juices. Sprinkle over the coriander and serve.

CHORIZO, SWEETCORN PUREE, FRIED EGG, PIQUILLO PEPPERS AND CORIANDER

As Lori will vouch, the corn in America is, for me, on another level – it is so sweet and juicy. The inspiration for this dish was on a trip to America where I had the most delicious side of creamed corn in New York at a Cuban restaurant. The comfort of this smooth, sweet, decadent purée was just indulgent. I then thought the corn would work really well with salty, spicy chorizo. I also love that sweetcorn comes into season at the end of August, just as most of the summer produce is ending, and this vibrant yellow comes to knock us out.

Serves 6

For the sweetcorn purée
120g/4¼oz unsalted butter
4 onions, sliced
3 cloves garlic, minced
3 bay leaves
¼ teaspoon cayenne pepper
6 heads/cobs sweetcorn or
    650g/1lb 7oz corn, kernels
    taken off and 4 husks saved
725ml/1 pint 6fl oz chicken or
    vegetable stock or water
salt and pepper

4 tablespoons olive oil
9 individual chorizos or
    550g/1¼lb chorizo, halved
    lengthways but not all the
    way through
6 eggs
1 x 390g/13½oz tin piquillo
    peppers, cut into strips
½ bunch of coriander, picked

Notes
A great way to prep the corn is in a bowl or tray with a big lip. Taking corn off the cob is a messy job – if prepped on a flat surface, half the corn goes flying all over the table and floor.

Start by making the purée. Melt 100g/3½oz of the butter over a low heat in a medium pan. Once foaming, add the onions, garlic and bay leaves. Season with salt, pepper and the cayenne. Cook till softened but not coloured – about 20 minutes.

Add the corn and four of the husks. Gently mix everything through for a few minutes. Add the stock and bring to the boil. Turn down to a simmer and cook for about 40 minutes. When the corn is fully cooked, turn off the heat and let cool for 10 minutes.

Remove the husks, making sure not to waste any of the liquid clinging onto them – I often squeeze the husks to extract as much flavour as possible.

Blitz in a liquidiser, slowly adding the rest of the butter in blobs. I like the purée to be super smooth and glossy, but it is also delicious a bit chunky. If it seems a bit thick, add in more stock or water – it should be the consistency of custard.

Preheat the oven to 160°C fan/350°F/gas mark 4. Put the oil and chorizo, cut-side down, in a large frying pan on a high heat. Cook so the chorizo goes crispy – about 1½–2 minutes on each side. When brown, put the chorizo on a baking tray and put in the oven.

Using the chorizo pan, fry the eggs in the chorizo oil. Turn to a high heat so the eggs go crispy on the bottom. Season. Add the piquillo pepper strips so they get coated in the chorizo oil.

By now, the chorizo will be cooked, so remove from the oven and pour all the juices into the egg pan. Place the warm purée on the bottom of each plate. Put 1½ pieces of chorizo on top and a fried egg. Drizzle over all of the juices from the egg pan. Scatter with the piquillo pepper strips and coriander leaves.

BLACKBERRY AND CREME FRAICHE BARS

On the weekend we always up our game on the sweet front. We tend to be much busier and have more people passing by who might just drop in for a coffee and a sweet treat. The great thing about this bar is that you can alter the fruit depending on the season – rhubarb, raspberry, apricot, redcurrant, gooseberry, blackberry... The tartness of the crème fraîche means that you can pretty much use any fruit you desire.

Makes 12 bars

For the base
185g/6½oz plain flour
50g/2oz icing sugar, sifted
170g/6oz unsalted butter, melted
pinch of salt

For the topping
4 eggs
270g/9¾oz icing sugar, sifted
4½ tablespoons cornflour, sifted
1½ teaspoons vanilla extract
225ml/8fl oz crème fraîche
1 x 225g/8oz punnet of
    blackberries

Notes
I always make the base the day before, leave in the fridge overnight and cook it first thing in the morning. I also make the bar on a Friday so it can set in the fridge overnight – this is a gooey bar, so the colder it is, the easier it is to slice.

Start by making the base. To a medium bowl, add the flour, sugar, melted butter and a pinch of salt. Mix well to form a dough. The pastry can be made up to a week in advance if left in the fridge.

Take a 23 x 23cm/9 x 9in baking tin and line with greaseproof paper.

Roll the pastry out directly into the lined baking tin using your hands, then take a piece of greaseproof paper, lay over the pastry and use a half-pint glass or jar to smooth over the top. Make sure the pastry goes right up to the edges of the tin as it will shrink a little once cooked. Prick the pastry all over with a fork. Place in the fridge and rest for at least 30 minutes.

Preheat the oven to 140°C fan/325°F/gas mark 3.

Make the topping while the pastry is resting. Whisk together the eggs, icing sugar, cornflour, vanilla extract and crème fraîche in a bowl.

When ready, bake the pastry base in the oven for about 25 minutes. You don't want any colour on the base and nor do you want to overcook the base – the base will be cooked again and if it is overcooked, it becomes crumbly and messy to cut.

When the base is ready, pour over the topping. Place the blackberries evenly over the top. I always make sure the top of each blackberry is on show. Put in the oven and bake for about 45–60 minutes. You want a slight wobble when you remove it from the oven as it will continue to cook.

Leave to cool completely in the tin and then cut into bars.

PEANUT BUTTER, CHOCOLATE AND SEA SALT COOKIES

We make our own peanut butter. It's very easy to make – we use unsalted peanuts in their skins and put 500g/1lb 2oz on a baking tray, sprinkle with salt and roast at 160°C fan/350°F/gas mark 4 until the skins start to separate and the peanuts lightly brown. Remove from the oven and leave to cool, peeling away the skins when the peanuts are still warm. The skins come away easily if you put the peanuts in a tea towel on a flat surface and rub the towel up and down for a minute. Blitz in a blender. Once ground, add a tablespoon of sugar, a pinch of salt and 2 tablespoons of plain olive oil and blitz until the peanuts release their oil and the mixture becomes thick and buttery. This will take about 10 minutes, so turn off your blender at 3-minute intervals and leave for a couple of minutes so as not to overheat the blender or the butter.

Makes 20 cookies

75g/3oz unsalted butter, softened
90g/3¼oz peanut butter
80g/2¾oz caster sugar
80g/2¾oz muscovado sugar
1 egg, beaten
80g/2¾oz plain flour
1½ teaspoons baking powder
100g/3½oz chocolate chips
sea salt, for sprinkling

Preheat the oven to 160°C fan/350°F/gas mark 4.

Cream the butter, peanut butter, caster sugar and muscovado sugar until light and fluffy. Slowly whisk in the egg. Using a wooden spoon, gently stir in the flour, baking powder and chocolate chips. Do not overmix.

Line a baking tray with greaseproof paper. Spoon out a tablespoon of cookie mixture, roll into a perfect ball, set on the tray and use a fork to lightly flatten the ball. Sprinkle sea salt on top and repeat to make the rest of the cookies. Bake for exactly 10 minutes. They will be soft when they come out of the oven but will harden up once cooled.

Notes
The cookie dough can be made in advance and either left in the fridge or freezer as a dough. It can also be weighed into individual cookies before chilling or freezing and then removed when ready to bake.

September

Disasters

Minor calamities survived make the best stories, however unfun they are when they're actually happening. Ask anyone in this business and they will tell you that anything that can go wrong probably will, and usually at the worst possible time. Accepting this as one of the realities of restaurant life and learning the art of resourcefulness is the only way to survive. We have, at various times, operated without gas (ours is bottled and although we always have a backup, occasionally, mysteriously, both bottles are empty); water; our Saniflo (I will spare you the details); all manner of machinery (toasters most frequently and you can't imagine what a havoc this wreaks). Our kitchen has flooded (something to do with a sump pump). Our shutters have jammed. We've washed thousands of dishes by hand. And thought our coffee machine was broken when it was actually turned off. Let's not even get started on cakes that haven't risen and rice that's turned to gloop.

Sometimes our disasters are self-inflicted, sometimes not. It doesn't really matter. They can never be solved by pointing fingers or assigning blame. (And you will not make yourself any friends if during one of these crises you dare utter, 'It wasn't me.') Whatever ingenuity or chaos we bring to these dramas tells us more about how we're doing as a team than we can ever see when the well-oiled gears are running smoothly.

Never did we love our chef Rachel more than on that busy Saturday when we went to change over the gas and found the spare was empty. 'Right,' she said, in that can-do Aussie way of hers, and started firing off changes. 'No fried eggs. We can still do the marinda tomatoes. I've got some ricotta in the fridge, let's do that with honey and walnuts.' And we were back in the game. In the meantime, one of our customers (because they can always tell when something's up) offered to run half a mile to the nearest builders' merchant and haul back a 47-kilo gas canister by trolley (they cannot be transported in closed vehicles) while his breakfast got cold. (Thank you Soheb!) It must be said that my son Julien has also done this. Our friend Avi too. I will risk saying that this rarely happens any more. We have all had enough fun with this particular charade.

Our first year, we were offered free use of the incredibly evocative Dalston Boy's Club as the setting for an autumnal Tuscan feast. The place reminded us of a haunted old theatre. At least it did when we first saw it. But in the bright light of day when we arrived to set up, it looked like our worst nightmare. There were great wads of fluff everywhere, as if an army of sofas had been eviscerated. Lipstick-stained wine glasses and ashtrays overflowing with cigarette butts. No water at all, which explained why the kitchen was piled to the ceiling with dirty dishes. I think I actually cried. But 50 people were coming for dinner and there was nothing to do but roll up our sleeves. By the time they arrived, there were candles and flowers everywhere. Cloth napkins and old, patterned crockery that Laura collected from her favourite brocantes in France. The room looked dreamy – so long as the lights were low and no one peered behind the curtains. At two in the morning we drove our dirty dishes home in the car and stayed up the rest of the night drinking wine and washing them.

There are many misadventures in the Towpath annals, but few as memorable as the night we catered a surprise birthday dinner for our friend Peter Pilotto, in the pop-up shop he and his partner Chrisopher's fashion label had opened in Kensington. We passed canapés and poured cocktails. There was an ikebana performance, during which we all watched flowers being misted and arranged with such quiet, measured intensity we could have been at a monastery in Japan. How it took until we were actually bringing the main course to the table for us to notice that something was missing is beyond me. But there were no plates. And by that I mean *none*. We thought they'd been hired. They thought we'd brought them from Towpath. It was my fault entirely. But as we've just said, self-flagellation doesn't actually solve anything in these situations. We ran down the street to the first hotel we could find and literally begged them to loan us 50 plates. And they did! They even helped us carry them back. What's more, Christopher (who was throwing the party for his partner) watched the whole drama unfold and thought it was hilarious. How do you become a beloved Towpath customer? Just like this.

CHOCOLATE SAUCE FOR HOT CHOCOLATE AND ICE CREAM

We have a large kid's community at Towpath and anyone who comes to visit will see the bar filled with drawings they bring us every year. All the kids love the hot chocolate sauce and, not only do the kids love it, so do the adults. We also love to drizzle the sauce over ice cream.

Ice cream is so important to us at Towpath, so even though there isn't a recipe in here (because it is so specific to our machine), it seemed a shame not to mention it.

In year two we decided that we wanted to serve ice cream. Jason came up with the brilliant idea of buying a soft-serve ice-cream maker. So we researched several manufacturers and found the 'electro freeze.' I remember Jason contacting them and saying that we wanted to make an all-natural soft serve. The owner of the company laughed, saying it wouldn't be possible as they only ever used powders and water. It would never set without stabilisers. We asked if we could come to the factory and test some recipes. He was extremely helpful and Jason went up to the factory, taking three different custard bases – one of 100 per cent full-fat cream, one half cream, half full-fat milk and one which was 100 per cent full-fat milk. Since the base sits in a cooled cylinder and is churned to order, anything containing cream (too much fat) turns to butter, but the full-fat milk base churned perfectly. The owner was flabbergasted. In Jason's excitement, he immediately ordered the machine.

In our naivety, we had grand visions of pushing the ice-cream machine out onto the towpath and serving customers straight from the pavement. What we didn't realise was that the machine weighs hundreds of kilos and is impossible to move. It now lives in the bar and every morning it gets switched on, woken up from its sleep and filled with many different delicious flavours. It took some messing around with initially to figure out what flavours worked and didn't work. Anything that can be infused in the milk works perfectly. It must be strained first as any bits will break the machine. Anything with a high-water content will produce an icy texture, so fruit flavours don't work. Our favourite flavours are chocolate, vanilla, fresh mint, fig leaf, malt, coconut, hazelnut, peanut, almond, sesame and orange and lemon peel.

This chocolate sauce is great as it lasts in the fridge for weeks and we have perfected the consistency so that it's ready to use straight from the fridge. It comes from Lori and is by far the most delicious and easiest to make of all the sauces we tested.

Makes 500ml/18 fl oz

185g/6½oz caster sugar
125g/4½oz cocoa powder,
    70 per cent or higher
1 teaspoon salt

In a pan, add 225ml/8fl oz water and the caster sugar and bring to the boil. Take off the heat and thoroughly whisk in the cocoa powder. I do this in stages.

Stir in the salt and leave to cool (unless you want to use straightaway).

Pour into a jar, cover and place in the fridge.

To make hot chocolate, take 2 tablespoons of the mix and whisk into 175ml/6fl oz of boiling milk. If you want it more chocolatey, add more (I do!).

MERGUEZ SAUSAGE, YOGHURT FLATBREAD AND PICKLED RED CABBAGE

Breakfasts on the weekend can be our busiest service and anyone who has come to Towpath will have seen how small the kitchen is. The way in which the kitchen works really only allows one chef to be in charge of the toaster and the cooking of the eggs. So we needed to come up with some dishes that could be prepared on the opposite side of the kitchen, far from the toaster and the already overworked chef on morning egg duty.

This is a perfect example. The sausages are actually mutton rather than lamb and are made by Swaledale, one of our incredible butchers based up in Yorkshire. They are sweet, smoky and spicy. The pickled red cabbage cuts through the richness of the sausage and in combination with a fluffy warm flatbread – the recipe comes from the amazing book *Saha* by Greg and Lucy Malouf – and a dollop of yoghurt, it is a grand meal in itself.

Serves 6

For the yoghurt flatbread

1 tablespoon quick yeast
½ teaspoon caster sugar
50ml/2fl oz tepid water
310g/10¾oz plain flour, plus extra for dusting
½ teaspoon salt
160g/5¾oz Greek or natural yoghurt
3 tablespoons olive oil, plus extra for oiling
6 tablespoons sunflower, vegetable or a neutral oil

For the rest of the dish

12 merguez sausages
2 tablespoons olive oil
90g/3¼oz rocket, washed and dried
180g/6¼oz Pickled Red Cabbage (see page 207)
350g/12oz Greek or natural yoghurt, thinned down with a few drops of water
1 lemon, juiced
salt and pepper

To make the flatbread, whisk the yeast and sugar in a small bowl with the tepid water until it dissolves. Put in a warm place until the yeast starts foaming.

Mix the flour and salt in another bowl.

In a jug, whisk together the yoghurt and olive oil. Mix the yeast mix and the yoghurt/oil into the flour mix and stir with a wooden spoon until a dough is formed. Knead the dough for 5 minutes until it is smooth and soft. You may need to add a bit more flour when kneading if it's a bit sticky. Put into a lightly oiled bowl (you can use the same one), cover with clingfilm or a tea towel and place in a warm place to prove. Leave until it doubles in size. The timing will depend on how warm it is, the humidity levels and where you place the bowl, but could take between 1–2 hours.

Remove from the bowl and knock back the dough. Divide into 6 smaller balls.

Lightly flour the work surface and roll out a ball into an 18cm/7in circle. Repeat, placing greaseproof paper between each flatbread.

Preheat the oven to 200°C fan/425°F/gas mark 7.

When ready to cook the flatbread, place a 23cm/9in frying pan on a high heat and add 1 tablespoon of sunflower oil. Once it is smoking, add the first flatbread to the pan. Let it brown for a minute and then flip over (the first one or two always takes slightly longer to cook, so cook those for 2 minutes on each side). Add a tablespoon of oil between cooking

Notes

A great thing to do is to make the flatbread dough the night before and prove it slowly overnight in the fridge. First thing in the morning, take the dough out. I also find it much easier to handle when it is cold from the fridge.

each flatbread. Don't be alarmed when the dough puffs up. This is a good sign. Repeat until all the flatbreads are cooked. Wrap the flatbreads in a tea towel to keep them warm and soft.

Meanwhile grab a baking tray and rub the merguez with the olive oil. Place in the oven and cook for about 8 minutes. Turn the merguez over and cook for another 8 minutes until brown.

To assemble, place a warm flatbread on each plate and add a generous handful of rocket so that it covers the bread. Put two merguez sausages on the rocket then cover with a generous handful of pickled red cabbage. Drizzle over some yoghurt and season with a tiny amount of salt and pepper. Drizzle all the delicious merguez oil over the top along with the lemon juice.

SEPTEMBER

PICKLED RED CABBAGE

I can never have enough pickles and you will see pickles popping up on the Towpath menu in all sorts of different combinations. With pickles, I always suggest making large quantities so they will last a while. I know that fridge space might be an issue but until you open them, they can be stored in a cool, dark space. They are so versatile and simple to make and once you start you won't be able to stop.

Makes 1 litre/1¾ pint

500g/1lb 2oz red cabbage, quartered and shredded to 0.5cm/¼in thickness (I find it easier to prep when the core is still intact, so remove the core at the end)
700ml/1¼ pints red wine vinegar
400g/14oz caster sugar
2 teaspoons black peppercorns
4 bay leaves
2 tablespoons black mustard seeds
2 star anise
1 sprig rosemary
1 sprig thyme
fine table salt

Notes
This is also great served on crostini rubbed with garlic and topped with goat's curd. Or even with grilled mackerel or smoked mackerel, onglet, smoked Hungarian sausages, duck rillette or just simply on a cheese plate.

In a colander with a bowl underneath, place a layer of shredded cabbage and sprinkle over some salt. The salt will be the seasoning of the cabbage so apply carefully. Toss well and keep repeating until all the cabbage has been salted. Leave for at least 2 hours.

While the cabbage is salting, add the rest of the ingredients to a saucepan. Bring to the boil, mix well so the sugar completely dissolves, then take off the heat and leave till fully cooled. The longer you can leave the pickling liquid, the longer the spices will have time to infuse – for a minimum of 2 hours, ideally.

Put the cabbage into a sterilised jar. Strain the liquid and pour over the cabbage. Seal the jar. Leave for a few days or up to 2 weeks before serving. It will keep indefinitely unopened and then once opened, in the fridge for up to 6 weeks.

TOMATOES, PEACHES AND TARRAGON

A delightful combination and so simple with the different flavours of sweet, savoury and tart. It's important to get perfectly ripe and flavoursome ingredients since they need to shine on their own. I like to use a more tart tomato here as it will be paired with a super sweet peach and I sometimes replace the peaches with nectarines if they are tastier.

Serves 4

10 marinda tomatoes, eyes
   removed and each cut
   into 8 wedges
3 peaches, perfectly ripe, halved,
   stoned and cut into
   small wedges
1 shallot, thinly sliced on a
   slight angle
10 sprigs tarragon, leaves picked
   and finely chopped
2 tablespoons riesling vinegar or
   any type of sweet white vinegar
4 tablespoons best olive oil
salt and pepper

Gently mix the tomatoes, peaches, shallot and tarragon together in a bowl and season.
   Pour over the vinegar and oil and toss gently.

Notes
This salad is great served with cured meats or chicken.
   To add a bit of richness to this dish, serve with mozzarella.
For extra crunch, toss in some toasted hazelnuts.

GRILLED POINTED CABBAGE AND ROMESCO

We recently catered a very close friend's wedding and this dish was one of the starters. I received so many messages complimenting me on this dish – I think it's the combination of the crunchy, slightly sweetened and buttery cabbage with the crunchy, sweet and smoky romesco that works so well. It's also so easy to make.

Serves 4

For the romesco

250g/9oz datterini tomatoes
3 cloves garlic, minced
1 tablespoon sweet smoked paprika
1 teaspoon cayenne pepper
2 tablespoons sherry vinegar
2 tablespoons olive oil
100g/3½oz ground almonds, lightly toasted
200g/7oz piquillo peppers or roasted red peppers (see Smoked Aubergine recipe, page 146)
salt and pepper

For the cabbage

2 large pointed cabbages or 3 small-medium pointed cabbages, outer leaves removed
4 tablespoons olive oil
1 lemon, juiced
best olive oil, to drizzle

Notes

Romesco will last in the fridge for over a week. It is delicious served with eggs, lamb, chicken, fish, any type of cooked greens, purple sprouting broccoli, asparagus, crispy potatoes, on top of a vegetable soup... the list is endless.

Preheat the oven to 200°C fan/425°F/gas mark 7.

Start by making the romesco. Place the tomatoes in a roasting tray with the garlic, paprika, cayenne, sherry vinegar, olive oil and some salt and pepper. Give the tomatoes a good toss and roast in the oven for 12 minutes. The tomato skins should start to split. If that hasn't happened, keep roasting for another 5 minutes. Leave to cool for 10 minutes.

In a blender or liquidiser, add the roasted tomatoes (making sure you scrape off all the goodness from the tray), toasted almonds and piquillo peppers. Blitz till smooth (though I like a little bit of texture in mine) and check the seasoning. Set aside until ready to use.

Fill a medium blanching pot with water and bring to the boil. Salt the water. While waiting for the water to boil, prep the cabbages – cut each in half, then if it's a big cabbage, cut each half into 3 wedges or 2 wedges if smaller. Put the cabbage wedges into the water.

Bring back to the boil and cook for about 5 minutes for the larger wedges and 3 minutes for the smaller wedges. Drain in a colander and leave for 5 minutes to get rid of excess water.

In a large, ovenproof frying pan, heat the olive oil until it is smoking. Add in the cabbage wedges, but do not overcrowd the pan (you may need to do this in batches) and brown each side. This should take a couple of minutes. Turn over and repeat on all sides to brown. Once all the wedges are browned, place in the oven and cook for about 8 minutes until the cabbage is completely cooked.

When ready to serve, place 3 wedges of cabbage on each plate. Season and drizzle with lemon juice.

Generously blob the romesco on top of the cabbage – about 2 tablespoons per person. Drizzle a tiny bit of olive oil over the top and serve.

A Long and Winding Road

If there's one thing I've noticed about humankind from my perch behind the Towpath counter, it's that we can't seem to help but want to know about each other. Epic dramas, daily musings, the *who what when where why* are all fodder for our abiding fascination with other people's lives. If you aren't that sort of person, skip ahead. Life is short! If you are, then for the record, here is a pocket version of the road that led me to Towpath.

I've so often thought that if at any time in my life someone had shown me a picture of my self-same existence 10 years hence, I would have had to squint very hard to find myself. 'Nope,' I imagine shaking my head, 'That's definitely not me!' Doing that job, married to that person, living in that country, not married to that person. And on and on. Very little has turned out as planned. But if I pull way back from the picture, far from my controlling ego and its little strategies, there does seem to be a strange logic to it all.

I was born in Los Angeles, into a family whose summer holidays were mostly of the camping in the High Sierras variety – all fishing, hiking, ghost stories and mosquito bites. I didn't set foot outside America until the summer before I turned 19, when I went to Florence to learn Italian. Which I did, in that time-honoured tradition by which you trade in the classroom for the real *avventura* of falling in love with an actual Italian (Jean-Louis, who was just that despite the French name). We met at his family's café, a stone's throw from the Ponte Vecchio. And so began my gastronomic education, which could so easily have come to an abrupt end when I insisted on asking for butter in a city renowned for its jewel-green olive oil, but instead ended up in marriage, two children, more restaurants (and eventually, though this is skipping ahead, a very amicable parting of matrimonial ways).

Jean-Louis followed me back to L.A., where a couple of years later he and his friend Antonio opened the 40-seat Locanda Veneta in West Hollywood, their very own version of *Big Night*. The simple, straightforward Italian-ness of the place struck a chord with a city starved for authenticity. At this point, the restaurant part of Jean-Louis and my family equation had little to do with me. I'd graduated from UCLA with a degree in Italian Literature and Political Science, gone on to law school and landed just the job I thought I wanted as a litigator in a groovy Westside law firm. My clearest memory of that period was the day I closed the door to my office and laid my head on my desk in tears, defeated by the realisation that I did not want to do the job that had taken me seven years of university to get. My last day as a lawyer ended at 6pm the night I went into labour with our first child, Julien.

Then came the early 90s when America became increasingly food obsessed and anyone who had a successful restaurant wrote a cookbook about it. Despite being repeatedly asked, Antonio and Jean-Louis had no interest in jumping on that bandwagon, mostly because they had opened a couple of other places by then and were too busy as it was. By then I'd had our daughter Michela and was happily homemaking, although my Italian was still much better than my cooking.

'Why don't *I* write a book for us?' I said one day. '*Va bene,*' they replied. What followed were several years in which I told people I was writing a book without actually ever being able to get beyond writing down ideas.

When Julien was six and Michela three, we moved from L.A. to a little farmhouse in Tuscany. Jean-Louis went back and forth between Italy and the States. I planted a garden, started to make bread and continued to say I was writing a book without actually writing one. One day I was outside hanging up the laundry, when I said to myself, 'Lori, you are either going to write this book once and for all or put it to bed and stop talking about it.' I made a deal with myself – I would write for at least two hours, four times a week for the next two months and then I would take stock.

I discovered that I actually liked writing. Not because it was easy to fill the blank page. It never is for me. But because I liked the way it made me look at life and think about things. Like the fact that what I loved most about Italy was the way the daily activity of keeping one's self and one's family fed was lived with such light-hearted generosity, creativity and joy, all of which had nothing to do with being skilled in gastronomic theatrics or having a big fancy kitchen equipped with all the latest gadgets. What matters in Italy is a warmth of welcome nurtured by a deep-grained sense of hospitality. And conviviality. *La dolce vita* is not about Ferraris and speedboats. It's about taking pleasure in something as ordinary as sipping a thimbleful of coffee in the sunshine. All this I wrote about with the enthusiasm of the newly converted. The resulting book was called *Italy Anywhere* and was published by Viking/Penguin in 2000. It was full of recipes, the most wonderful illustrations by my friend Heather and lots of little stories encouraging home cooks to spend less time following recipes than looking at the way Italians live their culinary lives and bringing that spirit home.

Those were the heydays of food writing. You got paid (true, never enough to get rich on) to go out into the world and poke your nose into people's gastronomic business, eat the most delicious things and come home to tell the story. I wrote for magazines like *Gourmet* and *Saveur* about everything from truffle hunting in Umbria to the lemons of Capri, Moroccan cooking adventures, Portuguese *piri-piri* and breadmaking at home – a home which at this point consisted of me and the kids, since irony of ironies, when Jean-Louis and I parted, he returned to L.A. while Julien, Micky and I stayed in Tuscany, which by now had come to feel like *casa*.

In the midst of all of this, I was offered another book to write, this time about Tuscany. The book's London-based photographer was Jason Lowe. He was talented, hilarious, and so refreshingly un-Latin, he slipped right under the radar. The next thing I knew I found myself once again in a relationship with a man who lived in a different country than me. We pitched ideas all over the place for projects that kept us working together. Eventually we even got married, though for the first couple of years he and his daughter Rae remained based in London and my kids and I in Tuscany. (Spoiler alert – although we opened Towpath together and had a good run, we are no longer married.)

Two writing projects from those days changed the trajectory of my life. The first was Jason and my book, *Beaneaters & Bread Soup*, which tells the gastronomic story of Tuscany through portraits of some very inspiring folk. I'd become fascinated by a certain type of artisan I'd met over the years there – keeping bees, making cheese, forging knives, weaving cloth – it didn't really matter so much *what* they did as their relationship to their work.

Whatever their work, however tedious and unromantic its daily demands, they seemed to come to it with a wholeheartedness that reminded me of Ursula Le Guin's description of love, which 'doesn't just sit there, like a stone, [but] has to be made, like bread; remade all the time, made new'. I knew I hadn't yet had work in my life that I'd met with anything approaching the

constancy, integrity, enthusiasm and glorious eccentricity I saw in the artisans I was writing about. But it made me happy that there were people out in the world with that kind of relationship to their work. And I loved the fruits of their labours.

A long walk across a very large country was the subject of another life-changing writing project (although not for the reasons I imagined at the time). I'd wrangled a commission from *Gourmet* magazine to write a story about something that I'd been dying to do – walk the ancient pilgrimage route to Santiago de Compostela in north-west Spain, with only the barest necessities in a rucksack on my back. That in itself was one of the first intriguing questions. What did I need so much I'd be willing to carry it for nearly 900 kilometres? Surprisingly little it turns out.

I came back a convert – not to Christianity, but to walking. To simplicity. And the belief that everything matters. Walking slowed me down to the pace at which we are made to go through life. My mind fell in sync, my eyes readjusted to the long view.

On an elemental level food was fuel and, for once, I'd both earned my hunger and been given every opportunity to satisfy it. White asparagus, wild borage, sharp ewe's milk cheese, sweet membrillo and red wine all came from fields we walked through by day. But mealtimes were also a kind of communion. 'However great the distance we walked alone,' I wrote, 'at the table we came back together and told our stories… we chatted about pilgrimy things – our aches and blisters, where we'd walked from and where we were headed. Sometimes we talked about what the miles might be teaching us – that we didn't "need" as much as we thought; the humility to take what was offered and be grateful; to trust that there would be shelter, sustenance and friendship when we needed it; and the steadfastness of purpose to put on our packs and walk, day after day, even when we didn't really feel like it.'

I could go on and on about the Camino de Santiago. In fact, I did. I came back so exhilarated that after I wrote the piece for *Gourmet* I kept on writing for a year, only this time from London where I'd come to live. I wanted to tell a story that wasn't about food. To unpack the lessons I'd learned from walking. I had the enthusiastic support of an agent and a wonderful editor. But I could never quite get my words to reach the height of my experience. And so I put the project down. This was disappointing in the way only failing at something you've tried your hardest to do can be. And disconcerting. I was in London with nothing of substance to do. I didn't know enough about the place to write about it, and I'd become a bit gun-shy of writing anyway. I was still a mother, but no longer on active duty. I had a few lovely new friends, though none of the tried-and-tested variety. And I was nearly 50, which felt a bit late in the day to reinvent myself.

Enter Jason with an idea. Three tiny kiosks were for sale on the canal across from where we lived and he wanted to buy them. I thought about it for a while and I came back with an idea of my own. If we were going to open a little café (one of the possibilities we'd bandied about), I was ready to be the one standing out there doing it. Of course, I had no real idea what that 'it' would require, but something was coming together in my mind and I was ready to try to make, as Antonio Machado says, 'sweet honey from my old failures'.

The Camino had made me into a walker. I believed in walking the way people believe in meditation, or eating from the five food groups. And unlike, say wine, I loved it *and* it was actually good for me. What little I felt I understood about London I'd learned through my wanderings. Urban isolation has a flavour all its own. Alone in a crowd on Oxford Street is different than alone on a mountaintop. More desolate. Possibly more common. The canal provided an unlikely refuge. I'd walked it from Little Venice to the Limehouse Basin, drawn to the murky ribbon of water slowly snaking through the city, with its narrowboats instead of cars, its moorhens, its coots and its gentle invitation to amble.

The Lilliput size of the kiosks appealed to my new-found appreciation of all things small and simple. I knew something interesting could be done with them – after all, *I Fratellini*, one of our favourite places in Florence, had been pouring wine and making the most delicious sandwiches out of something even smaller since 1875. I also liked the idea of finally being one of the people actually *doing* something, instead of someone on the sidelines with a notebook and a pen. I confess to spending a lot less time thinking about the food than about how we could create a place where people would want to slow down, to talk to each other or simply to stop, if only as briefly as a hummingbird on a blossom, before picking it all up again and going back into the fray.

So here we are. Ten years ago Towpath was my road out of writing. And now it is my road back in.

ROAST CROWN PRINCE SQUASH, RICOTTA AND CARAMELISED CHILLI SAGE BUTTER

The humble squash is a true sign that autumn is on the horizon. While September can still be warm and leave us with a few last balmy evenings, the days are starting to shorten, become crisp and cooler and you can feel the shift. This dish to me epitomises this time of year. The combination of the sweetness and earthiness of the squash with the crispy warmness of the sage work wonderfully as a pair. Add in a blob of rich, creamy and savoury ricotta and some caramelised sage and chilli butter and it warms the soul.

Serves 4

1 large or 2 medium crown prince
  squash, weighing around
  2kg/4½lb
2 tablespoons olive oil
Caramelised Sage and Chilli
  Butter (see page 179)
150g/5½oz ricotta
salt and pepper

Notes
Any type of pumpkin or squash could be used here. You will just need a robust variety that is happy to be roasted and doesn't have a high water content like spaghetti squash.

Preheat the oven to 210°C fan/450°F/gas mark 8.

Cut the squash into four. If you have one big squash, be very careful as the skin is super tough – I put a tea towel between my hand and the tip of the knife to prevent my hand going through the top of the blade. Remove the seeds and discard. Remove the skin. I find using a serrated knife the best option and if you get slightly further under the skin, it's much easier to remove – you want to remove the green colour under the skin. Cut into big wedges – I normally cut each quarter into three or four wedges lengthways.

Toss in the olive oil. Season and place on a large baking tray with the wedges standing up. Cook for about 25–35 minutes until the squash has browned and is fully cooked. This stage can be done in advance and kept in the fridge for 2–3 days and you can reheat without affecting the squash.

Make the Caramelised Sage and Chilli Butter (see page 179).

Plate up using one large platter or four individual plates. Place a bit of ricotta on the bottom so that it can secure the squash wedges, then layer up a few of the squash wedges and scatter some blobs of ricotta around. Layer up the rest of the squash and blob more ricotta over and around.

To finish, generously drizzle over the caramelised sage and chilli butter with lots of sage and lots of the butter. Season.

CONFIT DUCK LEG, LENTILS AND MUSTARD

Confit duck legs in the fridge can be very useful on the days when the weather trips you up. When the weather prediction is for pouring rain, I generally plan a smaller menu as it tends to be much quieter. But when I wake up, open the curtains and see a crystal-clear blue sky with the sun shining bright, I think uh-oh! Having things in the fridge that I can then pull out is invaluable. Once the duck legs are cooked and immersed in duck fat, they will last in the fridge for a couple of months, which then allows me to create a dish almost entirely on the spot. Because the duck keeps so well, I've given slightly larger quantities than you might be used to. It takes the same time to cook more and it means that you will have duck legs in the fridge for another time or to make Duck Rillette (see opposite).

Makes 8 confit duck legs

For the confit salt
50g/2oz coarse salt
peel of ¼ orange
peel of ¼ lemon
1 clove
½ teaspoon coriander seeds
½ clove garlic, peeled
1 bay leaf
1 teaspoon chopped rosemary
1 teaspoon chopped thyme
5 black peppercorns
1 star anise
25g/1oz granulated sugar

For the duck legs
8 duck legs, skin on
1 litre/1¾ pints duck fat (enough to submerge the legs)
Dijon mustard, to serve

Notes
I make green sauce by chopping half a bunch of parsley, mint and tarragon with a handful of capers and cornichons and mincing a clove of garlic. Add a teaspoon of Dijon mustard, a couple of chopped anchovies, olive oil, a teaspoon of the caper brine, and salt and pepper. Mix.

To make the confit salt, blitz everything except for the sugar in a Magimix until well amalgamated. Pour into a bowl and mix the sugar in by hand. If you don't use all the confit mix, it will keep in the fridge for months.

Take each duck leg and sprinkle the confit salt over each side. You will need about 1 tablespoon per leg.

Place in a tightly fitting container, cover and put in the fridge for 24–48 hours.

Preheat the oven to 130°C fan/300°F/gas mark 2.

Remove the duck legs from the container and pat dry with a tea towel – I don't rinse them as the curing salt should perfectly season the duck.

At the same time, put the duck fat in a pan and heat until melted. Put the duck legs in an ovenproof dish deep enough to hold the legs and the fat and that has a tightly fitting lid (use foil if necessary). Pour over the duck fat so the legs are completely covered. Cover with greaseproof paper and the lid. Place in the oven for around 2½–3 hours until the meat comes away easily from the bone. Check after 1½ hours and then every 30 minutes after that. Eat straightaway or leave to cool in the fat and place in the fridge for another day.

Preheat the oven to 210°C fan/450°F/gas mark 8. Remove four duck legs from the duck fat, making sure the remaining legs are covered with the excess fat. Heat a large, ovenproof saucepan on a high heat and, when smoking, add the duck legs, skin-side down, to start crisping up the skin. After a few minutes, turn the duck legs, place the pan in the oven and cook for about 15–20 minutes until the skin is really crispy.

Serve with warmed lentils (see page 155) and some Dijon mustard or green sauce (see Notes).

DUCK RILLETTE

Delicious on a hot summer's eve with a glass of wine, this is the most perfect way to use extra confit duck legs from the recipe opposite.

Serves 4–6

4 confit duck legs and their fat
2 teaspoons grated nutmeg
2–3 tablespoons sherry vinegar
4 slices bread, toasted
50g/2oz cornichons, drained
salt and pepper

Notes

The duck legs are also delicious in a salad. Take the skin off and crisp it in a very hot oven. Then shred the meat and put into a watercress, pickled walnut and beetroot salad with a lovely mustardy dressing. Sprinkle the crispy duck skin over the top!

.

Preheat the oven to 160°C fan/350°F/gas mark 4.

Take the duck legs from the fridge and put into a roasting tray with all the fat.

Place in the oven and heat until fat has melted and legs are warm but not too hot to touch – about 20 minutes.

Remove the legs from the fat and, taking one leg at a time, remove all the skin and any sinewy bits. Shred the meat off the bones. I find the fastest and simplest way is to first remove the meat with your hands, place in a bowl and then shred using your hands.

Pour in some of the duck fat to bind it all together. Start with 150–200ml/5–7fl oz and add more if necessary. This works much better if everything is warm-hot – it is very hard to mix properly if everything has cooled down too much. Use a fork to mix the fat through as this also helps to shred the meat. Season and add the nutmeg and some of the sherry vinegar. Taste and add more seasoning and vinegar if necessary.

If not serving straightaway, tightly pack in a tub or jar and pour some duck fat over the top to cover it. Make sure the rillette is totally covered in fat as it will preserve it – if it is properly covered with no air pockets, it will keep for 2 months in the fridge.

When ready to serve, remove what you need from the tub and bring up to room temperature. Skim off the fat from the top.

Serve with toasted bread and cornichons.

BRAISED LAMB SHOULDER

I first made this dish when I was working for Harry and Ali in Chassignolles. The restaurant only offered a set menu and cooking whole lamb shoulders was a great thing to serve to one big table – not only does it look spectacular, it tastes even better. I have such fond memories of making this dish there and it is one that I serve a lot when we do private parties.

Serves 6

2.5kg/5½lb lamb shoulder
olive oil
3 heads garlic, whole
half bottle dry white wine
150ml/5fl oz chicken or beef stock
   (or water)
salt and pepper

Preheat the oven to 130°C fan/300°F/gas mark 2.

Heat a deep roasting tray (large enough to hold your lamb) over a medium flame until hot.

Lightly rub the lamb with oil. Generously salt and pepper both sides. Place the lamb shoulder, fat-side down, into the tray and brown. Turn over and quickly brown the other side.

While the lamb is browning, blanch the garlic heads for 15 seconds in boiling water to remove the outer papery skin (from the outer head, not the individual cloves). Break the heads into individual cloves.

When the lamb has browned on both sides, add the white wine, bring to the boil and reduce until the alcohol has burned off (there will still be liquid in the tray). Add the stock, return to the boil and reduce for a few minutes. Make sure you scrape all the goodness stuck to the bottom of the tray as well. Add in the garlic cloves, another pinch of salt and pepper and cover with foil.

Braise the lamb in the oven for 5½ hours. Check after 3 hours – if the tray is bubbling, turn the heat down slightly. The lamb is ready when the meat falls off the bone.

Turn the heat up to 180°C fan/400°F/gas mark 6, remove the foil and braise for 30 minutes so that the lamb is crisp and brown on top. Take out the oven.

Use a pair of tongs to twist and remove the shoulder blade. Set aside all the bones to make a stock if you wish (see Notes opposite).

Transfer the meat and garlic to a heated serving platter. Pour the liquid from the tray into a jug, skim off some of the fat and pour the remaining juices over the meat and serve.

I love to serve this dish with Farro, Broad Beans and Peas (see page 64) or simply with roast potatoes or potato dauphinoise.

LAMB BROTH

Making a lamb broth is an utterly delicious way to use up leftovers from a lamb braise. You can make a stock from the bones, and the leftover juices from the braise is what gives this broth its rich flavour. So good that you might consider roasting a whole shoulder for four people and using the rest for broth. It's a wonderful one-pot meal.

Serves 6

500g/1lb 2oz crown prince
  squash, peeled, deseeded and
  cut into chunks
5 tablespoons olive oil
1 litre/1¾ pints lamb stock
  (see Notes)
500g/1lb 2oz picked braised lamb
  meat (see recipe opposite),
  plus all the remaining juices
12 confit garlic cloves (from the
  recipe opposite)
2 bunches of cavolo nero, stalks
  removed, leaves torn into pieces
100g/3½oz farro, rinsed and
  cooked (see page 64)
1 bunch of flat-leaf parsley, leaves
  only, chopped
salt and pepper

Preheat the oven to 210°C fan/450°F/gas mark 8.

Coat the pumpkin in olive oil, season and roast on a baking tray for 25–35 minutes until the squash colours slightly and is soft but not mushy.

Warm the lamb stock and juices in a large saucepan. When hot, add the braised lamb meat, confit garlic and roasted pumpkin. Warm gently for 5–10 minutes, then add the cavolo nero and the farro. Simmer for 5 minutes. Adjust the seasoning. Scatter each serving with chopped parsley.

Notes
Make a lamb stock from the bones by boiling them with garlic, carrots, onions, leeks, celery, peppercorns and bay leaves, plus any vegetables that need using up. Bring to the boil, skim off the fat and simmer in 1.5 litres/2¾ pints of water for 3–4 hours. Strain before using.

NAPOLI SAUSAGE RAGU

Most weekends we have the hearty Napoli sausage sandwich on the breakfast and lunch menu. It consists of Napoli sausages and lots of butter and ketchup on fresh bread. Sometimes we have sausages left from the weekend and so a great way to use them is to turn them into a ragu. I also make this dish from scratch as it is perfect to serve at Towpath on a crisp day. It is a comforting, nourishing dish and a regular on the menu both at the beginning and end of our season. Serve with wet polenta.

Serves 4

4 tablespoons olive oil, plus a
    nice glug for serving
6 brown or red onions, thinly
    sliced
4 cloves garlic, minced
2 bay leaves
sprig of rosemary
sprig of thyme
10 napoli sausages or any other
    coarse pork and fennel
    sausages
200ml/7fl oz red wine
2 x 400g/14oz tins whole plum
    tomatoes, blitzed or mashed
100g/3½oz Parmesan, grated
salt and pepper

Notes
We shot this recipe at Lori's house in Tuscany. When cooking in another country or even buying ingredients from other suppliers, the resulting dish can be quite different, for example, the sausages we bought in Tuscany were incredibly fatty. Delicious in flavour but once cooked, a lot of fat leaked out which I then skimmed off. This meant that the ragu would have benefitted from having more sausages.

Preheat the oven to 140°C fan/325°F/gas mark 3.

Add 3 tablespoons of olive oil to a saucepan over a medium heat. Warm and then add the onions, garlic, bay, rosemary and thyme. Cook for 20 minutes until the onions soften.

While the onions are cooking, brown the sausages in an ovenproof frying pan with the rest of the oil and place in the oven for 20 minutes. Remove from the oven and place on a tray. Deglaze the pan with the red wine to get all the goodness from the sausages and add the delicious red wine/sausage juices into the onion pan.

Cook for a few minutes and then add in the tinned tomatoes. Rinse the tin out with water and add that to the pan too.

Slice the sausages into 2cm/¾in-thick slices and add to the pan. Turn down to a simmer and cook for a minimum of 3 hours. The longer and slower you cook the ragu, the richer and fuller it will taste. Stir from time to time to scrape the bottom. If it's catching, add a glug of water and stir again. You want the ragu to reduce and thicken.

I always leave the seasoning right to the end. As the ragu cooks and reduces, the flavour will intensify so it's best to check the seasoning once it's finished cooking.

Serve with Parmesan and a drizzle of olive oil.

TREACLE BARS

These treacle bars have the same base as the Blackberry and Crème Fraîche Bars (see page 196) and are made in a similar way – the base is cooked first and the topping is then poured over and it is cooked again.

Makes 16 bars

For the base
1 cooked tart base (see the Blackberry and Crème Fraîche Bars on page 196)

For the treacle topping
400ml/14fl oz golden syrup
100g/3½oz breadcrumbs or panko breadcrumbs
70g/2½oz ground almonds
zest of 1 lemon
150ml/5fl oz double cream
1 egg, plus 1 yolk

Gently warm the syrup in a medium saucepan and when liquid, add the breadcrumbs, ground almonds and lemon zest. Mix well and remove from the heat.

In a separate bowl, whisk the cream, egg and egg yolk till well amalgamated. Pour into the syrup mixture and stir together well.

Pour the treacle topping over the cooked base, turn up the heat to 150°C fan/340°F/gas mark 3½ and cook for around 30–45 minutes and then check – the topping should still have a slight wobble. Remove from the oven and leave to cool in the tin.

As with the blackberry bars, I often make these a day ahead, so I can put them in the fridge overnight to make it easier to cut the next day, but these treacle bars are also delicious served warm straight out the oven with a blob of crème fraîche.

DAWNY'S CHEESECAKE

The one thing my mum isn't great at making is cakes – I have vivid memories of them always collapsing. But there was one thing she baked that was so delicious she didn't really need anything else in her repertoire. My dad loves this cheesecake so much that to this day he still hides it from us so he can eat it all himself. And I will still grab his plate when he's not looking and hide it from him.

This recipe is so very simple and pretty hard to mess up. It comes from Dawn's best childhood friend, Evie, who probably got it from a South-African Jewish cookbook. The only thing I would say is always to cook it in a 23cm/9in round Pyrex dish. My mum always insisted on this, but for years at Towpath I made it in cake tins and it never came out as good as hers. A couple of years ago, I finally ordered Pyrex dishes. What a difference it makes!

Serves 8–10

125g/4½oz unsalted butter, melted
200g/7oz digestive biscuits, blitzed in a Magimix or with a rolling pin to fine crumbs
2 eggs
170g/6oz caster sugar
500g/1lb 2oz cream cheese
1 teaspoon vanilla extract

Preheat the oven to 150°C fan/340°F/gas mark 3½.

Mix the melted butter and digestives in a bowl to form a crumb. Put most of the crumb in the base of a 23cm/9in round Pyrex dish (save a handful for sprinkling over the top) and press firmly. Put in the fridge to chill for at least 10 minutes.

Using a hand or electric whisk, whisk the eggs, sugar, cream cheese and vanilla extract together for a couple of minutes until light and fluffy.

Take the base out of the fridge, pour over the topping and sprinkle the remaining crumb over the top.

Bake for 35 minutes. It should still have a moderate wobble in the centre when you take it out as it will continue to cook as it cools down.

Serve warm or at room temperature, with some fresh fruit or poached fruit on the side.

October

A Conversation with Laura

LORI DE MORI: *Can you remember the first time you heard about Towpath as an idea?*

LAURA JACKSON: It was when you and Jason came to Chassignolles in France where I was working. It was put out there kind of whimsically. You guys asked me what I was planning on doing when I got back to London. And I thought, 'No idea!' I was enjoying not even worrying about it. My only plan was that I wanted to carry on cooking. Chassignolles was a seasonal place and I was working from the beginning of May until November. Not dissimilar to Towpath.

LDM: *When you first saw the kiosks on the canal, what did you think?*

LJ: That the idea of of opening a place there was kind of mad… but exciting! I had a feeling that it was going to be good. And it was something so different from anything I'd ever done. Skipping forward, I think that if we had continued running food out of the bar and cooking at your house across the canal, I wouldn't have stayed. Obviously there was a limit to what I could do with the cooking in the beginning. But when we acquired the kitchen, it changed everything really.

LDM: *What was it like cooking out of someone's house?*

LJ: (laughing). I think my parents thought we were completely insane. Not the cooking side. But I remember I would often stay the night because I was still living with my parents which was a 45-minute cycle away and I can remember my mum saying to me, 'I just don't think this is a good idea. Staying at their house, cooking at their house. It's not very professional. I understand you guys are close. But be careful.' I don't know, I feel that I can be super conventional and quite conservative in a lot of ways, but this just seemed like a fun thing to do and I was up for the challenge.

LDM: *In the beginning we all agreed we would open Towpath and try it for three months and then talk about it. At the end of three months, I remember you saying there was nothing you would rather be doing than cooking at Towpath.*

LJ: There you go! I think it was really exciting to be involved in something from the beginning and have the feeling that I could do what I wanted. You guys trusted me. Until then I'd always come into a kitchen and asked, 'What can I do, what are we making?' Of course you're learning so much that way, but it was exciting to have this side of it be all mine. And to have a customer! And see them return! I remember days where we were so excited because we'd had 15 customers in one day. Or the day we took £250 pounds and we were like, 'Oh my god, can you believe it, our best day ever!'

LDM: *Did you find that the constraints in our set-up also helped us in a certain way? Forced us to think out of the box?*

LJ: I think that's what you're really good at… something I've learned so much from you. Rather than say, 'This is what we want to do', it's more like, 'This is what we've got to work with. There's no kitchen on site. Just a tiny little bar where you're going to have to bend down and stir the stew in the urn while the customer wonders where you've disappeared to.' You can either get really stressed or just say, 'Let's figure out what we can do with what we've got.' That was what was so charming and unique about Towpath. And still is.

LDM: *What is it about cooking you like so much? How did you come to it and how would you describe your approach?*

LJ: Well I came to it in a slightly weird way. I'd finished my undergrad in physiology in Bristol. I'd come back to London and didn't really know what I wanted to do. I'd always thought I wanted to be a doctor. I don't really know why. I think maybe because my uncle was a doctor. I'd watched him in surgery, and I thought it'd be cool. I also think I didn't know what was out there. I'd applied for post-grad medicine in London and I had a year off before it was going to start. My

friends took the piss out of me at university because I was always thinking about food. But I was so bad at cooking. There were seven of us living in a house together and generally once a week one of us would cook dinner. When I think of the stuff I cooked. Terrible! Really bad! But I loved eating. Really loved it.

I went and did a cookery course so I'd know how to make an ok meal for myself when I was back at school. I loved the hands-on bit. It wasn't particularly creative because you were learning techniques and silly things that you would never really do. But I liked the idea that you start out with something and even if it's time consuming, it's quite a fluid process and you can get a result quite quickly – unlike Alex (Laura's husband, an architect), whose projects can take years to finish. I wouldn't have the patience for that. To see a transformation in a short space of time is quite satisfying for me, I suppose. Anyway, the course was meant to be a month, but I ended up doing the diploma which took six months and not going to medical school.

LDM: *Were you the star pupil?*

LJ: No! I was so bad at it. I think I failed our final exam twice. It was ridiculous. A nightmare. I was so nervous about it. And when you're cooking, being nervous is the worst thing. We were having to make puff pastry from scratch, three different meat dishes, a béarnaise, which, of course, split because I was over-thinking it. My puff pastry was a complete disaster – it didn't rise and it was all greasy and oozing butter.

LDM: *When you finished your diploma, were you keen to go work in a restaurant?*

LJ: Yes. I'd done some work experience. I even did a day with Jason. He was shooting an Italian cookbook. I didn't know that neighbourhood very well. I remember I had to find some ingredients and most of the local shops were newsagents that didn't have anything good. I was so nervous. I also did a month at Bibendum which wasn't really the kind of food I wanted to do.

LDM: *At that point, did you have an idea of what kind of food you wanted to cook?*

LJ: I knew what I liked. I knew I didn't want fancy. I'm embarrassed to say, but I think – don't laugh – I wanted to be cooking but not working all nights and weekends. (Laughter. Lots. As that's pretty much what she has been doing for the past decade.) I didn't want to do catering. But I didn't necessarily want the rush of a service. And I didn't want to work in a basement with no light. On Alex's recommendation, I went to speak to Leila (of Leila's wonderful café and grocery off Arnold Circus). She'd just opened and at this point it was only the grocery shop, not the café, and she did some catering. She wasn't hiring, but she'd helped set up a place in Primrose Hill and one of her friends was the head chef. This was Melrose and Morgan, which in the early days cooked everything on site. There was a massive table with quiches, tarts and big salads, a couple of meaty hot things. Sausages rolls. In the fridges there were fish pies and cottage pies to take home. You were cooking in the same room that all the customers were coming into.

LDM: *Who was your head chef?*

LJ: Rosie (she says, smiling). Rosie Sykes. I remember she interviewed me, and I brought my CV which basically had nothing food related on it. I actually knew very little. All the things I'd learned at cookery school were for dinner parties for four. That all went out the window. Rosie fundamentally taught me all my basic skills. She wasn't a scary, shouty chef. She was so enthusiastic and patient. And literally, there was never a single drop of waste in her kitchen. She was always looking at things that were left over and thinking, how can we turn this into something delicious? I think that's a really strong part of my cooking, which came from working with her.

LDM: *Where did you work next?*

LJ: At this point, I wanted to try to do service. I ended up at Rochelle Canteen. That was amazing. I learned so much there. It was a completely different energy and pace. Kevin and James, my head chefs, were so different from each other in their personalities and in the way they cooked, but both are amazing cooks. And there was an excitement to doing service and being in a small team. It was also fun sometimes cooking for Rochelle's catering events – wild parties in crazy places, with people spending mad amounts of money!
   And then I went to Chassignolles on holiday and I fell in love with it. So I wrote to Harry and asked him if I could work there the following summer. He knew the places and people where I'd worked.

LDM: *What's the backstory of the Auberge de Chassignolles?*

LJ: Harry Lester had the Anchor & Hope in London and he and his wife, Ali Johnson, wanted a change. He'd gone into Leila's one day and someone had told her just that morning about a little auberge for sale in the Auvergne. And you know what he's like, the next thing you knew he'd bought it and opened a little hotel and restaurant there.

LDM: *How did his cooking influence you?*

LJ: One of the things I loved about Chassignolles is that you would literally pick or forage for a lot of the things that you would use in your meal, so you were seeing things right from where they were coming from, all the way through to being delivered to the table. Having spent my whole life in a city, this was quite an exciting thing. Also, Harry's incredibly particular but also totally spontaneous. Sometimes he would just change his mind at the last minute, but I just loved his food. It was all about letting the ingredients shine and not messing around too much.

I cooked a lot with Harry, but he also left me to my own devices with his menus and his recipes. It was quite a good stepping-stone for Towpath because I was teaching myself a lot of things, but if I was confused I could always find him. It was a good learning curve for me. At Towpath, even now, I'm still teaching myself, but I'm less scared about it than I was.

LDM: *Who else do you take your inspiration from?*

LJ: In an ideal situation I like to have someone in my kitchen whom I can learn from so it's not just me teaching others. I still feel I have so much to learn. When it gets really, really busy, every second counts and it's hard to start messing around with new recipes. When you do things for the first time it takes a lot longer. Sometimes I feel I'm in a bit of a rut during the peak of summertime. I'm just churning out the same things. It's not that I don't enjoy making them. But I'd also like to do some new, interesting things. I loved having Davo (Davo Cook) in the kitchen. He came from Moro, which has a different school of cooking, and he

worked for an amazing Aussie guy who makes a lot of Lebanese and Middle Eastern food, and most of all he just has a real natural flair of his own. And I love working with Rach (Rachel O'Sullivan) who's super into Asian flavours. With them you can have a conversation as simple as, 'I've got this box of chard in today. Here's what I was thinking of doing with it. What do you think?' Straightaway I want to do their thing because I want to learn. It's amazing to have people like that in your kitchen.

LDM: *If you had to describe your style of cooking?*

LJ: You should describe it! (Laughing.) If you look at all the places I've worked – and maybe this isn't a good thing – they all have the same school of thought. Maybe I should have gone and experienced the whole Michelin star thing. But I like things super, super simple. Good produce. Homely, I would definitely say for me. Nourishing. Nurturing. It's never going to be too fancy. And that's why when people read this book they're going to realise how easy it is. Anyone can do it!

LDM: *In the current Towpath, what do you love the most about what you're doing or what you've created in your kitchen?*

LJ: I love, most of the time, how it feels like a family rather than a place where you go to work and it's all very polite and civil and that's it. It feels much more than that. Sometimes it can be too much, but I love that aspect of it because it feels comforting and it's not just about cooking. A lot of people say one shouldn't get too close to the people they work with, but I don't agree.

I love where Towpath is. Coming in before everyone else and doing some cooking and having a moment of calm and quiet. I think it's amazing to turn up on a Saturday morning early on a beautiful day when there's lots to do and no one's around yet. Even just standing outside before going into the kitchen is pretty special. And also – though when I'm really busy it can be totally annoying – I love seeing the familiar faces and being able to chat. In most kitchens, you'd either be far away or in a basement.

LDM: *What does our downtime do for you?*

LJ: It makes me realise how tired I am! Makes me realise I need to adjust a little bit each year, maybe not do so much. It gives me inspiration, time to mess around with new things. Gets me excited about starting all over again. Makes me petrified that I won't know how to cook anymore and no one's going to come back when we reopen! I think it's really good to have the downtime and take a step back and think about the whole year because, when you're in the moment, it's hard to think clearly about it all.

AUBERGINE KASUNDI

Kasundi originates from the Bengali region of India. Traditionally it was a fermented mustard paste that's as strong as Japanese wasabi and was so laborious and expensive to prepare, it was known as 'the queen of pickles'. It became a quintessential part of the royal meal and was served only in royal or upper-class families. Women from that elite were given permission to prepare it according to specific rules and rituals and only at specific times of the year.

We serve this as a weekend breakfast at room temperature on toasted sourdough with crumbled feta, chilli and lots of fresh herbs (coriander, parsley and mint). Although aubergine kasundi would be scorned upon by traditionalists, it is delicious and came to us from Rach.

Serves 6

about 250ml/9fl oz sunflower, vegetable or a neutral oil
500g/1lb 2oz aubergines, halved then quartered, cut into 3cm/1¼in wedges
1 tablespoon cumin seeds
½ tablespoon nigella seeds
1 tablespoon mustard seeds
3 red onions, finely diced
1 tablespoon garam marsala
2 tablespoons finely grated ginger
2 long red chillies, halved and finely diced, seeds in
3 cloves garlic, minced
1 x 400g/14oz tin whole plum tomatoes, blitzed or mashed
2 tablespoons muscovado sugar
2 tablespoons malt vinegar
salt and pepper

Heat 75ml/3fl oz of the oil in a large saucepan over a high heat until smoking. Add enough aubergine to cover the base of the saucepan but not so it's crowded. Brown for about 5 minutes on each side and then remove with a slotted spoon onto a tray lined with kitchen paper. Repeat with the rest of the aubergine, topping up the oil whenever necessary.

Using the same pan with the same oil, reduce the heat to medium and add in the cumin, nigella and mustard seeds. Cook until the seeds start to pop and hiss. Stir for a couple of minutes.

Add in the onions, garam marsala, ginger, chillies, garlic and season. Turn down the heat to low and stir well. Cook until the onions have become soft and sweet – about 20 minutes.

Now add in the tinned tomatoes, making sure to rinse the tin with water and adding that in too. Bring to the boil, then turn down to a simmer.

Add the aubergines, sugar and vinegar and simmer for about 30–45 minutes until the sauce has reduced. Stir from time to time. When ready, check the seasoning and leave to cool.

Notes

The kasundi will benefit from being made a few days in advance. Since there are lots of spices in this dish, the longer it sits, the more the flavours will infuse and enhance.

Kasundi is also delicious served with soft-boiled or poached eggs. I often serve it with lamb chops with lots of yoghurt drizzled over.

EGG AND BACON PIE

This is another favourite for the bar counter in between breakfast and lunch on busy weekends. It is one of Rosie Syke's recipes and is a great way to use up pastry ends. She says this is a real New Zealand staple. Rosie has spent a lot of time there as her mum is from New Zealand and it reminds her of her youth when they used to pack it up for many a picnic.

In the first few years of Towpath, I always made my own puff pastry as it is one of my favourite tasks. I insisted that I would never use ready-made puff pastry as you can always taste the difference. As things got busier and busier, I found that lovingly and painstakingly making puff pastry every week was neither time nor cost effective and so I had to bite my lip and start buying ready made. You can actually get really lovely pastry now and you don't even need to roll it out, but I still love making it on quiet days.

Serves 8

450g/1lb puff pastry
10 eggs
10 bacon rashers, smoked and
   streaky, rind removed
1 egg, lightly whisked with
   1 tablespoon full-fat milk
salt and pepper

Preheat the oven to 205°C fan/425°F/gas mark 7 and place a baking tray in the oven. You will also need a 27cm/10¾in round tart tin with a removable base.

If the puff pastry has not come in a roll, roll it out to a thickness of 0.5cm/¼in. Cut out one circle that's slightly bigger than the base of the tart tin and one that's the same size as the base.

Line the tart tin with the larger pastry circle and make sure that the edges are pressed in at the base and the pastry is coming up over the sides.

Crack the eggs directly into the pastry base, spreading them evenly across. Using a fork, lightly pierce each egg yolk. Season with salt and pepper.

Take the bacon rashers and bash them out to a thickness of 2mm/¹⁄₁₆in. Cover over the eggs. You may need to slightly overlap the bacon but make sure the surface of the eggs is completely covered.

Wet the rim of the pastry with water and lay the smaller pastry circle on top to form the pie.

Tightly press the edges together, trim the excess pastry, crimp the sides and cut a cross in the centre of the pie. Glaze the lid with the egg-and-milk wash.

Put the pie into the oven on the hot tray and bake for about 18 minutes. Check to see if the pie has browned – it may need 5 more minutes. Turn the heat down to 160°C fan/350°F/gas mark 4 and cook for 8 minutes until the pastry, eggs and bacon have cooked.

Take out of the oven and let cool for 5–10 minutes. Remove from the tart tin and cool for another 10 minutes on a wire rack. Serve with Rhubarb Ketchup (see opposite) or a side salad.

RHUBARB KETCHUP

I am a real fan of Heinz tomato ketchup and get really annoyed when I order something with ketchup and it comes with their homemade version, which tastes like nothing of the sort. This rhubarb ketchup is not trying to replicate Heinz but it is incredible how it tastes like a cross between Heinz ketchup and HP brown sauce. When I first made it with Rosie Sykes, I assumed that I was going to dislike it strongly as I do all other homemade ketchups, but I fell in love. Dip a flaky, savoury, salty pastry, such as an Egg and Bacon Pie (see opposite), a sausage roll or a pasty into this ketchup and you will be blown away. Thank you, Rosie, for changing my mind.

I make a substantial amount of this so it will last for a while – if sterilised properly, sealed well and stored somewhere cool and dark, the ketchup will last for years until opened. Once opened, store in the fridge – it will keep for several months.

Makes about 1.5kg/3lb 5oz

850g/1lb 14oz rhubarb, trimmed, cut into similar-sized batons and washed
250g/9oz cooking apples, quartered and cored, no need to peel
110g/3¾oz red onions, chopped
250ml/9fl oz apple cider vinegar
10g/¼oz salt
175g/6oz soft brown sugar
25g/1oz dates, pitted
3 cloves garlic, peeled
2 bay leaves
½ cinnamon stick
¾ teaspoon pepper
¾ teaspoon ground mace
½ teaspoon chilli flakes
½ teaspoon ground allspice
½ teaspoon ground ginger

Place everything into a large, heavy-bottomed saucepan and give it all a good stir. Turn the heat to high and bring to the boil. A lot of liquid will come out of the apples and rhubarb, so keep on a high heat but be sure to stir often as it will start to catch.

Once you feel this happening or when the liquid starts reducing, turn the heat down to low. Reduce by at least a third or until the fruit has completely dissolved – about 45–60 minutes.

Turn off the heat, then remove the bay leaves and the cinnamon stick.

Leave to cool for about 5–10 minutes and then blitz until completely smooth and you have a ketchup consistency.

Pour into sterilised jars, seal and leave for about 6 weeks before using. If you can't wait that long, leave for a couple of weeks and then taste to see if it's ready.

Notes
This recipe is a great way of using up excess fruit. You can replace the rhubarb with any other fruit – I've used plums, cherries and apricots and the result is just as delicious.

APPLE, CELERY, BLUE CHEESE, WALNUT AND BITTER LEAF SALAD

I could eat this salad endlessly, all day, every day. It's the combination of all the different ingredients that makes it so nourishing and moreish – the richness of the cheese, the crunch and sweetness of the apple, the nuttiness of the walnut, the bitterness of the leaves and the acidity from the apple cider vinegar. A dream combination. What a great way to start a meal on an autumnal day.

Serves 4–6 as a starter

1 head radicchio, core removed
   and leaves separated
1 head treviso, core removed and
   leaves separated
1 green chicory, core removed
   and leaves separated
4 inner celery stalks, cut on an
   angle about 3mm/⅛in-thick
2 spring onions or 1 large tropea
   onion, thinly sliced on an angle
100g/3½oz wet walnuts or
   toasted walnuts, halved
200g/7oz blue cheese, crumbled
1 large apple or 2 small ones
120ml/4fl oz apple cider vinegar
4 tablespoons olive oil
salt and pepper

Prep the leaves and wash and dry if necessary.

Place the leaves, celery, spring onions, walnuts (keep a scattering to finish the dish) and blue cheese in a bowl. Toss well.

Core and thinly slice the apple. Do this just before serving as you don't want the apple to go brown. Add the apple to the bowl and then season with salt and pepper.

I normally just drizzle the vinegar and oil over separately and taste, but you could also just mix it together in a jug and pour over.

Toss well again, check the seasoning and scatter over the remaining walnuts.

PUNTARELLE, ANCHOVY, CHOPPED EGG AND PARMESAN

Puntarelle is part of the chicory family and is bitter in taste with crunchy shoots on the inside and green dandelion-like leaves on the outside. I feel like it's a vegetable that's become on trend in the last few years, but it's something that's always been in Lori's diet, having lived in Tuscany for so long. I remember eating it years back in Rome, where the puntarelle salad originates. Lori reintroduced me to it right back when Towpath opened and it is a vegetable that I feel very strongly about. I love bitter things and I love the crunch of the inner shoots served raw in a salad as below or the leaves just simply sautéed. To me, it feels like a natural injection of health, a pick-me-up. It's in season usually from the end of October to the beginning of April.

I often serve this salad on its own, but it's delicious with roast beef, roast chicken or poached chicken tossed through it – just omit the eggs. Other uses for the leaves include wilting them down in soups or stews or blanched and then tossed with olive oil, lemon juice, chilli and anchovy.

Serves 4

1 head puntarelle, leaves removed and saved for another use
75–125g/3–4½oz Anchovy Dressing (see opposite)
4 eggs, hard-boiled, peeled and finely chopped
4 spring onions, thinly sliced on a small angle
100g/3½oz Parmesan, finely grated
½ bunch of parsley, picked and finely chopped
1 tablespoon merlot red wine vinegar or red wine vinegar with a sprinkle of sugar added
salt and pepper

Separate all the individual stems of the puntarelle shoot. Cut off the white base which is tough and incredibly bitter – you will feel where to slice by how easily your knife goes through.

Slice the stems into thin, long strips and soak in iced lemon water to crisp up. If left for long enough, the strips will start to curl. When ready to use, drain well in a colander and pat dry to get rid of any excess water.

Place the puntarelle, anchovy dressing, three of the chopped eggs, the spring onions, 80g/2¾oz of the Parmesan, the parsley and vinegar in a bowl. Toss well and taste for seasoning as the anchovy can make it quite salty. Add salt, if necessary, and pepper.

Place in a serving bowl or on four individual plates and sprinkle the rest of the egg and Parmesan over the top and a grind of pepper to finish.

ANCHOVY DRESSING

Makes 500g/1lb 2oz

1 egg, plus 1 yolk
1 tablespoon Dijon mustard
2 cloves garlic, minced
1 tablespoon lemon juice
1 tablespoon red wine vinegar
1 tablespoon water
1 x 45g/1¾oz tin anchovy fillets,
   drained and chopped – the
   oil can be used as part of the oil
   below
400ml/14fl oz sunflower,
   vegetable or a neutral oil

Using a Magimix, hand blender or whisk, combine all the ingredients except the oil until they are well amalgamated and form a smooth liquid.

In a continuous stream and with the motor running, slowly pour in the oil so that it forms a thick dressing. Make sure the oil combines properly otherwise the dressing will split. When the mixture gets too thick and it becomes hard to incorporate the oil, add in a splash more water to loosen it. You are aiming for a mayonnaise consistency.

Because of the saltiness of the anchovies, you shouldn't need to add any seasoning. Keep in the fridge and use within a week. Spread it on toast or add to fried eggs at breakfast. Mix through a green salad or toss it through purple sprouting broccoli.

AUBERGINE PARMIGIANA

This dish is a crowd-pleaser. The combination of tomato sauce, lots of melted mozzarella and Parmesan with fried aubergines is the universal definition of comfort food. Something that will instantly warm you up physically and mentally, giving you that big hug you need as the days become shorter and the darkness descends. But people love it so much that I can put it on the menu at any time of year. Occasionally, when the weather changes for the worse, I can be left with a substantial amount of aubergines and mozzarella. This is where the parmigiana comes in. Even if it's warm out, it never fails to please.

Serves 4–6

3 tablespoons olive oil
3 red onions, finely diced
4 cloves garlic, minced
bunch of basil, leaves picked,
    stalks saved
2 x 400g/14oz tins whole plum
    tomatoes, blitzed or mashed
sunflower or vegetable oil,
    for frying
1.5kg/3lb 5oz aubergines, sliced
    lengthways into 0.5cm/¼in-
    thick slices
2 x 250g/9oz balls buffalo
    mozzarella, torn into pieces
200g/7oz Parmesan, finely grated
salt and pepper

Notes

This is a great dish to prepare in advance if you have people coming round as it actually benefits from being cooked in advance. I always make the parmigiana the day before and leave overnight in the fridge to set. I then cook it and let it cool down completely, otherwise it can be a bit of a nightmare to cut into neat slices. I then warm it again when ready to serve. It is also equally delicious served at room temperature.

Start by making the tomato sauce. Heat the olive oil in a saucepan over a medium heat. When warm, add the red onions, garlic, basil stalks and season. Cook until soft and sweet – about 15 minutes.

Add the tinned tomatoes, making sure you rinse the tin with water and add all that goodness in too. Stir well and bring to the boil, then turn down to a gentle boil and cook for 1 hour. Season again and remove the basil stalks. You want the sauce to thicken, reduce and sweeten.

While the tomato sauce is cooking, fry the aubergines. At Towpath I fry the aubergines in the deep-fryer, but to fry the aubergines in a pan, put in a hot frying pan with generous amounts of oil (so it coats the bottom of the pan) and cook until brown. Once brown, turn over and brown the other side. You may need to do this in batches, as you don't want to overcrowd the pan. Once cooked, put the slices on kitchen paper to drain off all of the excess oil.

Preheat the oven to 210°C fan/450°F/gas mark 8.

To assemble, take a 20 x 28 x 6cm/8 x 11 x 2½in rectangular gratin dish. Start with a layer of aubergine slices, slightly overlapping them so they are tightly packed in. Season. Spread over a very thin layer of tomato sauce (this is important – the dish should be dense not saucy!) and season again. Dot some mozzarella over, sprinkle with some Parmesan and scatter over some basil leaves.

Repeat until you have four layers, finishing with mozzarella and Parmesan on top. Add double the amount of Parmesan on the top, but do not scatter the basil leaves on this time as they will go brown and soggy.

Notes continued

If you really hate the smell of frying, like my mum, then you can always bake the aubergine slices. Rub the slices with oil, season and place on baking trays, well-spaced out, in a hot oven – 200°C fan/425°F/gas mark 7. Roast until the aubergines have browned and are soft in the middle – about 30 minutes.

Do not worry if you have sauce leftover, but everything else should have been used up.

Place in the oven, with a tray underneath if the dish is very full. Cook for 20 minutes until brown and crispy.

Turn the oven down to 160°C/350°F/gas mark 4 and cook for another 15 minutes. Remove from the oven and leave to cool for 10 minutes.

Serve with salad or, if you want to be really indulgent, with crispy potatoes.

SMOKED HADDOCK FISH PIE

Another of Lori's favourites and a perfect dish for a cold day. This pie is inspired from the days when I worked at Melrose and Morgan, which was my first cooking job. Along with serving lots of fresh food, we had several fridges full of prepared food. Every week, I would make endless fish pies and cottage/shepherd's pies. I'm still surprised that I love making this, but I think it's the memory of it being one of the first things I learnt to cook that puts a smile on my face. I like to serve my fish pie with greens or a watercress salad.

Serves 6

1kg/2¼lb smoked haddock fillets, skin on
1 litre/1¾ pints full-fat milk, plus 100ml/3½fl oz for the potatoes
4 bay leaves
handful of peppercorns
1.2kg/2lb 10oz Desiree or Maris Piper potatoes, peeled
150g/5½oz unsalted butter, plus 100g/3½oz for the potatoes
1 large or 2 medium leeks, washed, and sliced
4 eggs
100g/3½oz plain flour
½ bunch of dill, finely chopped
1 lemon, juiced
salt and pepper

Notes

This is a great pie to make in advance as it will sit well in the fridge for a couple of days before cooking. Take it out of the fridge about 30 minutes before you put it in the oven and add about 15 more minutes to the cooking time once you've turned the temperature down.

Preheat the oven to 160°C fan/350°F/gas mark 4.

Put the smoked haddock, 1 litre/1¾ pints of the milk, the bay leaves and peppercorns in an ovenproof dish. Cover tightly with foil and place in oven for 20–35 minutes, but check if the haddock is ready after 20 minutes. The fish should be slightly undercooked as you will be cooking it again. It should come away easily from the skin but still be a bit translucent. Take out of the oven and remove the foil. Once you are able to touch, but while still warm, remove the skin and any bones, keeping the pieces as large as possible. Strain the milk and keep in a saucepan to use later.

While the fish is cooking, cut the potatoes into similar-sized pieces and run under cold water to remove all the starch. Place in a saucepan, cover with water and season. Bring to the boil and cook until soft. Drain in a colander and mash using a mouli.

Warm the 100ml/3½fl oz milk and the 100g/3½oz butter for the potatoes in a small saucepan and then stir into the potatoes for a creamy mash. Season.

At the same time, melt 50g/2oz of the butter in a saucepan over a low heat. Add the leeks, turn up the heat and sweat until soft and sweet. You don't want any colour, so once the liquid has evaporated from the leeks, turn down the heat and stir from time to time – this should take about 20 minutes. Season.

Soft-boil the eggs (for 6 minutes – you want them runny) and rinse under cold water to stop them from cooking further. Peel and cut into quarters lengthways.

Now make the béchamel. If the fish poaching milk is not warm, warm gently over a low heat. In another saucepan, melt the remaining 100g/3½oz butter on a low heat. Add the flour and, with a wooden spoon, stir continuously. Cook for about 5 minutes until the flour has cooked out. Add a couple of ladlefuls of the warm milk. Whisk vigorously as the sauce will thicken straightaway. Leave a couple of minutes between each ladleful to allow the sauce to thicken and the flour to cook – there is nothing worse than a floury béchamel.

Repeat until all the milk is incorporated. Stir the whole time as the flour can burn on the base of the pan. Bring slowly to the boil and cook on a low heat for 5 minutes, stirring. Season and add the dill.

Preheat the oven to 205°C fan/425°F/gas mark 7.

To assemble the fish pie, take a 20 x 28 x 6cm/8 x 11 x 2½in rectangular pie dish. Layer the leeks on the bottom, place the haddock on top. Scatter the eggs over and season. Drizzle over the lemon juice and ladle in the béchamel to cover the entire pie. You might have a small amount of béchamel left over. Leave to stand for 5–10 minutes. Finish with the mash and use a palette knife to smooth down the mash. With the round end of the palette knife, make indentations in the pie so it looks like the scales of a fish.

Bake for 20–30 minutes so it browns on top, then turn the heat down to 150°C fan/340°F/gas mark 3½ and cook for another 10–15 minutes.

LAMB MEATBALLS AND ROSE HARISSA TOMATO SAUCE WITH BARLEY COUSCOUS

A few years ago, Lori was asked by Belazu, one of our suppliers, to come up with recipes using their rose harissa and this is what she devised. I think it is a very easy and delicious meal – the kind of dish you could keep on eating forever – and it is a regular on the menu. Perfect for a busy day, as it can be made in advance and takes very little time to plate up.

Serves 4

For the tomato sauce
3 x 400g/14oz tins, chopped or whole tomatoes, mushed to a pulp
2 tablespoons olive oil
1 tablespoon rose harissa
salt and pepper

For the meatballs
100g/3½oz old bread, crusts removed and torn into pieces
125ml/4fl oz full-fat milk
2 eggs, lightly beaten
700g/1lb 9oz minced lamb
1 onion, diced
2 cloves garlic, minced
1 teaspoon ground cumin
1 tablespoon finely chopped flat-leaf parsley
1 tablespoon finely chopped coriander
2 teaspoons salt
50ml/2fl oz sunflower, vegetable or a neutral oil, for frying
200ml/7fl oz Greek or natural yoghurt, to serve

Start by making the sauce. Put the tinned tomatoes (rinse the tin out with water and add that too), olive oil and rose harissa in a saucepan and season with salt and pepper.

Bring to the boil, stir well and turn down to a simmer so it's just ticking over. Cook for 45–60 minutes to reduce and enhance the flavours, stirring from time to time to prevent it from catching.

While the sauce is cooking, make the meatballs. Start by soaking the bread in the milk.

In a big bowl, mix everything else together (except for the oil and yoghurt). Now squeeze the bread dry and finely crumble into the rest of the mix. Mix well and slap for a couple of minutes to help tenderise. Shape into 5cm/2in compact balls – you should end up with 20 balls. Place on a baking tray and put in the fridge.

When ready to cook, heat the oil in a large frying pan. Once the oil is smoking hot, brown the meatballs for about 2 minutes on each side. Do not overcrowd the pan otherwise they will sweat rather than go crispy.

If you are cooking them in batches, use a slotted spoon to remove each batch when ready and place in the tomato sauce.

Once all the meatballs are in the sauce, turn the heat down very, very low. Put the lid on and cook the meatballs slowly – this should take 15 minutes. Turn the heat off and leave the meatballs in the sauce.

When you are ready to serve, drizzle a generous amount of yoghurt on top and serve with the barley couscous (see opposite).

For the barley couscous

200g/7oz barley couscous or
  wholewheat or plain couscous
4 tablespoons olive oil
200ml/7fl oz boiling water
1 lemon, juiced
2 tablespoons roughly chopped
  parsley
2 roughly chopped tablespoons
  coriander
2 tablespoons roughly chopped
  mint leaves
2 spring onions, thinly sliced on
  an angle

To make the barley couscous, put the couscous into a
heatproof bowl with 2 tablespoons of the olive oil and
season. Give it a good mix so that all the couscous is
thoroughly coated. Pour over the boiling water and
cover tightly with clingfilm. Leave in a warm place.

After about 20 minutes, remove the clingfilm and
fluff up the couscous using a fork. Mix everything else
in and taste for seasoning.

MEAT LOAF

I first made this recipe when we decided to collaborate with the amazing Dario Cecchini from Panzano. Dario is a dear friend of Lori's and runs a beautiful if not mad butcher's shop/restaurant. Imagine turning up and hearing the butcher recite a long and passionate excerpt from *Dante's Inferno* or to hear opera music blaring through the little village.

We thought it would be a lovely idea to put on a Towpath dinner in the spirit of Dario. Dario would send me a whole load of his recipes. I would mess around with them, test them out, put my Towpath take on them and he would come over for the dinner. He would sing, recite poetry, blow his horn, dress in the colours of the Italian flag and I would pay homage to his dishes as interpreted by me. Initially, this was quite daunting as I didn't want to disrespect him or his dishes, but being the super passionate and enthusiastic man that he is, he loved everything. We decided that this would become an annual affair and we did it for three years, but we have been unable to coordinate over the last few years. I have faith, though, that it will happen again. Do not be disheartened by the colour and texture of the meat loaf. It almost looks like a loaf of bread – but trust me that once you bite into it with a blob of Dario's mostarda, your mouth will just melt away with the juiciness of it.

Serves 6–8

150g/5½oz onions, diced
1 clove garlic, minced
50g/2oz unsalted butter
800g/1¾lb minced beef
200g/7oz minced pork
40g/1½oz beef suet, finely grated
115g/4oz old bread, soaked in milk
    and when soft, really squeezed
    out
2 eggs, lightly beaten
2 generous pinches of chopped
    thyme
3 teaspoons salt
100g/3½oz breadcrumbs, or
    enough to coat the loaf
pepper

Sweat the onions and garlic in the butter over a low heat until they become soft and translucent. Season to taste and leave to cool.

Meanwhile, in a large bowl, mix the beef, pork, suet, bread, eggs, thyme, the salt and some pepper. Mix thoroughly for a couple of minutes to tenderise.

When the onion-garlic mixture is cool, add to the meat and mix well so everything is evenly distributed.

On a clean surface, flatten and bash the meat mixture. Repeat several times to tenderise, then form a very smooth, tight loaf. Leave to rest in the fridge on a lined baking tray for at least 30 minutes. You can also leave this overnight in the fridge.

Preheat the oven to 180°C fan/400°F/gas mark 6.

Once rested, take the meat loaf from the fridge. Pour the breadcrumbs into a tray and roll the meat loaf in the crumbs until coated. Wrap the loaf tightly in fresh greaseproof paper, making sure you put the fold on the bottom of the tray to prevent the paper from opening during cooking.

Cook for 50 minutes and then remove the greaseproof paper. Turn up the heat to 200°C fan/425°F/gas mark 7 and cook for an extra 10 minutes so the meat loaf turns a lovely golden brown.

Rest for 10 minutes and serve sliced with mostarda, chickpeas or cannellini beans and cavolo nero.

OCTOBER

BROWNIES

A staple on the Towpath sweets menu. When I was working at Rochelle Canteen, I was sent to spend two weeks in the pastry kitchen at St. John. It was an incredible experience and one of my first jobs was to make the brownies. I made them every day for those two weeks and continued making them at Rochelle where they were also on the counter most days. I love how rich and gooey the brownies are. There was no need for me to change the recipe as it's perfect in every way.

Makes 16

200g/7oz dark chocolate (70 per cent), chips or cut into chunks
150g/5½oz unsalted butter
3 eggs
250g/9oz caster sugar
50g/2oz plain flour
65g/2½oz whole, shelled hazelnuts in their skins

Preheat the oven to 160°C fan/350°F/gas mark 4.

Melt the chocolate and butter together in a bain-marie.

In a large bowl, whisk together the eggs and sugar.

In a slow stream, pour a couple of tablespoons of the melted chocolate-butter mixture into the eggs and sugar. Whisk well. This is to stop the eggs from curdling. Now add the rest of the chocolate-butter mixture and really whisk thoroughly. This stage is important as the mixture can split, but by continuing to whisk, the mixture should noticeably thicken. If that doesn't happen, then you will need to blitz the mix with a hand blender to bring it back together.

Use a wooden spoon to fold the flour and hazelnuts into the mixture.

Line a 23 x 23cm/9 x 9in baking tin with greaseproof paper (letting a little extra hang over the sides). Pour in the mixture and bake until the brownies still wobble a bit in the centre – about 15–25 minutes.

Leave to cool before cutting.

ARMENIAN SPICE CAKE

David Cook, known to us as Davo, was one of our extraordinary chefs who cooked with me in the second and third years of Towpath. He is truly one of the best chefs I know and I was overjoyed that he wanted to come work with us. Davo had been head chef at Moro for years and was running Bocca di Lupo when it first opened, and his cooking epitomises natural flair to me. He never ever followed a recipe and just instinctively knew what to do and his excitement, happiness and constantly moving hands were infectious. Davo now lives a quiet life in Queensland, Australia and I try to see him every year when I go out to Sydney, where he always teaches me new recipes. His mum, known to us as Mama C, is also a wonderful cook and this recipe originates from her. Davo made this at Towpath and everyone loved it so much it is now a regular feature on our sweets menu.

Serves 8

16 dates, pitted
200ml/7fl oz hot coffee
180g/6¼oz muscovado sugar
200g/7oz caster sugar
140g/5oz plain flour
140g/5oz self-raising flour
120g/4¼oz unsalted butter, cold
    and diced
330ml/11fl oz full-fat milk
1 egg, plus 1 yolk, whisked
1½ teaspoons bicarbonate of soda
¾ teaspoon ground cinnamon
½ teaspoon grated nutmeg
50g/2oz walnut halves, toasted
crème fraîche, to serve

Soak the dates in the coffee and leave for at least 1 hour. If you can do this 24 hours in advance, the dates will really take on the flavour of the coffee.

Preheat the oven to 140°C fan/325°F/gas mark 3 and line a 23 x 23cm/9 x 9in baking tin.

Drain the dates in a colander and set aside until ready to use.

Put the sugars, flours and butter in a bowl and rub in with your fingertips to form fine breadcrumbs. Take 250g/9oz of this crumb and lightly press into the base of the baking tin.

To the rest of the crumbs, add the milk, whisked egg and yolk, bicarb, cinnamon and nutmeg and mix till smooth using a wooden spoon.

Place the dates in the tin over the crumb layer. You should get 4 x 4 rows.

Pour the mix into the baking tin and scatter the walnuts over the top.

Bake for 1 hour and test with a skewer. You want the mixture to still slightly cling to the skewer in a fudgey-way rather than a runny way.

Leave to cool for 15 minutes and then serve with a generous blob of crème fraîche.

This cake is also delicious served cooled and even better with a strong coffee.

November

Sap Not Rising

When I was at university, I had a feeling I could never quite make sense of. It arrived at the end of every academic year, irrespective of whatever marvellous thing I'd planned to do with my summer holiday, and its intensity was directly proportionate to how hard I'd worked. What I expected, and what seemed perfectly reasonable to wish for after all that sustained effort, was elation. What I felt instead was its dull, lumpish cousin, deflation. On a more poetic day you might call it melancholy. The bittersweet sadness that comes with endings – no matter how anticipated or longed for.

While our closing date is set for the Sunday nearest to Guy Fawkes Night, the end of Towpath evenings is a moveable feast that has more to do with us standing on the canal with a finger to the wind than the actual calendar. Even ten years in, we are easily fooled by a few days of sunshine and can never quite fathom the sand running out of the hourglass and months of cold, dark days throwing a blanket over our shenanigans. We only truly start to believe it when we can feel it in our bones.

There's a certain conversation Laura and I have every year when a warm September spell has the canal swarming with humanity. One of us says, 'Do you think maybe we should keep doing dinners a little longer this year?' And the other replies, 'Let's wait a bit and see.' And what we see is always the same thing. A sometimes sudden, other times almost imperceptible shift in the season. Summer holidays are over, the kids are back marching along the towpath in the mornings on their way to school. There's a certain nip in the air and the damp, musky scent of flowers past their bloom and leaves beginning to turn. From one day to the next, people start asking us when we are closing for winter. We can all sense an ending, even if we can't put our finger on it.

At this point, Laura and I usually start talking about how good it would be to keep some sort of weather diary, which would eventually become a kind of Towpath Almanac we could consult every year to help us chart our course. But we never do. In this we are more like the birds who don't start flying south because it's written in a calendar, but because some internal clockwork signals that the time has come.

Life is suddenly easier when we don't have so many shifts to fill – it takes a lot of people to keep Towpath afloat through an endless succession of breakfasts, elevenses, lunches, teatimes, aperitifs and dinners. It doesn't seem to matter how many people we hire, there will always be a sunny week where we know we'll be rammed, and it's all – but never enough – hands on deck.

We careen through summer, our little Towpath like some tinny car on the autobahn, speedometer needle juddering in the red, until suddenly it's over and we downshift to the saner rhythms of Dolly's *Nine-to-Five*. This coincides nicely with the return to university of the handful of Towpath helpers who'd asked to work every hour god gives and suddenly have more important things, like particle physics or cultural anthropology, to think about.

Although we still have weeks before we tuck up for winter, there's the unspoken feeling that whatever flowering and fruiting the year holds has mostly happened. The harvest is in. And we are tired. All that furious pedalling, however exhausting, created an energy of its own, and now that we've slowed down, its light has dimmed. And we feel a bit flat. A bit whatever the opposite of sap rising is.

None of this is helped by the last Sunday in October's turning back of the clocks, that dubious gift that gives us a single morning's extra hour of sleep in exchange for months of unnaturally (at least to those who haven't been born into them) long, dark nights. The sun stays low in the sky all day, no longer even skimming the top of the buildings that face us on the other side of the canal. On a clear day, it still shines on Towpath for a few hours in the morning, then again for less than half an hour as it traverses a gap between buildings and, finally, briefly, just before dusk, which descends in the early afternoon and leaves the canal properly dark and desolate by the time we close at 5pm. If we ever needed our own personal  reminder that we are on a moving planet, tilting this way and that on its journey around the sun, this is it.

It isn't as if our customers desert us when the season turns. Bright mornings are still lively. Loads of regulars come for one last lunch. And then there's always a handful of people who 'discover' Towpath right before we close, and are bereft at the thought of living without us until March. Their enthusiasm puts a little spring in our steps. But by 3.30 the canal feels eerily deserted. A bit of a wasteland. It's as if our whole workday has been compressed into something much smaller, and nice as it is to get out early, there's something oddly dissatisfying about it all.

How do we keep ourselves from plodding through the days until the end of the season? We are tired, true. Be we are none of us plodders. There are two things really – one last dinner and our final night of fireworks, the latter of which has been a Towpath tradition since very early days (and hence deserves a chapter all its own).

The Last Dinner (which I am refraining from calling the Last Supper, as that carries all the wrong connotations) is a relatively new experiment. It began in 2018 when we thought, wouldn't it be nice to get our Towpath 'friends and family' round the same table. They've been buzzing around each other all year long, so much so that some of them have already become out-of-school friends of

ours or each others. Who are they? An amorphous group whose primary identifying characteristic is an eagerness to eat Laura's cooking and/or stand at the bar talking with us, however inclement the weather. Any of its number is more likely to avoid Towpath during a ferociously sunny weekend than when it's raining horizontally. Which means that we can invite them all for an al fresco dinner in November certain that no one will ask, 'What will we do if it rains?' They already know. We

will wrap ourselves up, drink wine, fill our bellies and try to stay dry. Then we'll go home to sleep in our warm, cosy beds. This is not Glastonbury with its muddy tents. If anything, a bit of weather will make it all more of an adventure.

This year the meal fell on a Friday and Laura decided on a loosely based Shabbat dinner, a nod to our shared Jewish heritage and some beloved old family recipes. We began with potato and onion latkes with sour cream and apple sauce (the recipe passed down to my dad from my great-grandmother Pearl, whom we all only ever knew as Baba). Then there was Laura's mum's chopped liver and chopped herring, scattered with egg and gherkins, and looking attractively 1970s *Time-Life* cookbook photo-ready on the plate. There were golden loaves of challah, the braiding of which was perfect, though not quite as self-evident as Laura's aunt had assured her it would be. This was followed by kneidlach and chicken broth (also known as matzo-ball soup). Laura lamented that the balls were too hard. According to my mom, when you make them for loads of people this is unavoidable. No one else seemed to notice. The main course was tzimmes – beef brisket with sweet potato, potato, carrots and prunes – Laura's version of her mum's recipe (from her own mum as well as Claudia Roden and a South African Jewish cookbook writer named Myrna Rosen). A bowl of tangerines would have sufficed for dessert, but in keeping with the food-to-get-you-through-a-Siberian-winter theme, we finished with Lokshen pudding (sweet noodle kugel) and poached quince. We did not, you will be happy to know, serve the syrupy Manischewitz wine of my American childhood Passover seders, but more bottles than it would be polite to tally of a spicy red Grenache from the Ardèche.

As it happens, it *did* rain a bit during dinner. Our friend Enrico (whose chair was wedged happily between captivating dinner companions, though awkwardly between our open awnings) gamely held an umbrella in one hand while eating with the other. Another friend John had presciently worn a raincoat and gallantly positioned himself as a sort of shield for the rest of his table.

It was very late by the time everyone left, and a handful would be back for breakfast in the morning. It's naïve to think that the problems of the world could be solved if we just all sat around the table and ate dinner together. But it would be a good start.

EGGS BHURJI

This is another of Rachy rach's recipes. She revolutionised our breakfast menu and this is a breakfast dish that you don't seem to find anywhere else and one that people love and are disappointed when it's not on the menu. Its origin is Indian and Rach loves to cook dishes inspired from India, Asia and the Middle East. It is a great one to serve when having guests round as the base should be made in advance, so the flavours can infuse. Then when you want to eat it, all you have to do is add some eggs and seasoning and serve. Traditionally it is served with roti or naan or even with rice in South India. At Towpath we serve it with toast, lime drizzled over the top, fresh coriander and spring onions.

This dish reminds me of another important chef who helped me run the ship for the last two years. His name is Marky Mark. When Rach decided to move to Ramsgate, I needed someone to help me run the place. My old head chef from Rochelle Canteen, the legendary Kevin McFadden, highly recommended Mark, and since then Mark's support and ability to cook the most incredible food was second to none. He has now moved back to Portsmouth – he is already greatly missed.

Serves 4

For the base

3 tablespoons olive oil
3 onions, thinly sliced
2 cloves garlic, minced
60g/2¼oz ginger, minced
2 green chillies, finely diced
   (save some to finish)
15g/½oz fresh turmeric, peeled
   and grated
1½ tablespoons cumin seeds,
   toasted and finely ground
½ lime, juiced
salt and pepper

For the eggs

8 eggs
4 tablespoons coconut milk
   (or full-fat milk)
2 tablespoons unsalted butter (or
   a neutral oil), plus extra for
   buttering the toast
4 slices sourdough bread, toasted
4 sprigs coriander
2 spring onions, thinly sliced on
   a small angle

Start by making the base. Heat the oil in a medium saucepan and when hot, add the onions. Stir for a couple of minutes, then turn the heat to very low.

Cook for about 5 minutes, until the onions start to soften and then add the garlic, ginger, chillies, turmeric, cumin and season with salt and pepper.

Cook until the onions have completely softened and the spices have infused – this should take about another 25 minutes. When they are ready, check the seasoning and add half the lime juice. Leave to cool, so the flavours enhance and get to know each other.

When you are ready to serve, whisk the eggs with the coconut milk, and season, but only salt lightly and add more salt once the eggs are cooked, if necessary.

In a large frying pan, melt the butter or heat the oil on a low heat. Once it is foaming or hot, add the onion base and stir to warm through for a couple of minutes.

Pour in the egg mix and stir constantly to prevent the eggs from overcooking or sticking to the bottom of the pan. This should only take a matter of minutes as you want the egg mix to be quite loose. Turn off the heat, but continue to stir as the residual heat will cause it to carry on cooking.

Check the seasoning, butter the toast and place a piece on each plate. Add the egg mixture to each plate, drizzle over the rest of the lime juice and scatter over the coriander sprigs and spring onions.

TOASTED CHEESE SANDWICH WITH QUINCE JELLY

Like most utterly simple things, this recipe is as good as the raw ingredients you begin with. Get your hands on the best artisan sourdough bread – we get ours from e5 Bakehouse. We've also experimented with different Cheddars, but even in blind tastings nothing compares to Montgomery Cheddar. If you can't find it, use the best farmhouse Cheddar you can find.

Makes 2 sandwiches

2 spring onions, sliced
300g/10½oz Montgomery
  Cheddar, grated
4 slices day-old sourdough bread
  (fresh is fine but harder to cut),
  buttered on the outside
Quince Jelly, to serve (see
  overleaf)

Heat a heavy-bottomed skillet (cast iron is good if you have one) over a medium heat.

Mix the spring onions in with the cheese and heap half of this between two slices of bread that have been buttered on the outside. Do the same with the other two slices. Cook each sandwich on both sides until the cheese has melted and the bread is golden and crispy.

Serve with Quince Jelly.

QUINCE JELLY

It must be said that making jelly is not the easiest of all culinary exercises. It definitely has a mind of its own. As English quinces generally come into season towards the end of the Towpath year it has become a ritual that every year, once Towpath closes its shutters to customers, I will come in and start making batches and batches. It really is a labour of love (when making it in such large quantities). If you take your mind off it for 2 minutes, you could turn around and find it completely overflowing at any given time – an absolute nightmare when cleaning the stove as it literally sticks to everything. So I can't turn on it, leave the kitchen and come back in a few hours. I have to nurture it and be patient. It's actually incredibly therapeutic as it gives me plenty of time to reflect on the year.

When I first started making quince jelly, I would carefully strain the quinces through muslin only extracting the clearest liquid. I realised that my yield was so small that one day I decided to really mush the quince through a large colander. The resulting liquid was not clear but the yield was so much more. Just before jarring, I would strain the jelly through a fine sieve and this resulted in a perfectly clear quince jelly with much less waste. These tips are important when making 160 litres!!!!

Don't bin the unused quince pulp, it makes a delicious cordial (see Notes, below).

Makes 1 litre/1¾ pints

3 lemons, sliced
2kg/4½lb quinces
1.2–2kg/2lb 10–4½lb caster sugar
    (this will depend on how much
    liquid you have)

Notes
To make quince cordial: cover the quince pulp in water. Bring to a boil and simmer for 2–3 hours. Strain through a sieve. Add sugar to taste. Gently heat the cordial until the sugar has dissolved. Chill and add a dash to a glass of prosecco or mix with fizzy water.

To a large saucepan, add the sliced lemons to 3 litres/5¼ pints water.

Wash the quinces, then quarter them, making sure to cut through the core and pips – the pectin is in the pips and this is what helps set the jelly. As you cut each quince, add it to the lemon water to keep the fruit from oxidising.

Bring to a boil, uncovered, and reduce to a simmer. Cook until the quince is very soft – about 1–1½ hours – adding additional water if necessary to keep the fruit covered in liquid. Strain through a colander and really mash the quince with your hands to remove all the liquid. Save the quince pulp and put to one side.

Measure the resulting liquid, so you can measure how much sugar you need. I use a ratio of 60 per cent sugar to the liquid. Add the sugar to the liquid.

Put a saucer into the fridge to cool to test the jelly. Bring the quince liquid and sugar up to a high boil in a heavy-bottomed pan (copper is the best if you have one). Skim all the bright white scum off the surface while the liquid boils. Keep an eye on the liquid as from time to time it will try to overflow. You want the liquid to be moving but it does not have to be a roaring boil. The jelly should take around 30–45 minutes to set.

In the meantime, sterilise your jam jars. Place the jars and lids in hot, soapy water. Rinse in hot water. Place in an oven preheated to 120°C fan/275°F/gas mark 1 until absolutely dry and ready to fill.

Do your first jelly test after 30 minutes. Put a spoonful of the quince mixture onto the chilled saucer and place immediately back into the fridge. Leave for 5 minutes and then test. It has set when you can run your finger through the mixture and the little trail from your finger remains. If the liquid runs into it, continue to boil the liquid. Chill your saucer once again and check again in another 10 minutes.

When the jelly has reached setting point, strain the mixture through a fine sieve, then pour into hot, sterilised jars. Seal and leave to cool. Unopened, this will keep for years in a cool, dark place. Once opened, refrigerate – it will last for 6 months.

CAULIFLOWER CHEESE

It's 5pm on a rainy, cold afternoon in mid November and we've just arrived at Lori's house in Tuscany. Towpath has been closed for about two weeks now and it has been that weird transitioning period from having a crazy, hectic life to suddenly not really knowing what to do with myself, and also knowing that I have lots and lots of writing to do for the book. We planned to make a trip to Lori's to write in an inspiring place and have our two photographers (and dear friends), Joe and Scott, come with us for a few days to take some pictures for the book in a calm and thoughtful way.

We spent the morning in San Casciano, Lori's local town that has an amazing greengrocers, butchers and delicatessen. When we arrive I feel like royalty. Everyone is so excited to see Lori. Kisses and hugs from everyone, excitement on their faces when she walks in the door and interest and slight confusion on why we are buying so much stuff for just the four of us. In the delicatessen there are over three generations working there, from grandma right down to granddaughter. Everything we choose provokes a question, 'Why are you choosing this? What are you going to do with it? Have you ever tried this? This is really similar but I think would work even better.' The passion and love for what they are selling and making is on another level. Don't think you can do this trip quickly – be prepared for at least a five-minute conversation on each thing you pick up. It is truly a magical experience, and so opposite from anything you experience in London, you almost can't quite believe it's happening. And I don't even understand Italian and still feel the love and dedication they give.

Several hours later, after we have done all our shopping, we head back to Lori's for the last two hours of light. This is our first shot.

Serves 4

1 litre/1¾ pints full-fat milk
2 bay leaves
8 black peppercorns
½ onion
2 cloves garlic
1 or 2 cauliflowers
   (about 900g/2lb in weight),
   outer leaves and tough base of
   stem removed
100g/3½oz unsalted butter
100g/3½oz plain flour
1 teaspoon cayenne pepper
200g/7oz sharp Cheddar,
   I use Montgomery's Cheddar,
   grated
salt and pepper

Put the milk, bay leaves, peppercorns, onion and garlic all together in a saucepan and bring to just below the boil. Remove the pot from the heat and let the mixture infuse until everything else is ready to go.

Bring a large pot of water to the boil. Add salt, then drop in the whole cauliflower. When the water returns to the boil, boil for 4 minutes and then drain.

In the meantime, melt the butter and stir in the flour. Using a wooden spoon, stir continuously to make sure the flour doesn't form lumps or stick to the pan. Cook for about 5 minutes so that the flour is cooked.

Strain the infused milk and start whisking in the milk slowly, a ladleful at a time. This allows the flour to cook while thickening the sauce. When all the milk is incorporated, stir for another 5 minutes. Taste to check that the flour has completely cooked out.

Stir in the cayenne pepper and half the Cheddar and season.

Cut the cauliflower in half or quarters depending on size. Place in a roasting tray so that it is very snug. Sprinkle with salt and pepper.

Pour over the béchamel, sprinkle over the rest of the grated cheese and leave to sit for at least 20 minutes. You can also do this in advance and leave overnight in the fridge.

Preheat the oven to 210°C fan/450°F/gas mark 8.

Bake for about 20 minutes – you want the cheese to be browned on top. Once brown, reduce the heat to 150°C fan/340°F/gas mark 3½ and cook for an additional 15 minutes.

Serve with a crisp green salad. I always serve the salad with a lemony olive oil dressing as this cuts through the richness perfectly.

CAVOLO NERO, FARRO AND PARMESAN

This is a very warming, comforting autumnal dish – that instant hug I love so much. It was first cooked in the Towpath kitchen by Rachy rach and this is my interpretation. The cavolo nero pesto is a great thing to have in the fridge as it quickly turns a simple dish into something delicious. The amount below will give you leftovers, so please dollop on eggs for breakfast, toss through a pasta, spoon on top of any vegetable broth or on the side of meat or fish. Since the pesto uses Parmesan and a lot of dishes that I cook at Towpath contain Parmesan, I am always left with lots of rinds. This is the perfect dish to make a Parmesan rind stock. It is super flavourful and adds a great depth of flavour. All you have to do is take the Parmesan rinds, cover with water and cook for a few hours.

Serves 4

250g/9oz farro
1 tablespoon olive oil
50g/2oz unsalted butter
4 shallots, thinly sliced
150g/5½ oz cavolo nero leaves,
    roughly chopped
1 teaspoon chilli flakes
4 cloves garlic, minced
150ml/5fl oz white wine
½ lemon, juiced
150g/5½ oz Cavolo Nero Pesto
    (see overleaf)
200ml/7fl oz water or stock of
    any variety (I use a Parmesan
    rind stock, see recipe
    introduction)
150g/5½oz Parmesan, grated
salt and pepper

Rinse the farro thoroughly. It is always surprisingly starchy, but the water should run clear when all the starch is removed.

Cover with cold water in a pan and bring to the boil. Skim off the scum, then turn off the heat. Drain in a colander and rinse under cold water to remove any excess starch.

Repeat this step again – cover with water, bring to the boil and remove any scum.

Turn the heat down to a simmer for about 20–25 minutes until the farro is cooked but still has a bit of a bite. Season with salt and give it a good stir. Drain again, rinse with cold water to get the final bits of starch off. Give it a good shake in the colander to get rid of any excess water. Leave aside until ready to use.

Melt the olive oil and butter in a pan on a low heat. Add the shallots and the cavolo nero. Sweat down till softened but not coloured – about 5 minutes.

Add the chilli flakes and garlic and mix well, then add in the farro. Mix well and cook for a few minutes.

Turn the heat up and add the white wine. Bring to the boil and keep stirring to prevent it from catching. When it reduces, turn the heat down and add the lemon juice and pesto.

Mix well to make sure the farro is evenly coated with the pesto. Stir and cook for a few more minutes. Pour in the water or stock. I like to keep this dish veggie, but adding chicken stock will enhance the flavour. Slowly bring to the boil and cook for about 5 minutes.

Stir in 100g/3½oz of the Parmesan and check the seasoning. Serve with the remaining Parmesan on top.

CAVOLO NERO PESTO

Makes about 675g/1lb 8oz

3 bunches or 300g/10½oz
  cavolo nero with stalks removed
  (I find that the bunches can
  vary in size so it's best to weigh)
175g/6oz Parmesan, grated
2 teaspoons chilli flakes
3 cloves garlic, minced
½ lemon, juiced
200ml/7fl oz olive oil
salt and pepper

Fill a large saucepan with water and bring to the boil. Wash and drain the cavolo nero.

Fill a bowl with iced cold water to prepare for the cooked cavolo nero.

Once the pan of water is boiling, salt the water and then add in the cavolo nero. Cook for 3–4 minutes once it has come back to the boil.

Drain in a colander and immediately place in the iced cold water. This will prevent the cavolo nero from losing its lovely green colour.

Remove from the water and really wring out the cavolo nero in small batches. Just like spinach, you will be amazed at how much water it releases.

Roughly chop through the cavolo nero and place in a food processor. Add the Parmesan, chilli flakes, garlic and lemon juice. Blitz to form a paste and then slowly pour in the olive oil with the motor running.

Remove from the food processor, taste and season if necessary.

Fireworks

From the very beginning, we were never able to simply call it a day at the end of our Towpath year without some sort of festivities. The first closing party of record was a simple affair. There were no fireworks. It was December (the one

and only time we stayed open so late in the year). We invited our friends around to the bar, ate up all the remaining cheese sandwiches, drank all the red wine, then rolled down the shutters and didn't come back until a couple of freezing days later when three heroic volunteers (Lucie, Aida and my daughter Micky) returned to clean up the congealed mess.

Our closing night has evolved over the years, but for the most part it looks something like this:

There is always mulled wine – Laura's take on Nick Strangeway's recipe, which steeps red wine with clove-studded citrus that has been sprinkled with muscovado sugar. For those like our friend Jeremy Lee, who calls vin brulé 'a bad use of good wine' or even worse 'a bad use of *bad* wine', we have our usual bottles.

Something to eat, different every year, but always warming – think chilli con carne, pulled pork buns, jacket potatoes, merguez sausages.

Music, occasionally live – we've had folksy acoustic as well as raucous rock and rolly, though lately we've had more fun blasting our favourite playlists with Alex Capps DJ'ing from the coffee machine, steam wands full tilt, transforming the bar into London's tiniest, smoky disco.

A fire, sometimes two, on the raised woodchip patch by the bridge we all call 'the beach'. Child-friendly, warming fires less suited to burning effigies than to lighting sparklers, roasting marsh-mallows and sitting round for hours once the fireworks are over.

Decorations, which started out as a bit of bunting, but have grown to include a dozen oil lanterns that we hang from the apple tree outside the kitchen. Candles galore and, thanks to Laura and Alex, whose wedding celebration paraphernalia we inherited, a spool of LED lights long enough to wrap around all four kiosks, and miles of coloured plastic bucket lights which festoon the beach and the old sycamore tree overhanging it.

Fireworks. Proper ones – which we've always gotten from Kimbolton, the last remaining firework manufacturer in the UK. They've ceased trading, alas, and it's hard to imagine another company so willing to try to indulge our preference for shimmery, crackly, slightly hallucinogenic pyrotechnics, rather than LOUD and garish ones. We will miss them.

The evening kicks off at around 6:30pm, which at this time of year has the benefit of being on the child-friendly side while still feeling like the middle of the night. The hour and a half between Towpath's regular closing and the party's first arrivals has all the energy of a frenzied, maniacal barn raising. All the while we compulsively watch the sky and consult a variety of ever-changing, mostly unreliable weather reports, unsure until the very last moment whether we're throwing an enormous shindig or awaiting the arrival of a few intrepid friends to huddle under the awnings with us while it chucks down rain.

Most years (but by all means not all) we've won our bet with the weather gods and by 7.30pm our stretch of the canal is packed beyond imagination. There is a notable absence of dogs, for whom this is an especially traumatic time of year. Joe Woodhouse and Alex Bank have long disappeared with a couple bottles of wine and all of the fireworks, which they've arranged in some sort of logical firing order on the far side of the bridge or, even better, directly across from Towpath on the rooftop of

some very dear and trusting friends of ours. There's a flurry of Mission-Control-at-Cape-Canaveral-style communications between Alex and Laura until finally the sky above us begins to shimmer and flare. We know the show is over when the boys come stand on the edge of the roof with their arms held up to the sky like rock stars. Or superheros. Which they are.

As for us, well, there is nothing more beautiful to behold at the end of a long year than a sea of faces tilted up towards the night, illuminated by a confetti of light, fire and friendship. Something about the scene feels like a return to childhood. To innocence. Whatever community we've managed to create from our little perch beside the water has come together this one last time before disbanding until spring. We can't think of a nicer way to say farewell.

PEPOSO

This recipe is inspired by Lori's friend, Mario Mariani, a potter from the Tuscan town of Impruneta. Traditionally this stew is baked in the cooling embers of a wood-fired kiln at the end of the firing day, when the heat is perfect for a slow-cooked stew and so you make use of the residual heat left over from firing a kiln. When Mario makes this stew, he invites the whole community over for dinner at a long table he sets up in the yard outside the kiln. Since Towpath doesn't have a wood-fired kiln/oven, I have amended this delicious stew while still bringing out the flavours. I like to serve it with polenta or boiled potatoes and some greens like cavolo nero. It is the perfect warming stew.

Serves 4

1kg/2¼lb beef chuck, neck or any cut of beef suitable for slow braising, cut into 6cm/2½in chunks
250ml/9fl oz red wine
3 tablespoons olive oil
6 cloves garlic, minced
1 x 400g/14oz tin peeled Italian plum tomatoes, crushed
1½ tablespoons crushed black peppercorns
300–500ml/10–18fl oz chicken stock (you can also use water)
salt

Marinate the beef overnight in the red wine (or for longer). This will make the meat more tender and juicy.

Heat the oil in a large, heavy-bottomed casserole. Drain the wine from the meat and save. Once the casserole is hot, brown the meat on all sides. Don't overcrowd the pan otherwise the meat will sweat rather than brown, so cook in small batches if necessary.

Once all the meat is browned, return it to the pan. Add the garlic, tomatoes (making sure to use a little water to gather everything out of the tin), the crushed pepper, the reserved wine and enough stock so the meat is just barely covered. Season with salt.

Bring to the boil and simmer, uncovered, for 3½ hours or until the meat is super tender but not falling apart. Stir from time to time to make sure it's not catching on the bottom. Check the seasoning, adding more salt if needed.

BUDINI DI RISO (ITALIAN RICE CAKES)

I remember tasting these during a Towpath field trip to Tuscany. They were just a perfect combination with a coffee in the morning. In Tuscany you will often find these cakes encased in pastry, but I prefer these. They are gluten free and a great alternative to all other sweets we have up on the counter. These normally come out on the weekend and the recipe is inspired by Patricia Wells – I love the passion of her writing and the simplicity of her recipes.

Makes 12

750ml/25fl oz full-fat milk
90g/3¼oz risotto rice
2 generous pinches of salt
100g/3½oz caster sugar
60g/2¼oz unsalted butter, cut
   into small pieces
3 egg yolks, plus 2 egg whites
zest of 2 lemons
2 tablespoons lemon juice

Pour the milk into a saucepan and heat on low until just before the boil. Add the risotto rice and salt, stir well and simmer gently for 12 minutes (keep an eye on the pan as it's easy for the milk to over or under boil).

Stir in the sugar and butter. When the butter has melted, simmer for another 12 minutes. Leave the mixture to cool completely.

Preheat the oven to 180°C fan/400°F/gas mark 6.

Pour the cooled mixture into a bowl. Use a wooden spoon to mix in the egg yolks, lemon zest and juice.

In a separate bowl, whisk the egg whites until they form soft peaks. Gently fold the egg whites into the rice mixture.

Line a muffin tin with paper or reusable silicone muffin cups, spoon in the mixture and place in the oven. Bake till light brown on top and a skewer inserted into the middle comes out dry. This should take about 20 minutes. Cool in the tin for 10 minutes, then remove and serve or let cool completely.

Notes
At Towpath I always cook the rice mixture the day before and leave to cool until I can put in the fridge and leave overnight. This means I can come in first thing in the morning, cook them straightaway and serve them fresh out the oven.

Postscript

We are always asked what we all do during the months that Towpath is closed. After we've scrubbed the kiosks and everything in them within an inch of their lives, made detailed lists of things to do before we reopen in spring, and lovingly examined every plate and bowl for cracks and chips (we all have our favourites in circulation and oh how we mourn the ones we must retire). When finally the shutters are rolled down for the year, we are like puppies off the lead. Playful, sleepy, delighting in what it feels like to simply wake up and have a sniff around. Some of us eventually head off to other kitchens or dining rooms. Pick up a guitar and write songs. Set out on exotic travels or far-flung trips to see family. But one thing always – somewhere near the beginning of our downtime, Laura and I go to Tuscany.

You probably think that (in the nicest possible way) once Towpath closes for winter, we can't wait to see the back of each other, at least for a little while. We have, after all, spent most of our waking hours in each other's company for the past eight months. But only in a manner of speaking. The kitchen and bar are separate realms and when we're busy we only spend time together in the harried, semi-distracted fashion of a married couple with a houseful of toddlers. Which is why in the summertime we try to meet regularly at the Ladies Pond for a swim and a walk through the Heath. And in winter we take ourselves to the Tuscan countryside for a bit.

Coming back to the farmhouse that my kids' father and I restored thirty years ago is a bit like opening a time capsule. Favourite drawings from primary school are still around. *New Yorkers* from when Obama was president. Our days are not so noteworthy, except in their simplicity. A little yoga followed by coffee and yoghurt with muesli, maple syrup and fruit, remarkable only in that for once it's me making breakfast for Laura and not the other way around. And then it's usually on foot through the woods to the town of Mercatale or a short drive to San Casciano, the site of much of my own gastronomic education, to see what we want to bring home to cook.

Tuscans are deeply suspicious of artifice at the table and so ingredients are everything. Nowhere is this more evident than at the market. Imagine having to ask for everything by name. You will hear whole conversations about which particular loaf of bread someone wants at the baker's. Be given several opinions as to the best cut of meat to use for *peposo*, a local potter's stew made with red wine and peppercorns. You won't pick your own vegetables – you tell the greengrocer what you want. And it's never as straightforward as simply saying something like, 'artichokes'. Do you want smooth-skinned *morelli* for eating raw or their small, rougher cousins to slice up for a pasta sauce? Or perhaps the even smaller ones for preserving in oil (a labour of love if ever there was one) or the giant *mamme* for eating whole? Remembering all the while that there's not an artichoke to be had for love or money when they're out of season.

The level of culinary discourse is so naturally high (among both men and women, and in every socio-economic class, by the way) that it's an education in itself to just stand around, watch and listen to people doing so naturally what we've all tried so hard to learn. It's no different at the table. Italians love to talk about food while they're eating. And they are never falsely complimentary – if they think your soup's *sciocco* (lacking salt or, even worse, flavourless!), you're going to hear about it.

Once we're back home, we spend the rest of our day (except for napping or more walking) in the one big room that has everything in it we need to be happy. At its heart (no surprise here) is *la cucina* with its sturdy cooker, wooden cabinets painted green, row of thick Neapolitan tiles, rough terracotta floor and open shelves holding a lifetime's accumulation of bowls and platters. An old wooden haberdashery counter with a pale marble worktop upon which countless loaves of bread have been kneaded looks out onto the rest of the room. It took a friend to tell me how much the Towpath bar has taken on the feel of this kitchen. Not only because of their similar shape, but because they both answer to the same guiding principle – if a thing can be both useful and lovely to look at and handle, why shouldn't it be? Think of the homely beauty of a carved wooden spoon or a glazed terracotta bowl. Of tea towels and aprons worn soft through use.

But where the Towpath counter looks out onto the canal, the view from the kitchen is of a big wooden table, two ancient leather armchairs, stacks of books, bowls of onions and garlic, and of apples and lemons, wildflower posies and a fireplace big enough to cook in. Which we do – toast bread for bruschetta, grill *bistecca* and sausages, roast chestnuts and occasionally even stuff artichokes with olive oil, garlic and parsley, wrap them in foil and tuck them in among the embers until they're charred on the outside and tender and juicy at their hearts.

The room's windows and doors open out into the countryside. Early mornings are dreamy, the hills blanketed in mist and everything covered in a fine layer of frost. During the day the light pours in or rain slaps against the windows. At night we close the shutters and light the fire. In case you're wondering, we hardly speak about Towpath at all and, even then, only in the most practical terms: 'What shall we do about those sockets behind the cooker? Shall we repaint the kitchen floor?' We never find ourselves trying to figure out some way to stay open 12 months a year or (as many have suggested) brainstorming how to replicate Towpath someplace else during winter. We pour our hearts and energy into it eight months a year. And then we recharge. Which won't keep next year's reopening from hitting us like a freight train. It always does. And somehow we'll get ourselves back up to speed again.

This year's downtime in Tuscany has a little more structure than usual as we're testing recipes for this book, cooking for four what Laura usually cooks for 40. But even that's not really why we've come. Italy is about resetting our compass and renewing our friendship.

Recipe Index

Index

Thank Yous

This whole book has always felt like a long and rambling love letter to the many people who've helped Towpath exist in the world in all its particular and improbable beauty.

To the first Towpath team, who joyfully leapt into the unknown (and occasionally into the canal) with all their talent, energy and creativity: Jason, Amanda, Micky, Rae, Joe, Scott, James, Toby, Lucie, Mike, Aida, Coco, Cheri and Sam. And to all the lovely people who followed them, sprinkling their own magic into the mix. There can never be thanks enough.

Endless gratitude to all of you (and your children and your dogs) who've braved the weather, indulged our eccentricities and given us a hero's welcome every spring when we return. With love to Boo (and Andrew & Erin) for the best hugs ever; Charlotte for rose elixir; Dan, Nicola, Danielle and all the DTS peeps for countless acts of helpfulness; Christopher & Peter; Dennis & Misia for morning set-ups and daily dégueulasses; Ed for drawing our favourite Towpath blackboards; Enrico for just about everything; Fergus & Rebecca; Fleur & Brodie; Hilary for a cascade of blossoms; Irah, for being our first Towpath baby (and Tali, Dani, Romy & Maya for being themselves); James & Paul; John for morning book chat; Matt & Bella for braziers, flowers and so much more; Norman for his sheer presence; Peter & Parinaz for making us feel like we're their home away from home; Richard for keeping the conversation flowing; Rob for gardening, dishwashing, incredible helpfulness and generosity of spirit; Rose for her delightful Towpath animation; Roshinee & Alexander for letting us set off fireworks from their rooftop; Sonjay, Sophie for making us her first destination when she's back from the wilds; Susanne for being our number one fan as we are hers; Tracey, Mabel & Harry; William & Sandhini… and Steve, Mary, Colin and Jodie who will forever be missed.

Our suppliers inspire us daily, and our work is lighter and happier because of the delights they bring us. With special thanks to Charlie at Allpress, Ben at Ben's Fish, Carlo at Caves de Pyrene, Ben at e5 Bakehouse, Giacinta & Alberto, Raef & Kit at Gergovie Wines, Leila for being such an all-round inspiration, McKanna Meats, Alessandro at Piansa, the whole Neal's Yard Dairy team, Bora at Newington Green Greengrocers, Northiam Dairy, Jenny & Kevin (whose hair looks like a fluffy chick) at North Eggs, George at Swaledale and Alex & Damiano at Tutto Wines. Thanks also to lovely Paul at Alclear who keeps the critters away.

This book simmered slowly in our imagination for years before it was brought to life by many helping hands. Heartfelt gratitude to:

David Godwin for the enthusiasm and exuberance he brought to every step of this project. And Philippa for ushering us beautifully along the way.

Margo Baldwin (for handing us her card after a long lunch at Towpath), Rosie & Matt for making Chelsea Green Publishing the perfect home for this book. More than ever we are inspired by what Chelsea Green stands for and the integrity with which it walks its talks.

Muna Reyal for joyful collaboration and her wise and skilful hand.

Will Webb for the care and talent he brought to designing the beautiful book you hold in your hands.

Katie Read for all her efforts to get the good word out.

Anne Sheasby for helping make sure that we dotted our 'i's and crossed our 't's.

Anna & Harry for just being you and designing an elegant and simple website, taking Towpath into the technological world after 10 years!

Jimmy for his lovely photo of Sophie von Hellermann's painting. Thank you Sophie for allowing us to use your beautiful painting.

Joe Woodhouse & Scott MacSween for years of documenting and participating in Towpath life, tiling the walls as well as taking the pictures. For being impeccable friends and capturing the true spirit of Towpath.

Jojo Tulloh for introducing us to David, for writing such beautiful words about what we do, and for being a true and treasured friend.

A sisterhood of cooks and writers have especially inspired us over the years. Their values, sensibilities and skill in the kitchen and/or on the page have encouraged us to bring our best to what we do: Rosie, Rachel, Leila, Margot, Kitty, Olia, Anna, Jojo, Hattie, Melissa and Christopher of Canal House – and also, known to us only on the page, but no less inspiring, M.F.K. Fisher, Laurie Colwin and Madhur Jaffrey.

LAURA GIVES SPECIAL THANKS TO:

Harry Lester and Ali Johnson – the time I spent at Chassignolles was my happiest and I learnt so much on so many different levels. If I hadn't have worked there, my path wouldn't have crossed with Lori and Jason and led to the creation of Towpath. So thank you all round.

Em – the biggest heart I know. For helping me along the way, opening my eyes to leading life in a happier and calmer way. Giving me the tools to see the world differently and in a better way.

Mum – even though you will deny it, all my recipes are inspired by yours. Thanks for your constant support throughout my whole career and special thanks for tirelessly going through all my recipes, testing and editing with me.

Thanks to all my testers in the Adelaide hills, it was a fun weekend of testing.

Alex T. for his meticulous testing and enthusiasm.

Sarah and Sara for testing in lockdown and giving me a good reason to pester you and feel like I'm still at work.

My sister for helping edit, my brother and dad. Benji and Marais.

Alex, my constant support, my rock. My love.

LORI GIVES SPECIAL THANKS TO:

Mom for holding me up in the air when I was an infant and saying, 'You will be enthusiastic!' And dad for your willingness to believe in something just because I did.

Julien and Michela. I love who you are, and who you are becoming.

Rae and Emily, you bright lights.

Roberto Piccolo, with love.

My SWW's, soulful witnesses to everything.

Enrico, Sophie and Hilary. You've made London home.

Finally, Laura and Lori would like to thank each other – a friendship and a livelihood shared – who could ask for more?

PICTURE CREDITS

Scott MacSween: 4; 7 April, May, June, August, September, October, November; 22; 38–41; 43; 47; 55–57; 63; 67–69; 72–74; 79; 83; 86; 87 top; 88–89; 96; 100–101; 103; 105; 106 bottom; 111; 114; 127; 129; 131; 132–137; 139; 140; 143; 147; 149 top and bottom right; 151; 156; 159; 162–165; 167; 172–174; 180; 198–199; 201; 203; 210; 213–15; 224; 226–227; 229; 232; 235; 254–257; 259; 268–271; 275; 279

Joe Woodhouse: 7 March and July; 9; 10; 12–13; 15; 16; 21; 24–26; 30; 33; 35; 36; 45; 49; 50; 53; 58; 66; 70; 77; 81; 82; 85; 87 bottom; 90; 95; 99; 102; 104; 106 top; 108; 112; 117; 118; 120; 123; 125; 138; 144; 149 bottom left; 153; 154; 161; 169; 170; 178; 183; 184; 187; 190; 193; 194; 205; 206; 212; 217; 219; 221; 223; 238; 241; 243; 245; 247; 249; 250; 253; 258; 261; 263; 265; 266; 272

Lori De Mori: 2; 19; 29; 37; 107; 150 Alex Bank: 28; 97; 285
Fuschia Kate Sumner: 208

About the Authors

LORI DE MORI is the author of four books about Italian cooking and food culture. Her writing has appeared in the *Best Food Writing Anthology*, *Gourmet*, *Saveur*, *Bon Appétit*, *Food & Wine*, the *Independent*, the *Telegraph*, *Olive* and elsewhere. Her last book, *Beaneaters & Bread Soup* was shortlisted for both the Guild of Food Writers and the André Simon Food Book of the Year. This is her first book about one of her own culinary adventures.

LAURA JACKSON cooked at Rochelle Canteen and at the Auberge de Chassignolles in France before coming to Towpath. She's drawn chefs like Rosie Sykes, Davo Cook and Rachel O'Sullivan to cook with her in Towpath's kitchen. Her food is seasonal, honest, unfussy and comforting – and so delicious people have been known to come for breakfast and stay through lunch. She delights in making everything from pickles to ice cream herself. And takes her inspiration where she finds it – so long as it's about making the ingredients shine.